RELIGIONS OF THE ORIENT

A CHRISTIAN VIEW

RELIGIONS OF THE ORIENT

A CHRISTIAN VIEW

JOHN A. HARDON, S.J.
Bellarmine School of Theology
Loyola University, Chicago

LOYOLA UNIVERSITY PRESS
Chicago 60657

© 1970 Loyola University Press

Library of Congress Catalog Card Number 71-108377

ISBN 0-8294-0185-7

Printed in the United States of America

CONTENTS

PREFACE

Religions of the Orient—A Christian View is intended as a textbook for classroom or private study use. It is the outgrowth of several years of teaching the non-Christian religions and will hopefully introduce Christian students to the religious wisdom of the Afro-Asian world.

The four religions covered in the book represent almost ninety percent of the affiliation in these living faiths of mankind. They are treated analytically, rather than with a great deal of factual detail. No previous knowledge of the respective religions is necessary to profit from this study. For those who may wish to supplement the present volume with further, informative matter on the Eastern religions, the author's paperback, *Religions of the World* (Doubleday), is recommended.

Although written to be studied, *Religions of the Orient* can also profitably be read as a concise analysis of the main features of man's religious quest outside of Western society.

Study aids are provided in the form of Historical Outlines, Topics for Discussion and Questions for Examination, Glossary of Terms, and a carefully Select Bibliography.

The author is grateful to the publishers from whose copyrighted books quotations were used in writing the manuscript. Complete data on the sources quoted are given in the reference section.

Special thanks are due to Mrs. Warren Joyce for her expert assistance in preparing the book for publication.

CHALLENGE OF THE
ORIENTAL WORLD

There have always been good reasons for learning about the religious culture of other people. Natural curiosity makes us want to know how others think and live, and the appetite for knowledge is never stronger than when the object of research is the soul of man in its relationship to the ultimates of human existence.

But this is not the main reason why Christians today should take seriously the mandate of the Second Vatican Council to learn as they have never done before about the non-Christian religions of the world, especially in Africa and Asia.

The really urgent motives for making such a study can be expressed in three words: nearness, prejudice, and need—where nearness has to do with the rapid shrinking of the globe, prejudice accounts for our tragic ignorance of what half the world believes, and need is a weak word to describe the grave urgency of sharing with this other half of the human race what we, as Christians, undeservedly possess but which they, as non-Christians, will never

1

take unless we first learn to appreciate what they are and respect their own great treasures of religious faith.

Speaking of nearness, we are still using such words as miles and days to measure the distance between ourselves and the Eastern hemisphere. But space and time are no longer obstacles to communication of thought or of transportation across the seas.

Science in the past generation has conspired to bring people of all nations and cultures into easy and almost instant contact with one another. Within hours I can fly from Chicago to Cairo, or from Toronto to Bombay or Tokyo; and in split seconds I can watch on television what is happening on the other side of the globe.

But this very nearness has terrifying implications. If we are getting that close to others physically, we must also draw closer to them spiritually. For we have only one option: either to develop into a world community or advance into world conflict. Experience tells us that if two people, say a husband and wife, are not in love, cohabitation can become a torment and they want nothing more than to be separated as completely and as quickly as possible. Nearness is not the same thing as intimacy.

Apply this to the people of the Orient whose culture is their religion. Everything they do is permeated with the sacred and all their actions, even the seemingly most trivial, are expressions of belief. Institutions of government, as for example the Constitutions of India and Pakistan, reveal a profoundly religious attitude. Social customs, like the caste system among Hindus or Chinese ancestor worship, ethical standards and moral persuasions, literature and political aspirations—in a word, every aspect of life and thought—has centuries of religious faith behind it and reflects sacred traditions that reach back in antiquity to three and four thousand years before Christ.

Oriental culture, so deeply religious in its foundations, is daily nearer to us—physically—but it is still as far removed psychologically as it was in the days of Magellan. Europeans have been in the Far East as nations some four centuries and Americans less than one hundred years; and they already have to their credit more devastating wars with the Orientals than the whole past history of Asia.

I believe that America's presence in Vietnam is morally justified. But I also believe that a major factor in producing the tension between Americans and Asiatics is the distance, not of space but of spirit, between us. We do not know the Orient and we are doing very little to learn it, notably about its religious principles that fill Asia like the atmosphere which people breathe.

The same with Africa. Ask the average North American what is the dominant belief of that continent and he will probably say primitive religion. If you further ask him what is primitive religion, he will tell you it is a combination of magic, sorcery, and cannibalism. It never occurs to him that the principal religion of the Africans is Moslem and that Islam has a world affiliation of almost five hundred million adherents for whom Allah is the one true God.

We are profoundly ignorant of how this myriad of humanity in Afro-Asia thinks about the deep issues of man's existence, and ignorance here is more divisive than distance and space could ever be. Two things are furthest apart when they are separated in spirit. No wonder we still use expressions like, "As mysterious as a Chinese riddle," or "As dark as an African jungle."

Prejudice naturally follows on ignorance. What we do not understand we first fear, then dislike and, unless the ignorance is dispelled, dislike grows into all kinds of rejection.

Let us look at the stereotypes of the four major non-Christian religions of the world—Hinduism and Buddhism, Confucianism and Islam—and compare them with the reality.

Take Hinduism. Pronounce the word and what are the first associations that come to mind? Yoga acrobatics that some Western fadists take up to improve their bodily posture; Indian fakirs that make a specialty of walking on broken glass and swallowing naked swords; and Pariahs that live an animal existence and are just a shade above the lower species from which they have recently derived by reincarnation.

What is real Hinduism? On the testimony of its own believers, Hinduism cannot be defined. It is more a variety of approaches to the Reality that stands behind life than a single religious system. Or it may be described as a league of religions whose common denominator is a desire for union with the Infinite or Brahman, who is the ground of all being and the basis of all life.

This is Hinduism at its best. It is also the Hinduism about which most Westerners know the least. Yet this is the side that must be known if we are to begin looking at India as something more than colonial prey, or that even now is called a backward country because it lacks the material wealth—the bathtubs and can openers —that affluent Americans enjoy.

The same with Buddhism. Immediately we hear the name and we picture dark temples with strange buddhas sitting on pedestals, or Zen cultists squatting on the ground for hours lost in dreamy speculation or, more recently, monks committing suicide by burning themselves to death in protest against an alleged persecution by oppressive Christians.

Because we did not know Buddhism we mistook fanaticism for faith, as happened in Vietnam, and became willing victims of Marxist propaganda. We were sold the idea that checking the Vietcong would be religious discrimination and, by the time the truth was discovered, we were embroiled in a war that may develop into a world conflict.

But true Buddhism is so akin to Christianity that, as you read its sacred writings, you are lost in admiration at its balanced outlook on life and its deep understanding of human nature. The doctrine of deliverance preached by Buddha has close analogies with the teachings of Christ, and Buddhist charity has elements that remind one of nothing so much as Christ's sermon on love at the Last Supper.

Confucianism has its own distorted image in our society. The Western picture of Confucius, at best is that of a strange Chinese philosopher, and at worst is that of a man who coined clever phrases that are used in magazine ads to give the product an Oriental flavor. Confucian proverbs like, "The cautious seldom err," or "The rich fool is like a pig that is choked by its own fat," are about the only thing the average American (or European) knows of the genius who shaped the ethical standards of more than half of Asia for the last twenty-five hundred years.

So, too, Islam. The typical idea we have of Moslems is of the infidels who persecuted Christians and provoked the Crusades. To this day, the names "Moslem" and "heathen" are synonyms in our vocabulary, and a familiar term of reproach is to call someone a "Turk."

Yet Islam is unique among the religions outside of Judaeo-Christianity because it professes belief in one personal God, creator of the universe and just Judge of the living and the dead.

The Arabic word for God is *Allah*, to distinguish the Supreme Deity from the numerous pseudogods that were worshiped in Arabia in Mohammed's time. Koranic attributes of God are rich and varied. He is the Hearer and Seer, Bestower and Reckoner, Pardoner, Keeper and Guide. The titles applied to him have been gathered into the ninety-nine "most beautiful names of God," which the pious Moslem repeats daily on his lengthy string of beads.

Finally we come to our third reason for growing in the knowledge of Eastern religions, beyond the importance of keeping pace with a shrinking world and avoiding the mistakes (and tragedies) which prejudice has brought about.

The people of Africa and Asia are in desperate need, and we can help them, if only we come to know them well enough to sense this need and are generous enough to fill it. At mid-century we won a military victory in the Far East and promptly began to impose our own pragmatism on a nation that needs nothing more badly than religious principles on which to build its populous civilization.

Teeming China, now under Communism; southeast Asia restless with hungry millions while nearby Australia is almost empty and waiting to be tilled and filled; thirty-eight new countries came into existence in Africa since 1950 and are looking for a place under the sun.

All of this is happening, but when most Westerners hear about it they are as little impressed as if they were reading the sports page. Maybe less. They get very emotional about the World Series while the starvation of thousands in Biafra is only interesting if sad news.

From the Oriental and African point of view, the progress of science has indeed brought the Christian West close to the largely non-Christian East. Too close it would seem. We have made our physical presence felt in ways that were unknown in all previous history. Until recently Westernization had little effect on the mainstream of Hindu and Buddhist, Chinese and Islamic thought. Wider familiarity with European and American literature, contact (often imposed) with Western peoples through the period of colonialism, the late war and its aftermath, have brought into Eastern circles a sympathy for Occidental ideas whose effect is bound to be far-reaching.

Everything depends on what kind of Western influence will be operative. This, in turn, depends on what knowledge of the East has shaped the influence and who in the West is exercising it.

There are forces in Afro-Asia that are not true to the culture of its people, and ideas that are alien to the best interests of India,

China, Kenya, and Nigeria. There are ideologies in Europe and America that are not consistent with the true spirit of the Vedas and Upanishads, or of Buddha and Mohammed.

All of this points up the crucial value, on our part, of having the right people know the right things about the East and of sharing the truth accordingly. Will it be a naturalistic humanism in the West that scarcely knows God and looks upon Christ as a myth, influencing the Orient in its direction? Or will it be a valid Christianity that sees in Oriental religions so much that is good and wants to build on this the edifice of a new and better world?

HINDUISM

The symbol of Hinduism is the sacred syllable, *OM*,
enshrined in a continuous circle surrounding fifteen prongs. *OM* is
the name of Brahman, the Absolute, in three letters—A U M—each
representing a personification of Brahman, as Brahma (Creator),
Siva (Destroyer), and Vishnu (Preserver). The unbroken circle stands
for the Wheel of Existence, or endless reincarnation to which everyone
is fatally subject. Fifteen prongs typify the multiplicity of things
emanating from Brahman and yet caught within the cycle
of birth and rebirth.

If it is a truism that all wisdom came from the East, it is certainly true that all the wisdom of the non-Christian Orient had its roots in Hinduism, the oldest religion of the East.

The name itself does not mean much. *Hindu* is simply the Persian word for "Indian," and literally identifies a person who accepts the dominant religious culture of India, whose beginnings reach back to the third millennium before Christ.

Its followers currently number about eighty-five percent of the five hundred millions who live in the peninsula bordered on the north by Pakistan and the Himalayas, and on its two sides by the Arabian and Indian seas.

A popular myth about Oriental religions is to suppose they are not scriptural faiths. One reason for this prejudice may be that we know so little about the literature of the East, whether secular or sacred, and naturally assume that its belief and worship are on the same nonliterate level that we associate with most Asiatics. How few Americans know that India had a cultivated language long before the time of Abraham or that English and French are linguistic descendants of Sanskrit, in which all the sacred writings of ancient Hinduism were composed.

Hinduism has its own scriptures which are still the mainstay of Hindu thought and the principal source of religious life and practice. Of unknown authorship, they are commonly dated from 2000 B.C. to A.D. 400.

Three sets of sacred writings contain all the essentials of Hinduism and, in fact, cover the whole span of religious development through which the religion passed in its forty some centuries of existence. It is reputedly the oldest living faith of mankind.

The principal Hindu scriptures are the four Vedas, the Upanishads, and the Bhagavad Gita. Each deserves a brief explanation because of its contribution to the essence of Hinduism.

Vedas means "knowledge," and already suggests something of the thrust of Hinduism as a religion with intellectual preoccupation. Among the four Vedas—the Rig Veda, Sama Veda, Yajur Veda, and Atharva Veda—the first, Rig Veda, is basic to a correct understanding of the Hindu faith. It is also the most ancient and, to that extent, most representative of original Hindu beliefs and attitudes.

The *Upanishads* are also called Vedanta, or "end of the Vedas," because they come at the close of Vedic literature. Their more familiar title means "to sit down before," that is, a teacher. As speculative commentaries on the more simple Vedic writings, they also imply that Hinduism is something that needs to be studied. It is decidedly intellectual.

On a more popular level, the *Bhagavad Gita* (or simply *Gita*) is part of a larger work, the epic *Mahabharata*, which runs to more than a hundred thousand couplets. The Gita itself is still fairly long. Gandhi is said to have memorized its contents of 30,000 words. A mixture of religious sentiment, warlike legends, and philosophical reflection, the Gita has become "India's favorite Bible," to permeate the collective consciousness of the people as no other piece of Hindu writing.

As might be expected, the Hindu sacred literature touches on every aspect of faith and worship, and has produced an enormous volume of commentary and interpretation. Sometimes as you read these works and their interpreters you wonder if there is any thread of agreement running through this library of religious thought. The

9

hundreds of Hindu sects, a hundred or more subcastes, and thirteen major languages in modern India (each with numerous dialects)—all with their traditions and different understanding of the Vedas, would suggest anything but coherence and the practical impossibility of isolating any kind of unity.

Unity is not the right term to use in speaking of Hinduism. In our sense of uniform doctrine, there is none in Hindu culture and any attempt to find it is illusory.

What may be found and what can be of great value for believers in another religious tradition is the main concern of Hinduism, what occupies most of its time and on which most has been written.

The great Hindu preoccupation is with Being; not this or that form of Being; not, as in Western society, the practical application of various kinds of being that impinge on human life—but Being.

How did Hinduism come to concentrate on this (to us) strange concept, strange at least as part of religion since we think of it mainly as belonging to philosophy? That will be our first question.

How does Hinduism understand Being, what are its implications for Hindu faith, worship, and moral conduct? Our second question.

Finally what can Christians learn from the Hindus in their approach to Reality? Or to put it differently, what adjustments in Western thought about Being and Existence have to be made if Christians hope to enter into effective dialogue with the disciples of the Vedas and Upanishads?

IN QUEST OF REALITY

Historical Hinduism began with the mythology of the Rig Veda. This oldest document of Indian literature consists of more than a thousand hymns arranged in ten circles or books. Prayers of petition and praise addressed to the gods are the dominant theme.

A Hindu commentator, Yaska, writing about 500 B.C., classified the chief Vedic deities into the gods of earth (four of them), the gods of the air (also four), and the gods of the bright heaven (eight in number). Out of these sixteen deities, only six are really significant because they were later on to develop, each in his own way, into the Supreme Being. The six to remember are Varuna and Indra, Agni and Soma, Rudra and Vishnu.

Each of these gods corresponded to some force in nature. Among them Varuna was the highest cosmic deity; Indra was the god of war; Agni of fire; Soma of rare vegetation; Rudra the lord of cattle; and Vishnu represented earth, sky, and what is beyond.

A typical hymn addressed to Rudra, who later became Siva—the great god of the Himalayas—brings out the nature worship of primitive Hinduism.

> Most healing are the remedies thou givest;
> By these for a hundred years I'd live!
> Hatred, distress, disease drive far away,
> Rudra, dispel them—away, on every side.
> May we not, Bull Rudra, provoke thy wrath
> By bowing down to thee, by praising thee ineptly,
> By invoking thee with others.
> Raise up our men with healing remedies,
> Best of physicians—so do I hear of thee.
> O Rudra, where is thy caressing hand,
> The hand that heals, the hand that cools,
> The hand that bears away god-given hurt?
> Great Bull, forbear with me.[1]

This is pure mythology. Yet, already in the world of the Rig Veda, which may have been as early as 3000 B.C., there are traces of what future Hinduism was to be: a constant search for meaning in the universe of space and time.

One of the remarkable features of Hinduism is that it did not develop in the same way as the religion of other ancient peoples. The Egyptians and Babylonians, the Greeks and Romans never graduated beyond their mythologies. And their religions died. The best that the Greeks could do was finally to have Zeus become leader of all the gods on Olympus, and the Romans did no better. Their pantheon had not radically changed even to the fall of the Roman Empire. They, too, settled for having Jupiter rise to the leadership among his peers, and that was all.

Not so Hinduism. Something like the henotheism of the Greeks and Romans can also be seen in the rise of Indra to his position as "king of the gods" at the expense of Varuna, comparable to the ousting of Kronos by Zeus in Greek mythology. But this was hardly more than an episode in the history of Hinduism.

As far back as the late Rig Veda period a new concept entered the religion of India. The gods remained but they became less and less important as the prophets of Hinduism began looking for a unifying principle of the universe. They saw polytheism as a scandal which raised many problems and solved none.

Three hymns toward the end of the Rig Veda face the historic question of how the world was made. Commonly called creation hymns, they lay the groundwork for all future Hindu speculations on the first problem of Being: How did everything come to be?

In the most important of these hymns, the poet tells how inadequate he found the gods of mythology. He was groping for a real God whom men could worship not because they had always done so, but because he deserved man's homage as the Author of the universe.

As it stands, the hymn is ambivalent, suggesting the need for a clearer understanding of Reality. Yet it remains as a monument of the ancient Hindu desire to find a single, ultimate explanation of true Being.

> He who gives breath, who gives strength, whose command all the bright gods revere, whose shadow is immortality, whose shadow is death: Who is the God to whom we shall offer sacrifice?
>
> Who through his might became the sole king of the breathing and twinkling world, who governs all this, man and beast: Who is the God to whom we shall offer sacrifice?
>
> Through whose might these snowy mountains are, and the sea, they say, with the distant river (*Rasa*), of whom these regions are indeed the two arms: Who is the God to whom we shall offer sacrifice?
>
> Through whom the awful heaven and the earth were made fast; he through whom the other was established, and the firmament; he who measured the air in the sky: Who is the God to whom we shall offer sacrifice?
>
> Whom heaven and earth, standing firm by his will, look up to, trembling in their mind; over whom the risen sun shines forth: Who is the God to whom we shall offer sacrifice?
>
> When the great waters went everywhere, holding the germ (*Hiranyagarbha*), and generating light, then there arose from them the sole breath of the gods: Who is the God to whom we shall offer sacrifice?
>
> Who by his might looked even over the waters which held power (the germ) and generated the sacrifice (light), Who

alone is God above all gods: Who is the God to whom we shall offer sacrifice?

May he not hurt us, Who is the begetter of the earth, or he, the righteous, who begot the heaven; who also begot the bright and mighty waters: Who is the God to whom we shall offer sacrifice?[2]

Sometimes called the Hymn to the Unknown God, it was addressed to *Ka* (who), or the creator whom men do not know. This attitude has not substantially changed, except that three thousand years of meditation have enriched religious literature in the search for this Being.

Elsewhere in the Vedas, the process of creation was further explained. In bold language believers were told that the visible world, including man, came from some kind of Primal Being, but only by having this Being divide himself into as many parts as the creation he produced. Nothing was left to the imagination in identifying which part of Primal Being corresponded to which part of man as an individual or of mankind as a society. "A thousand heads had Primal Man," the Vedas said, "A thousand eyes, a thousand feet."

It was in this context that the foundations were laid for that most distinctive of Hindu beliefs, the caste system with its terrifying implications for the people of India. The act of producing the world by this Primal Being was understood to be a sacrifice; indeed, it was the paradigm of all the sacrifices that man would ever be called upon to make.

The Vedas asked into how many parts Primal Being was divided, into how many portions he offered himself in sacrifice. Into four parts, they declared, each corresponding to a part of himself.

What was his mouth? What his arms?
What are his thighs called? What his feet?
The Brahman was his mouth,
The arms were made the Prince,
His thighs the common people,
And from his feet the serf was born.[3]

Each of the four products of Primal Being represents one of the four basic castes of India: the Brahmins are the divinely appointed priests; below them are the Kshatriyas or soldiers and bearers of arms; below them are the common people, the Vaishyas, who engage in commerce and trade; and below them are the serfs, the Sudras, whose duty it was to serve the other three.

Here we have a profound insight into the meaning of sacrifice. Man is expected to surrender his own will and desires in response to the cosmic sacrifice made by the Source of all creation when he brought the world into being. He made the world at an awful cost to himself, literally parting with something of what constituted his entirety to bring beings outside of himself into existence.

Time and again the act of creation by Primal Being is described as a form of asceticism and a desire to share. On man's part no less is expected of him. He, too, must be ready to divide himself as the price of existence.

Viewed in this light, the caste system became what it has remained ever since: an absolute commandment laid upon men to accept their lot in life in humble sacrifice to the One who, in creating them, first sacrificed himself.

If the acceptance of one's place in the caste system thus became the first duty of the Hindu religion, it was also grounded on the first principle of the Hindu faith. All being is subject to the same law of self-sacrifice—Primal Being when it brought the rest of the world into existence, and man when he submits to the kind of existence in which he is born.

That was only the beginning of Hindu reflection on the concept of Being: to ask and to answer where the empirical world came from.

When the Upanishads came along, as commentaries on the Vedas, they further explained the origin of Being and its relevance to man. Primal Being became Brahman and everything else was related to it.

As the Upanishads describe Brahman, it is both changeless Being beyond space and time, the material cause of the universe, and the efficient cause as well.

Moreover, man is pictured as composed of two elements, a body with spatial limitations and a soul that is not rooted in space or time. Then ambiguity set in and the dilemma it posed has not yet been resolved. If Brahman is eternal and therefore outside of time, what should be said of man's spirit? Is the soul one with Brahman or distinct from Brahman? If the two are one, how could the Upanishads talk of creation? If they are distinct, why should the Upanishads speak of them as one?

A bit of vocabulary must be inserted here to clarify this critical problem. The word *Brahman* can mean either Absolute Reality, where Brah'man is neuter with an accent on the first syllable; or Brahman' is one of many human persons endowed with something of the power of Absolute Being, masculine gender, with the accent on the second syllable. This is not semantics. It touches on the heart of Hinduism.

You can read fifty writers on the Hindu religion and no two of them are quite agreed on what Hinduism is. Their disagreement stems from how they interpret the meaning of the word *Brahman*, and this, in turn, depends on what passages in the Upanishads they use and which they consider fundamental.

There are Upanishads that speak of Brahman in such pantheistic fashion that no room is left for doubt. There are others, and they are the majority, that never talk this way.

The most uncompromising text in the Hindu Bible on absolute monism occurs in the relatively late *Mandukya Upanishad*. In context, the author is trying to show how illusory is the whole cosmos, including mankind, compared with the one and only Reality, Brahman. He uses the analogy of sleep.

We know from experience how naturally we "emanate" an "objective" world in our dreams. Things that do not exist outside the imagination become as "real" as life, during sleep.

Something like this is true of Brahman, where (as always) the microcosm is an exact replica of the macrocosm, that is, our world is a reflection of the world of Brahman.

The world that we consider so real is really and only Brahman's dream. And just as we can distinguish varying degrees of subjective projection of ourselves into apparent objectivity, so with Brahman, the Absolute.

On the lowest level of subjective projection is the waking state; next in line is the dream; after that the dreamless sleep, where a person and his state of oblivion are one.

But there is one more stage of projection, beyond waking consciousness and beyond dreams and dreamless sleep. That is self-consciousness. We experience this in our lives. Brahman experiences this in Its life. Brahman's experience of Self is the finest description of how indistinguishably Brahman and the world are one. They are one as we and our Ego are one. If we seem to project self when we think of ourselves, this is not illusion; but neither is the thinking subject distinct from the object thought. No less must be said of Brahman and whatever else is conceivable besides.

No wonder this classic Upanishad dares address the sacred word *Om* to the universe at large. As the unique name of the Deity it is inscribed on Hindu temples and pronounced in every ritual prayer. Yet here it is applied, without qualification, to all the world.

> This syllable "Om" is this whole universe. And the interpretation thereof is this: What was and is and is yet to be—all of it is Om;
>
> And whatever else the three times transcends—that too is Om. For all this world is Brahman. This Self is Brahman.[4]

Language could not be clearer. Everything past, present, and future is Brahman; everything in the cosmos and whatever transcends it three times over, all is Brahman.

Unfortunately, this pantheistic image of Hinduism is the best known. But there is another side, more akin to the true spirit of the Indian people, which is not so well known. One reason may be that, as so often happens, those who believe are silent and not communicative; those who do not believe but merely speculate, are vocal and aggressively articulate.

Along with unqualified pantheism, the Upanishads give the Hindu believer plenty of evidence that Brahman can be conceived in two different ways. If there are passages describing Brahman as Absolute Being, there are others that speak of Brahman as man's participation in that Reality and intimate that he should seek to be united with the Author of his being.

On the one hand, therefore, Brahman is presented as the Highest and Supreme Being, than whom there is no greater.

> It is the unseen Seer, the unheard Hearer, the unthought Thinker, the ununderstood Understander. Other than It there is no Seer. Other than It there is no Hearer. Other than It there is no Thinker. Other than It there is no Understander. It is your Athman (Self), the Inner Ruler, the Immortal.[5]

At the same time, this utterly transcendent Being is declared to be distinct from the world and, what is most significant, distinct from the human beings in whom It dwells. The Sanskrit original allows us to translate the pronoun for Brahman as "He."

He who, abiding in all contingent beings, is other than all contingent beings, whom all contingent beings do not know, whose body is all contingent beings, who controls all contingent beings from within—He is the Self within you, the Inner Ruler, the Immortal.

If this still sounds ambiguous, the real distinction between Brahman as God and *Athman* as each person's Ego becomes clear from that most characteristic of Hindu doctrines, the belief in reincarnation.

REINCARNATION

Nothing more completely separates Hinduism from the religions of Semitic origin, especially Judaism and Christianity, than its implicit faith in the transmigration of souls.

This doctrine is alluded to in the Vedas and explicitly taught by the Upanishads. Though greatly developed in the past three millennia its essential features are the same as when they were first expressed in the year 1000 B.C. Synonymous terms are rebirth, transmigration, and metempsychosis—with only minor nuances in meaning and implication.

There are three parts to the doctrine of rebirth: its cause, its nature, and its possible escape. The cause and the nature are found in the Upanishads; but full details on the manner of escape had to wait until the Bhagavad Gita for general revelation to the believing Hindus.

What brings on reincarnation (*samsara*)? A distinction should be made between the general cause affecting the whole world, and the particular reasons affecting any one individual.

On a cosmic scale, reincarnation is simply a statement of the law of the universe: everything is in a constant state of change, but the change is only of the external or phenomenal part of things. Their inner essence or what may be called their noumenon remains the same. Relative to human beings, the Athman or Self is eternal and somehow distinctive for every person. This perdurable Ego remains substantially unchanged, while undergoing frequent change of residence, we might say, from one material habitation to the next.

Coming down to each individual person, three classes of people are envisioned by the Upanishads. The first class are those who in a previous existence (call it bodily habitation) relied on faith in the eternity of the Athman or Self. They succeed in stopping the

17

process of change and are liberated from the round of birth and rebirth. The second group are people who in their previous life had faithfully performed the duties of worship, almsgiving, and asceticism. They are reborn as men or women and start their life over again in human form. The third category is ignorant of this process of rebirth or how to be freed from it. They become reincarnate as less than human beings, and are condemned to existence as insects or reptiles.

How can this third class ever hope to escape from either further rebirth or extinction. One theory suggests that their life as animals is transitory, and they are reborn (after the animal stage) once more as men or women with prospects of final emancipation.

What exactly is reincarnation, or the "wheel of existence," from which every believing Hindu who understands his religion wants to escape? It is the nearest thing in Hinduism to what a Christian might call the law of retribution. But with one grave exception. The more pantheistic a Hindu's faith, the more he conceives of *samsara* as all happening outside himself; that it is Brahman, the Absolute, who undergoes these apparent transformations; that really nothing actually changes but only seems to; that the sensibly perceptible world of space and time is all illusion (*maya*); and that what looks like punishment for misbehavior (or misbelief) is simply the unfolding of predetermined law (*karma*) which the uninformed think is somehow affected by their own decisions or use of free will.

On the other hand, as a Hindu favors a theistic view of the universe, he sees in reincarnation an inexorable law, indeed, still called *karma*; but a *karma* in which he is not a helpless spectator but a true actor. His activity in any given stage of existence is partly responsible for his next stage of existence. Reincarnation on these premises is partly inevitable and partly conditional. The process itself is inevitable, but the direction of the process is not all fatalistic; men have a part in shaping their own destiny—even if that destiny is not the final one.

One passage in the Upanishads is classic. It corresponds in importance to such texts as "Without me you can do nothing," or "Upon this rock I will build my Church" in the Christian Scriptures. It occurs in the *Katha Upanishad*, written rather late in the Vedic period and revealing the historic struggle in Hinduism to decide whether God is an impersonal Absolute or a personal Being toward whom man is tending.

Present-day commentators among Hindus translate the passage in two different ways, depending on their theory of ultimate Reality. It is worth giving the context first, since it has bearing on the actual words and their interpretation.

The Upanishad is a dialogue between a man called Naciketas, the seeker after knowledge, and Yama, the god of death. Naciketas opens the dialogue with a direct question: "Other than righteousness (*dharma*), other than unrighteousness, other than what's done or left undone, other than what has been and what is yet to be—this that thou seest, tell it forth!"[6] Naciketas wants a clear answer to the question: "What further secret is there to man's life than good or bad behavior? What is finally man's destiny?"

Yama comes to the point immediately. He identifies in one word (and a synonym) what is the goal of man's existence.

> The single word announced by all the Vedas, proclaimed by all ascetic practices,
> The word in search of which men practice chastity, this word I tell thee now in Brief: "Om"—this is it.
> The Imperishable Brahman this, this the Imperishable Beyond. Whoso this Imperishable comes to know—what he desires is his.
> Depend on This, the ultimate:
> Who knows that on This [alone all things] depend—in the Brahman-world is magnified.[7]

So far, the matter is clear enough. The goal of human life is to come to the knowledge of Brahman, addressed as "Om." The intellectual possession of Brahman, therefore is the end of man's existence and the fruit of a good moral life.

Having settled what is man's destiny, Yama next explains where this Brahman abides. He is inside every man; he is that inner Self or Ego which existed before a man was born, and lives on after a man apparently dies.

Here ambiguity enters. If the Brahman toward whom man is tending is the Self, how is this Self to be understood? Is it the Ego pure and simple, or is it a reality distinct from the Ego, yet so closely bound up with a man's own being that it may be called by the same name? Let us hear the description that Yama gives of this Self, alias Brahman, which he said was the ultimate of human striving.

19

> More subtle than the subtle, greater than the great, the Self is hidden in the secret place in creatures here.
>
> The man without desire, all sorrow spent, beholds It, the majesty of the Self, by the grace of the Ordainer.
>
> In bodies bodiless, in things unstable still, abiding, the Self, the great Lord all pervading—thinking on Him the wise man knows no grief.[8]

These lines do not fully answer the question of whether Brahman is really distinct from a man's own being; but they strongly suggest that the two are not really (ontologically) one.

Now comes the decisive passage, on which all Hindu theology is divided, and which gives the clue to understanding what Hinduism is all about. We should see it in two translations, first the monistic and then the theistic.

> This Self can be obtained neither by verbal explanation, nor by reflection, nor by much revealed lore. Only the one who desires Him can obtain Him: the Self reveals His own truth.[9]

Hindus who prefer a theistic view of existence translate the passage differently, after agreeing that Brahman cannot be reached by any mere effort on the part of man.

> This Self can be obtained neither by verbal explanation, nor by reflection, nor by much revealed lore. By him alone can He be won whom He elects; to him this Self reveals His own true form.

Put side by side, the difference is startling. Given a pantheistic theology, men are said to strive for their destiny, but this striving is only make-believe. They do not literally desire to reach Brahman, but Brahman is gradually realizing himself. In Western philosophical terms, a la Hegel, successive rebirths are the dialectical process by which Reality (Brahman) develops into ever more perfect Being.

In theistic terms, however, there is a real and not merely nominal distinction between the Self in me and the Self which is me. The former exists independently of my mind and would exist though I were not around. The former exists only because of the former, and its being is incomplete or imperfect. It needs to be fulfilled by that other Self, which is truly Other because its existence is not mine; and yet may be called "Self" because I depend on it so completely.

The key word in this whole context is the verb *elects* or *chooses*, referring to Brahman's choice of those who eventually reach their goal. A Brahman that freely chooses is a personal God on the assumption that freedom to do this or that is what best describes (from our experience) what personality is. Choice or election also clinches the fact that Brahman is not the person whose destiny is reached by reaching Brahman; the two are really distinct, even as chooser and thing chosen are not the same thing.

MONOTHEISM

If that were all there was to the Hindu concept of God, it would be unsatisfactory. The heart of its faith would be a question mark. Is Brahman truly God or only a monistic Absolute? It is inconceivable that millions of Hindus since the Upanishads were written could have sustained on such uncertain fare.

Hinduism is not, fortunately, what some American or European authors make it out to be. No doubt there are ambiguities in the Vedas and the Vedanta, and the beliefs of many pious Hindus are strange and obscure to say the least. But Hinduism is not only a collection of contradictory statements in its sacred books, nor only the ignorance of many of its followers. It is also the heights to which it attains and the peaks that those who understand it best are invited to scale.

One such height is the most famous single piece of writing in Hindu literature, on a par with Plato's well-known passage in the *Symposium* where he asks if it is possible for anyone to reach Beauty Itself, simple, pure, and undefiled.[10] I quote the dozen verses from the *Svetasvatara Upanishad* without apology. They are more powerful than any argument to prove that for two millennia India had access to great spiritual wisdom and deep foundations on which Christianity might have built. But Christians did not know it, and even today are ignorant of the fact.

Unlike elsewhere, Brahman is here once again (as in the tales of the Vedas) spoken of as *Deva* (God) and not merely the *Athman* (Self). He is called *Bhagavad* (Lord), and he stands above the pantheon of the gods.

> He is the Beginning, the efficient cause of the conjoining [of soul and matter], seen as beyond the three times [past, present, and future], without parts too.

21

Worship Him who takes on all forms, becomes becoming, the adorable God who dwells in your thoughts, primeval.

Higher and other is He than [world-]tree, time and forms. From Him the world evolves, fully diversified. Righteousness He brings, evil repels, Master of good fortune, immortal, self-subsistent, of all the home and ground.

Of lords supreme Great Lord, of gods the highest God, of kings the highest King—utterly beyond! So should we know Him—God, Lord of the worlds, adorable!

There is naught He needs to do, He works not with any tool; like unto Him is none, none greater than He is known. Manifold is His exalted power, as manifold revealed. His works of power and wisdom inhere in His very nature.

No one in the whole world is His master, no one His ruler; no outward sign has He. He is the cause, Lord of the senses' lord. No one begot Him, no one is His lord.

The One God, in all contingent beings hidden, pervading all, of all beings the Inmost Self. Of all works (*karma*) the overseer, in Him all beings dwell. Witness, observer, absolute, alone, devoid of attributes.

Eternal among eternals, conscious among the conscious, the One among the many, He disposes over desires. He is the Cause, He can be comprehended in theory (*samkhya*) as in spiritual exercise (*yoga*). Knowing this God a man is from every fetter freed.[11]

It would be easy to point to other texts in the Upanishads that speak in less coherent terms, and numerous passages in which Brahman is anything but the one God who dwells in man as Creator and awaits man as Destiny. Yet authentic monotheism is part of the Hindu tradition and for too long has been overlooked by Western writers on the Orient.

INCARNATION AND DEVOTION

The Vedas and Upanishads are not all there is to Hindu literature. This is so true that for the average believer, say nine out of ten of the four hundred million Hindus in India, these two oldest and most extensive scriptures are quite unknown.

There are several reasons for this. The language in which they were composed is not the vernacular. It was Vedic and Sanskrit, which might be compared with Hebrew or Greek for the average

Jew or Christian in his use of the Bible. Moreover, the Vedas are too archaic to have much impact on present-day living, and the Upanishads too speculative to affect the ordinary conduct of ordinary people. Add to this the fact that for centuries most of the Indian subcontinent was illiterate and even today illiteracy is high.

If the people were to be Hindus at all, it would have to be on some other grounds than their knowledge of the Rig Veda or the *Svetasvatara Upanishad*. These documents are a challenge to the most sophisticated intellectual; they are no less cryptic to most believing Hindus.

It was the Bhagavad Gita, the *Song of the Blessed One*, that supplied this deficiency and is still the most influential piece of writing in Hinduism.

The Gita has been called "India's favorite Bible," and permeates the collective religious consciousness of the people as nothing else in Indian history. As Mahatma Gandhi lay dying, felled by an assassin's bullet, his last words were a repetition of the holy name of Rama, ". . . one of the *avatars* (earthly descents) of Vishnu. It was the Gita which prepared Hindus to identify Vishnu with the God who created the world."

Built into the Gita are two religious systems, theism and pantheism, which the author (or composer) carefully coordinated. Various theories have been proposed to explain the two irreconcilable strata. One is that the poem was originally theistic and professed belief in a single transcendent Deity, distinct from the universe; this was later edited to satisfy monistic philosophers in the Brahmin tradition. More likely, however, the Gita was first a kind of Upanishad cast in poetic form to meet the needs of the masses. Its dominant thesis is not only theistic but monotheistic, and represents the high point of popular religion in India about the year 200 B.C. Clustered around this central theme, and maybe superimposed by several writers, are various theories of being that range from complete pantheism to a mitigated henotheism, which postulates one chief deity among numerous lesser gods and goddesses.

The Gita is clothed in the form of a story timed on the eve of a great battle, featuring Arjuna, a reflective warrior who hesitates about opening hostilities because of the slaughter which this will produce. While brooding over the death of so many people, including his loved ones, the god Krishna appears and rebukes him for his scrupulosity, "that leads neither to heaven nor to honor."

23

After this opening of the dialogue between Arjuna and Krishna there follows a complete synthesis of Hindu theology that covers every possible angle. In one sense, the Gita is a *Summa theologica* of Hinduism which restates what the Vedas and Upanishads had been saying for a thousand years. In it we find all the ambivalence and frank contradiction over which the knowledgeable Hindu merely shrugs his shoulders and wonders that the Western mind is so concerned with consistency and logic.

In another sense, however, the Gita adds the final capstone to what a Christian might call the Hindu deposit of faith. It is immaterial whether we say that the pantheism (and mythology) of the Gita are merely descriptive of what some Hindus have always believed, but the normative doctrine is monotheism; or whether we take the unlikely minimist view and insist that everything in the Gita is on the same unqualified level.

No matter. The Bhagavad Gita is so detailed and so clear in teaching the existence of one only God, and how man can reach him that it must be taken as a valid picture of what Hinduism objectively is—in spite of the vagaries and incredible deviations among Hindus from the basic theme of the Song of the Blessed One.

Long before the Gita was composed, the Upanishads had already taught that Brahman was "the One God, in all contingent beings hidden." What the Gita did was to teach that this unique God is personal in a unique way; and that he is to be attained, above all, by the loving devotion of mankind.

The unique personality of God is taught by the Gita not so much in words as in the empirical fact that Krishna, appearing as a human being, affirms that he is the Lord (*Bhagavad*) and God (*Deva*) of the universe.

Hindu mythology had numerous gods and goddesses who spoke and acted in human fashion centuries before the Gita. But they were never identified with the one single God about whom the later Upanishads wrote so eloquently. Here was an innovation.

The climax of the Bhagavad Gita comes in the eleventh chapter, in the extensive theophany where Krishna reveals himself as the incarnate God and inseparable friend of Arjuna. The term Krishna uses is "supreme form as the Lord." The moment it dawns on Arjuna that the man he had been talking with so casually is God himself, he breaks forth in a torrent of exclamation. Words fail him to express all he wants to say, that this, this man is the Lord of creation.

Full just it is that in praise of Thee
The world should find its pleasure and its joy,
That monsters by terror tamed should scatter in all directions,
And that all who've won perfection should do Thee homage.
  For why should they not revere Thee, great as is thy Self,
More to be prized Thou than Brahman, Thou the first Creator
Gods' Lord, the world's abiding home, unending,
Thou art the Imperishable, Being, Not-Being and what
    surpasses both.
  How rashly have I called Thee comrade, for so I thought
    of Thee,
How rashly said, "Hey Krishna, Hey Yadava, Hey comrade!"
Little did I know of this thy majesty,
Distraught was I . . . or was it that I loved Thee?
  Sometimes in jest I showed Thee disrespect
As we played or rested or sat or ate at table,
Sometimes together, sometimes in sight of others;
I crave thy pardon, Lord, unfathomable, unfallen.
  Things never seen before I've seen, and ecstatic is my joy;
Yet fear and trembling possess my mind.
Show me, then, God, that same human form I knew,
Have mercy, Lord of gods, Home of the universe![12]

Krishna consoles the terrified Arjuna by admitting that he has, indeed, revealed himself in a way never done before. "I showed thee this my all-highest form," Krishna says, "glorious, all-embracing, infinite, primeval—which none has seen before save thee."[13] For ten chapters of narrative Krishna seemed to be just another man; then suddenly the flash of revelation—"This is God!" Then, just as suddenly, Krishna reverts back to his human state and Arjuna sees again only the man he knew.

But the revelation is not yet finished. On the heels of showing himself to be the infinite God, Krishna tells Arjuna something that had never been heard before.

For two thousand years the Vedas and their commentators had been preaching *moksha*, deliverance from the endless cycle of birth and rebirth through successive lives. But never once did they promise anything more. Even when they talked of reaching Brahman, the promise was a misty dream and, so it seemed, was more in the nature of absorption in the Absolute than attainment of eternal bliss.

Now Krishna speaks another language and tells Arjuna what the Hindus had scarcely surmised and, until this revelation, could never have believed was true. What Krishna tells him is so strange that some scholars, with some plausibility, hold that it must have entered the Gita from outside the stream of Hindu tradition, most probably from Christianity. Krishna is talking through Arjuna to all mankind.

> Right hard to see is this my form
> Which thou hast seen;
> This is the form the gods themselves
> Forever crave to see.
> Not by the Vedas or grim ascetic practice,
> Not by the giving of alms or sacrifice
> Can I be seen in such a form
> As thou didst see Me.
> But by worship of love (*bhakti*) addressed to Me alone
> Can I be known and seen
> In such a form as I really am;
> So can my lovers enter into Me.
> Do works for Me, make Me thy highest goal,
> Be loyal in love (*bhakta*) to Me,
> Cast off all other attachments,
> Have no hatred for any being at all;
> For all who do this shall come to Me.[14]

Is it any wonder that Hindus, who know their religion, complain that those who do not know it underestimate its greatness?

These closing verses of the eleventh chapter of the Bhagavad Gita have had a library of interpretations written about them. Needless to say they give us a different image of Hinduism than is commonly portrayed, and they bring out the one feature that is least often connected with non-Christian religions, namely the primacy of love.

CHRISTIAN APPRAISAL

The main reason for entering on the subject we are studying was to discover facts and insights that are not commonly known among Christians, and in this way to begin to bridge the intelligibility gap that still separates us in the West from the cultures of the Orient.

As we look back on what we have so far seen about Hinduism, what do we learn? I do not mean about Hinduism, but about religion itself and, therefore, about the Judaeo-Christianity that we profess to believe.

If it is true that divine grace is not foreshortened and that the salvific work of Christ has affected all of mankind, how has this grace been operative among people whom for so long we have looked upon as pagans? What can they teach us of the meaning of God and of man's striving for communion with the Source of his life and being?

These questions need some explanation, since we are not accustomed to going outside of Christianity to learn anything about religion. But Christian revelation does not cease to be normative just because we find evidence of religious truth among people who are not Christian.

What is some of this evidence in the religion of those for whom the symbol of faith is a perfect circle—representing the dreaded wheel of endless reincarnations, within which is inscribed the sacred name "Om"—standing for the Absolute Being which is Brahman?

Two dimensions of reality

The first great insight afforded by Hinduism to anyone who takes the trouble to examine it at close range is its preoccupation with Being. Nothing else is so prominent in Hindu thought and nothing is more constantly spoken of in its sacred literature than "Being" as Reality.

It is not only Being, however, that is so dominant, but concern to distinguish between two levels or forms of being that are so often taken for granted (when they are not confused) in the Western world of thought.

Nowhere surely do we see the distinction between the sacred and the profane more boldly drawn: between Being (in capitals) and being (in small letters); between Absolute Being that never came into existence because it has always been, and relative being that had its beginning in time and that, of itself, would lapse into the nothingness from which it came.

The whole history of Hinduism, from the earliest Vedas to the latest commentary on the Bhagavad Gita, is the story of Being. Hindus have never been satified with taking reality for granted. Where others would settle for living with things as they are, or

27

struggle to remove the painful elements of life in order to improve themselves by reducing labor or increasing the amount of pleasure to be enjoyed—not so the Hindus.

Their craving for more than forty centuries has been to get behind the mask of apparent reality, hidden by the material world, and somehow reach the really Real world that is not perceptible in space and time.

The Sanskrit vocabulary of the Upanishads is studded with words that try to express this dichotomy—and for the Hindus it is a genuine dichotomy—between what seems to be real and what is truly real, between what the senses perceive and what only the mind can conceive.

Always implicit in the Hindu religion is that what we see, touch, and taste is less than true; that truth is not accessible to the eyes and ears; that true Being is attainable only by a mysterious power that resides in every man—his Athman or Self—whose nature is in the same order of reality as the Brahman who can never be sensed but can only be known.

Even the extremes to which Hinduism has gone to stress this cleavage between the world of matter and spirit becomes intelligible once we realize what the Hindus believe is at stake: nothing less than self-deception about the whole purpose of man's existence. Is it only to have lived a few short years and experienced sensations in one's body, or is it eventually to have one's deepest Ego united with the supreme Deva (or God) in whose knowledge lies man's final destiny?

Knowledge as the basis of religion

Correlative with their preoccupation with Being, true being and not its illusory counterpart, Hindus place an emphasis on knowledge that should strike a familiar chord in the soul of Christianity.

We have seen something of what this means in the history of Hinduism. The very term for the first of its scriptures, the Vedas, means communication of truth from Brahman "like smoke emanating from wood." Absolutely speaking, the Vedas are the ideas in the Eternal Mind, while their verbal expression (the written or oral scriptures) are only human efforts to capture some of these ideas in capsule form.

So, too, the Upanishads are literally commentaries that a person learns by "sitting down before a teacher." Again the assumption is that knowledge comes from outside the human person, originally the mind of Brahman and proximately from other minds that have grasped the revelation that Brahman made to enlighten mankind.

There is such insistence on the objectivity of revelation in Hindu thought that no one could mistake it.

At the same time, Hinduism raises the paradox of making this very Brahman, who is the source of all human knowledge about true reality, so intimately joined with each person that sometimes the two seem to be one. Indeed, the two are simply one in those schools of Hindu philosophy which identify Brahman (the Absolute) with Athman (the Self).

But monistic Hinduism is neither typical nor dominant, in spite of what some interpreters would have us believe.

It brings out, however, something of the genius of the Hindu religion in pointing up the intimacy of revelation, or better, of the near-identification that occurs as the mind of Brahman penetrates ever more and more deeply the mind of the man who believes in what Brahman has revealed.

Otherwise than sense experience, which touches only the rim or edge of man's person, religious knowledge enters recesses of his being and quite transforms them into the object which is known. In this connection, Hindu theologians are accustomed to distinguish between two kinds of self: one they capitalize, and the other they leave (in English translation) in small letters—much as happens when writing about being. The first Self is actually Brahman, yet called "Self" because he permeates every pore of the mind that knows him; the other self is the person's own Ego, which is called self because it constitutes his individuality.

As might be expected, the object of this knowledge is both a distinction and a Reality. The distinction is to learn the difference between true Being which never changes and lesser (if not spurious) being whose nature is always to be changing. The Reality to be known is Brahman, which is at once the source of human knowledge and the goal toward which it tends.

A word of explanation about the Hindu concept of change. So much attention is paid to the idea of change that its implications should be briefly spelled out, if only better to understand what kind of knowledge is the main object of Hindu thought.

Hinduism, no less than other religions, takes into account the fact of man's death. Yet, unlike most other religions, it has focused on death as a cardinal principle of its faith. When a man dies, says Hinduism, what looks like a drastic change from living body to lifeless corpse is not so great a change at all. Better not even call it change, since the real reality which ultimately makes a man what he is, the Athman or Brahman in him, is the same after death as it was before.

Depending on how theistic a Hindu is, he will lay greater or less stress on the unchangeableness of this Athman or Brahman in man. But even where he clearly distinguishes Brahman as transcendent God from Athman, the contingent self, he never lets go the principle that death does not change a man. What changes is of little value, only the flesh that wrapped the soul during its short span of present existence. What does not change is the eternal reality that has another form of existence awaiting it, but not another being, once the present flesh is lost.

This attitude may well scandalize Western observers who place so much value on material things and whom perceptive Hindu writers describe as "men living in a dream." By Hindu standards everything that changes is no better than a dream compared with the unchanging Being that dwells in the innermost core of man. The trouble is that this unchangeable Reality is also invisible and impalpable—and for that reason so many people act as though it were not real.

Here is almost a one-sentence summary of what Hindu writers —since before the time of Christ—have been warning their people to avoid: "Do not be misled by appearances; compared with material things that have size and shape, only the spirit is real. What has weight and mass and can be measured is doomed to disintegrate into the elements from which it came; only knowledge and the knower can be said to grow and they will never die."

It is also in this context that Hinduism talks of freedom and of liberation from the endless cycle of births and rebirths, the awful *samsara* that hangs over the Orient like a cloud.

Where Judaeo-Christianity speaks of deliverance from sin, and of Christ as man's Savior from the consequences of disobedience to God—Hinduism has a different tongue. It uses words that sound the same but have quite a different meaning. Liberation in Hindu parlance is freedom from the oppressing ignorance which mistakes mirage for reality, or *maya* for Brahman. In more prosaic terms, the Hindu idea of salvation is liberation from the blindness of calling unreality real, and then acting on the error. In practice it means that a person who believes only in things with extension in space is enlightened to know about things which have no such limitations— who ever measured the size of thought or the power of an idea to project itself into the spaceless regions where Brahman dwells? It also means that men who are prone to believe only in what exists in time are delivered from darkness to see that true Reality had no beginning and will never end.

Love as the best means of salvation

With all its emphasis on knowledge as the basis of religion, Hinduism teaches (as we have seen) the sublimity of love as the highest and best way of achieving *moksha* or deliverance from the endless "wheel of existence."

By the time the Bhagavad Gita was written, Buddhism had already broken with Hinduism and consequently it is not certain whether the author of the Gita borrowed this doctrine of the primacy of love at least partly from Buddha or one of his disciples. More likely the idea was native to Hinduism and what we now call the Buddhist theory of charity did not originate with Buddha but came from the Bhagavad Gita.

In order to appreciate what the Hindu *bhakti* or loving devotion can teach Christians we must go back a moment to what has already been seen about the Hindu theory of world origins. According to the cosmogony of the Vedas, Primeval Being brought the world into existence by dividing part of himself in the act of creation. Later Upanishad theorists explained that this should not be taken literally, as though Primeval Being physically parted with a piece of his substance every time he brought something else besides himself into being. Rather, they explained, it means that Brahman emanated his own essence, sending it forth into the cosmos which except for him, would not even be.

As happens so often in other phases of Hinduism, so here the character of this creative emanation is more or less theistic—according to different schools of thought. The most authentic of these schools, which is based firmly on numerous texts in the sacred books, explains the emanation in terms that are close approximations to the "creation out of nothing" in Judaeo-Christianity. Certainly by the time of the Gita, *Bhagavad* (the Lord) is unequivocally said to be the efficient cause of all things.

We return to our theme. If man's noblest action with respect to God is to love him, and in loving comes to see him, and seeing him is delivered from the deathless cycle of rebirths—this is valid only because in loving God, man responds to God's previous love for man.

Recurring throughout the Gita is Krishna's insistence that he is the first maker of the universe, with the implication that he made (and continues making) through no duress but only because he wants to.

> I am the father of this world,
> Mother, ordainer, grandsire, all that need be known.
>> It is I who pour out heat, hold back the rain and send
>> it forth.
> The source of all am I; from Me all things proceed.
>> I am the Self established in the heart of all contingent
>> beings;
> I am the beginning, the middle and the end of all contingent
> beings too.
>> What is the seed of all contingent beings, that too am I;
> No being there is, whether moving or unmoving,
>> That could exist apart from Me.
> Whatever being shows wide power, prosperity or strength,
>> Be sure that this derives from but a fragment of my glory.
> But where's the use for thee to know so much?
>> This whole universe I hold apart,
> Supporting it with but a fragment of Myself, yet I abide
>> unchanging.[15]

Krishna piles verse upon verse telling Arjuna how completely the world derives from him, depends upon him, and is destined for him. "Of weapons," he says, "I am the thunderbolt . . . Among the letters of the alphabet I am the 'A' . . . Among chants the Great Chant am I . . . I am Death that snatches all away, and the origin of creatures yet to be . . . Of those who subdue the rod of chastisement am I, and the statecraft of those who seek the upper hand; the very silence of hidden, secret things am I, and the wisdom of the wise."[16]

If Krishna is the Lord of creation and the origin and goal of man's life, it behooves man to respond in kind. This response is the most precious single vocable in the Hindu language, *bhakti*. It is at once love and devotion, gratitude and generosity. It is above all an act of sacrifice.

Pantheistic interpreters of Hinduism find the concept so baffling they cannot bring themselves to admit what the text of the Gita demands. They prefer to find metaphors in all the passages where men are bidden to love the Lord in return for his loving them. They resort to symbolism to avoid unpleasant theological conclusions.

But this is not metaphorical language. Time and again, from every angle conceivable, men are told to love *Deva* (God) with ardent devotion analogous to Deva's love for them.

What is this love that men are bidden to show? It is manifest in good works, done solely for God. What is the fruit of this love for God? It is to receive still more love from Him.

> Let a man feel hatred for no contingent being,
> Let him be friendly, compassionate,
> Let him be done with thoughts of "I" and "mine,"
> The same in pleasure as in pain, long-suffering.
>   Content and ever integrated,
> His self restrained, his purpose firm,
> Let his mind and soul be steeped in Me,
> Let him worship Me with love (*bhakta*);
> Then will I love him in return.
>   I love the man who has no expectation,
> Is pure and skilled, indifferent,
> Who has no worries, and gives up
> All selfish enterprise, wrapt up in (*bhakta*) Me.
>   I love the man who hates not, nor exults,
> Who mourns not nor desires,
> Who puts away both pleasant and unpleasant things,
> Who's loyal, devoted and devout (*bhaktimat*).
>   I love the man who is the same
> To friend and foe, the same
> Whether he be respected or despised,
> The same in heat and cold, in pleasure as in pain.
>   Who's put away attachment and remains
> Unmoved by praise or blame, who's taciturn,
> Contented with whatever comes his way, of steady mind,
> Homeless, but loyal, devoted and devout.[17]

As though this were not enough, Krishna adds another litany of persons who are the opposite of devout, whose selfishness makes them unaware of God and whose conduct betrays their lack of love.

> Their minds unhinged by many a foolish fancy,
> Caught up in delusion's snare,
> Obsessed by one thought only: "I must satisfy my lusts."
> Puffed up with self-conceit, unbending,
> Maddened by their pride in wealth,
> They offer sacrifices that are but sacrifice in name
> And not in the way prescribed—the hypocrites!
> Selfishness, force and pride,
> Desire and anger—these do they rely on,
> Envying and hating Me
> Who dwell in their bodies as I dwell in all.
> Birth after birth in this revolving round
> These vilest men, strangers to all good,
> Obsessed with hate and cruel, I hurl
> Into devilish wombs.
> Caught up in devilish wombs,
> Birth after birth deluded,
> They never attain to Me;
> And so they tread the lowest path.
> Desire—Anger—Greed;
> This is the triple gate of hell,
> Destruction of the self.
> Therefore avoid these three.[18]

This is the last word that Hinduism has to say on love, and also the last on hate. Those who love God by their devotion to him show this love by avoiding desire, anger, and greed. All three are forms of self-love, and all three keep a man entering and leaving countless wombs instead of reaching his destiny.

Notice the warning about knowing the truth, which is that love of *Bhagavad* (the Lord) and not of *Athman* (self) guarantees final *moksha* or liberty. Yet some insist on "clutching at false conceptions." They are "puffed up with self-conceit" and "live at the whim of (their) own desires."[19]

So Hinduism ends where it began, with the praise of knowledge, based on objective truth, which sets a man free. This is the contrary of ignorance, born of subjective fancy, which enslaves.

BUDDHISM

The symbol of Buddhism is essentially a wheel
with sixteen spokes or, from another viewpoint, a disk with as many
emanating rays. Seen as a wheel it represents the basic Hindu belief
in reincarnation, or cyclic time, from which escape is promised
by following Buddha's Four Noble Truths multiplied by the
sacred number four. The same wheel also typifies the movement
of Buddhism through the world, advancing the wisdom of Buddha
to all nations. Taken as a disk, it symbolizes the sun which sheds
its light over all mankind, comparable to the radiation everywhere
of the brightness of the Enlightened One.

The best way to approach Buddhism is to think of it as an offspring of Hinduism. Since the founder of Buddhism had been a Hindu and his teaching was a reaction to the faith he had earlier professed, a follower of the Buddha is actually the disciple of a great—indeed the greatest—Hindu *guru* whose quest for deliverance from endless reincarnations led him to discover the religion that now bears his acquired name.

As a derivative of Hinduism, Buddhism would naturally have much in common with its parent, and these similarities we shall see. But the two religions are not the same.

Where Hinduism began as folklore and gradually developed into a complex speculative system, almost to the point of becoming a philosophy, Buddhism had a different beginning and has ever since been the opposite of metaphysical. It started as a practical religion, born of its founder's burning thirst for knowledge of how to escape the "wheel of existence." It has never ceased being that:

a religion whose preoccupation is not with thought but with action, whether personal and moral, or collective and ritual.

Still again, where Hinduism might be called the "Religion of Being," Buddhism would qualify as the "Religion of Deliverance." Correspondingly, where the Hindu is above all a thinker, the Buddhist is before everything else a doer. This is strikingly illustrated in the symbol of Buddhism, which at first glance looks very much like the Hindu circle with "Om" inscribed in its center.

Buddhism has a wheel, too, and the full name for its sacred design is *Dharma Chakra*, which means "Wheel of the Law." It is pictured as the disc of a wheel symbolizing the sun which shines everywhere indiscriminately. So, the belief goes, does *Dharma* or the Law of Buddha which has been universally effective in all lands of the earth. The spokes of the disc stand for a wheel that suggests motion or progress. Just as the wheel moves a cart, so Buddha set in motion his Four Noble Truths to revolutionize all human history.

Compared with Hinduism, the Buddhist faith has spread far beyond its birthplace at Benares in northern India. It has become, by all odds, the most universal religion of Asia. It has also made progress, in the sense of internal development, more than anything conceivable in Hinduism. Yet both these features, its widespread influence and its innumerable sects and interpretations, make Buddhism very elusive and much more difficult to identify, let alone classify, in contrast to the more localized Hindu ancestor.

Before we enter on a more detailed analysis of Buddhism and its meaning for Western thought, we should clarify one point on which a great deal that we are going to say depends. Far less even than Hindu writings, Buddhist sacred literature cannot be dated except in the most approximate terms. Complete manuscript texts of Buddhist scriptures are extant only from the Middle Ages of the Christian era, over fifteen hundred years after the events and teachings of Buddha reportedly took place. Moreover, the earliest Buddhist claim to anything having been written about Buddha and his doctrine puts the date somewhere between 30 B.C. and 15 B.C. or about four to five centuries after Buddha's death. "Before this time," so runs the Buddhist chronicle, "the wise *Bhikkus* (monks) handed down the texts of the three *Pitakas* and also the *Atthakatha*. At this time, the *Bhikkus* who perceived the decay of created beings, assembled and, in order that the religion might endure for a long time, they recorded [the above-mentioned texts] in written books."[1]

The late dates for any kind of sacred Buddhist writing, and their continued accumulation of legend and lore from many sources for upward of a thousand years makes it next to impossible to speak of Buddhism as anything but an eclectic religion. It has borrowed and absorbed on all sides, including Confucianism and Christianity. As a result we cannot talk about Buddhism as a closed religious system on a par with Hinduism.

Yet, Buddhism is distinctive. We can prescind from where it got what it now professes, and ignore the many unsolved problems about Buddhist history to concentrate on what directly concerns us here, namely the characteristic elements of what people called Buddhists now believe. But one more proviso. It touches on a crucial factor of modern history.

Until the rise of Islam in the seventh century, Buddhism was the partial religion of most of Asia, including Japan, China, India, and far into the southeast beyond Java. From about A.D. 700 a series of dramatic changes in religious posture began to take place. During the next thousand years Buddhism was more and more challenged for prominence; its very existence was threatened in one country after another. Japan developed a strong national religion called Shinto; China adopted the philosophy of Lao-Tze (Taoism) and the moral principles of Confucius; India reactivated its once dormant Hinduism; southeast Asia came under the militant influence of Islam. And all the while Christianity was making its own progress in Indochina.

By the twentieth century, the religious map of Asia had drastically changed. Lands like Borneo, Java, and Sumatra had become dominantly Moslem. India was once more strongly Hindu. Japan was predominantly Shinto. China settled for a Universism that was part Confucian, part Taoist, and decreasingly Buddhist. The former Indochina, and present Vietnam, acquired the largest concentration of Christians in Asia.

This forced Buddhism into two extremes: the practical syncretism with other Oriental faiths in China and Japan, and the intense fundamentalism under pressure from monotheistic Islam and Christianity in Burma, Ceylon, Thailand, and northern Vietnam. Symptomatic of this trend, Burma adopted Buddhism as the state religion in 1961 and Ceylon in 1966 abolished Sunday as a legal holiday, substituting *poya* days—which mark the four phases of the moon in the Buddhist lunar calendar.

The significance of all this for our purpose is twofold. It is unrealistic to speak of Buddhism in univocal terms, as though almost anything said of it is what all Buddhists believe or practice. It is also unhistorical to call practically anything uniquely Buddhist, as though it derived unilaterally from Buddha. Hovering over both factors is the astonishing change occurring everywhere in Buddhist circles, across the spectrum of faith and worship, either toward amalgamation with other religious cultures or toward isolation within its own inherent creed.

FOUR NOBLE TRUTHS

Where Hinduism claims no single person as its founder and traces its beliefs to the teachings of no historical persons, Buddhism from the beginning was a religion of discipleship. Its adherents were the followers of one man, whom posterity has come to call the Buddha, the Enlightened One.

It is immaterial that conflicting dates are given for the life-span of Buddha, ranging from 563 B.C. to as late as 326 B.C. What seems certain is that Buddha really lived and that the main outline of his original teaching has come down to us with some degree of accuracy.

His personal name was Siddhartha and the surname, Gautama. Since he belonged to a sub-clan of the warrior or Kshatriya caste, he was also called Sakya-Muni. The name Buddha came to be applied to him by his followers because he had attained bodhi or enlightenment. A synonym which he preferred was Tathagata, that is, one who had reached the summit of enlightenment and realized it himself.

After some years of apparently happy married life, Gautama left home and family in search of the secret of release from the prospect of repeated *samsaras* or reincarnations. The quest took him years, and in the process he tried every known method suggested by the different schools of Hindu thought. He tried, in sequence, all the honored paths of escaping what the Vedas said was every man's destiny. He worked specially hard at the mortification of his body and inflicted on himself every manner of ascetical indignity. But the harder he tried the further seemed the prospect of achieving what he sought.

Then gradually one night came the light. According to legend, he was sitting under a tree on the banks of a river near a place now called Bodhgaya. The vision came in three stages. It began by his

39

resolution to try concentrating his attention as he had done once before, only this time with greater effort. He fell into a trance.

During the first part of the night he reached the faculty of recalling his past incarnations, going back hundreds and thousands of previous lives. It was a terrifying spectacle of memory. During the middle of the night, he arrived at the insight of how reincarnation takes place, how a person changes habitat from one life to another. Finally as morning drew near, he discovered the secret of how to avoid any further rebirth, for himself and others. Henceforth he was the Buddha, the One-who-had-seen.

In view of the wide range of later developments in Buddhism, we should keep the essentials in focus. These essentials are agreed upon by all Buddhists and may be found in the earliest accounts of what Buddha preached to his followers.

The clearest account of Buddha's inaugural sermon contains all the basic elements of historic Buddhism. The story relates that his first audience was five ascetics looking for guidance, and the place was the Deer Park at Benares, the holy city of the Hindus, in the Ganges Valley of northern India.

Buddha had discovered that there are Four Noble Truths to explain how *samsara* can be escaped. No one has improved on his own description of each truth. He addressed the men as Bhikkhus, a common title for ascetics in his day, which he later adopted for the members of his monastic community.

> This, O Bhikkhus, is the Noble Truth of Suffering: Birth is suffering; decay is suffering; illness is suffering; death is suffering. Presence of objects we hate is suffering; separation from objects we love is suffering; not to obtain what we desire is suffering. Briefly, the fivefold clinging to existence is suffering.

> This, O Bhikkhus, is the Noble Truth of the Cause of Suffering: Thirst, that leads to rebirth, accompanied by pleasure and lust, finding its delight here and there. This thirst is threefold, namely, thirst for pleasure, thirst for existence, thirst for prosperity.

> This, O Bhikkhus, is the Noble Truth of the Cessation of Suffering: It ceases with the complete cessation of this thirst— a cessation which consists in the absence of every passion,—with the abandoning of this thirst, with the doing away with it, with the deliverance from it, with the destruction of desire.

This, O Bhikkhus, is the Noble Truth of the Path which leads to the cessation of suffering: that holy eightfold Path, that is to say—Right Belief, Right Aspiration, Right Speech, Right Conduct, Right Means of Livelihood, Right Endeavor, Right Mindfulness, Right Meditation.[2]

These four principles stand at the head of all Buddhist cultures, no matter how far removed they may seem to be from the original teaching of the master. Each has a wealth of spiritual meaning for anyone who takes the trouble to learn, which is not easy, on premises that are as Oriental as the Pali or Sanskrit languages in which they have come down to us.

Buddha resisted every attempt by his disciples to have him prove these Noble Truths. He had seen their validity in vision; others were to accept what he told them, or else stop calling themselves Buddhists. He came to preach a faith and not to teach a philosophy.

The goal he promised those who believed in him was Nirvana, which again he never cared to define. Pressed to give a rational account of his doctrine, he told a parable that says a great deal about Buddhism as a simple, unreasoning faith.

It is as if a man had been wounded by an arrow thickly smeared with poison, and his friends and kinsmen were to get a surgeon to heal him, and he were to say, "I will not have this arrow pulled out until I know by what man I was wounded, whether he is of the warrior caste, or a Brahmin, or of the agricultural, or the lowest caste." Or if he were to say, "I will not have this arrow pulled out until I know of what name of family this man is; or whether he is tall or short, or of middle height; or whether he is black or dark or yellowish; or whether he comes from such and such a village or town or city; or until I know whether the bow with which I was wounded was a chapa or a kodanda, or until I know whether the bow string was of swallow-wort, or bamboo fiber, or sinew, or hemp, or of milk-sap tree, or until I know whether the shaft was from a wild or cultivated plant. . . ." Before knowing all this, that man would die.

Similarly, it is not on the view that the world is eternal, that it is finite, that the body and soul are distinct, or that the Buddha exists after death that a religious life depends. Whether these views or opposites are held, there is still rebirth, there is

41

old age, there is death, and grief, lamentation, suffering, sorrow, and despair. . . . I have not spoken of these views because they do not lead to absence of passion, that is, to tranquillity and Nirvana.[3]

In Buddha's view, reincarnation was as obvious as the fact of sickness and death. He expected his disciples to be equally sure that the method he proposed for escaping endless birth and rebirth was true. Buddha never argued and, to this day, there is an elaborate Buddhist religion but no Buddhist philosophy.

TO LIVE IS TO SUFFER

The first great truth in Buddha's tetralogy is more absolute than some Western writers would have us think. He did not merely say that no human life is without suffering, nor that suffering is the common lot of all men. He stated in categorical terms that to live is to suffer or, if possible, even more categorically that existence equals pain.

The moment the principle is enunciated we find ourselves in a different world from that of the Vedas or Upanishads. Buddhism begins within man's consciousness and it never leaves the realm of subjective introspection. Hovering over this interior psychic world like an atmosphere is the awareness of suffering.

Gautama wanted to make sure his disciples were not distracted from this awareness, otherwise all the rest of his doctrine would be irrelevant. It was only on the premise of a man's deepest realization of the miseries of life that he would seriously undertake the difficult path which led to emancipation, where emancipation in Buddha's new vocabulary meant deliverance from the subjective experience of present existence.

Notice the change in focus. Buddha equated as the starting point of his system the faith in reincarnation with the fact of suffering. He assumed that it makes little difference at what stage in the cycle of rebirths a man finds himself. All men, without exception, are miserable.

He also understood that most people want to hide the fact of their misery; they either try to drown their sorrows by indulging in pleasure, at one extreme; or they try to dull their wretchedness by practicing asceticism, the other extreme. He opted for the golden mean, which did not mean some indulgence balanced with some discipline, but burrowing inside the human psyche to discover why every one suffers. In other words, suffering may be relieved by debauchery or mortification, but it cannot be removed in that way.

To remove suffering we must get at its root cause, which is the second Noble Truth. But before going on to the second, the first Truth must be firmly known.

In order to insure certainty about the fact of suffering, Gautama bade his followers contemplate the sordid aspects of life. He encouraged counteracting like with like, that is, the tendency to one kind of pleasure as a palliative for pain should be overcome by the precise opposite of the pleasure being sought. Thus if a man was prone to sexual pleasure, he should be exercised in exposure to bodily horror. The most highly recommended, first suggested by Buddha, was a visit to the cemetery or charnel house where all the senses will experience the condition of a decaying corpse.

While looking at the foul state to which a body is reduced soon after death, he will be disinclined to indulge the same body when still alive. He sees the body "bound up in skin and soaked in blood, covered with hide, overspread with masses of flesh, all overlaid with a thousand veins."[4] He sees it as nothing but a collection of bones, joints, tendons, skin with pores that are constantly exuding impurities, a haven for worms, a home for disease, where filth oozes from the eyes, ears, nose, and lower extremities.[5]

Buddhist literature abounds in classifications of suffering, but finally reduces it to two main categories, one theoretical and the other practical.

On the theoretical side, suffering is the subjective state which may arise from one or all of three situations. It may be ordinary suffering as physical pain or mental anguish. Or on a deeper level, it may be the result of drastic change, from enjoyment to its deprivation. Or finally, suffering at its worst is the "state of conditionedness," which means the condition of not being free, when a man is either prevented from acquiring what he wants or is forced to accept what he does not want.

Each of these states has its own scale of intensity. Plain endurance may be greater or less, and always in Buddhist belief physical pain is much lower in depth than suffering in the mind. In the same way, the suffering caused by change for the worse will be less severe when the previous enjoyment was not so great, or the loss gradual and not so sudden, or the deprivation partial and not complete. So, too, the lack of freedom may be more or less painful; less painful when a man's wants are frustrated and worse when he is constrained against his will; less painful when the frustrated ambition is of something not so ardently sought and more grievous when frustration involves an object on which one's whole heart had set; less painful when coercion is only mildly against a man's wishes and heaviest when submission demands the acceptance of what a man hates.

In practical terms, Buddha reduced suffering to "the five-fold clinging to existence," which meant the grasping for bodily form or shape, pleasant feeling or sensation, attraction of the will, internal fantasies and mental consciousness. More prosaically expressed, suffering arises in the five areas in which happiness is commonly sought: in the body's external senses, in sensual feelings, in volitional experience, in the imagination and deep inside the mind.

The key word here is evidently "clinging to existence," by which Gautama understood suffering existentially. We suffer, he would say, because we insist on finding happiness in these five faculties of our being. So much for the fact. But why do we suffer? On the answer to this question rests the Buddha's second Noble Truth.

CAUSE OF SUFFERING

Faced with the fact that all men suffer, Buddha asked himself why. He said the reason was because they gave in to illusion. Their desires betrayed them constantly in seeking for satisfaction, when fulfillment of desire was ruled out.

Before going any further, it will help to isolate the exact principle that Buddha was advocating. He was not merely saying that people suffer because, quite naturally, they often do not get what they want. Or they crave things too strongly, or look for achievement too quickly. Moderation in all things is a Greek proverb; it is also Jewish and Christian prudence. But it is not Buddhist morality.

In orthodox Buddhist theory, the whole litany of things mentioned makes us unhappy because we are plagued by the blind thirst (tanha) which drives us madly to seek what the universe cannot give. Note what we are saying: what the universe cannot give. It is therefore not delayed enjoyment or incomplete happiness, or expecting more than is available. This thirst is mad because it craves things which cannot be had.

Not a few writers, both Oriental and Western, have tried to soften the impact of this cardinal premise of classic Buddhism. One reason they give is that so many Buddhists nowadays do not seem to subscribe to its devastating implications. But that is beside the point. Buddhism is a system of thought whose principles are found in the authentic and original Buddhist scriptures. Twenty-five hundred years have brought many changes in religion and practice, and many Buddhists now are only slightly affected by the basic principles of their traditional faith. The same could be said of many Christians. Yet Christianity is not to be measured by the fidelity of its adherents but by the fundamental doctrines which the founder of Christianity taught are to be followed.

Moreover, just as in Christianity, so in Buddhism a large body of believers has remained substantially faithful to the teaching of the Enlightened One. They may differ immensely in their interpretation of what the Buddha meant, but they agree substantially on what he said. It is this agreement that allows us, or anyone, to talk about Buddhism at all, and be able to cut through the variety of schools and sectarian divisions. They have at least a common starting point.

This common starting point is the affirmation of two unqualified negatives: the denial of a real world of permanent essences or natures, and the denial of the perduring Ego or self.

Buddha borrowed both negations from certain Hindu sources, which he finecombed to support his main thesis.

Instead of one world with stable natures, Buddhist scriptures maintain that everything is a becoming, without beginning or end. Early Buddhist exegetes proposed a theory of evolution that put the whole universe through a process of birth and rebirth, a sort of cosmic reincarnation. In the limitless expanse of space, they argued, an infinite number of worlds come into existence and pass away through beginningless and endless time. A single cycle for reincarnating the world takes a *kalpa* or aeon. Once asked how long that would be, the Buddha gave a simile. Suppose there was a towering mountain peak, four leagues in size—height, width, and length the same. One solid block of rock without a crack. Suppose a man came along once every hundred years and gently wiped that mountain with a fine piece of cloth. The mountain would have long been worn away before a single *kalpa* will have passed.

Equally unstable, or better unreal, is the human self which people foolishly try to satisfy. Buddha called it *anatta* or the doctrine that there is no permanent self or soul in man. He searched through

45

the Upanishads and found there numerous passages asserting the Self or Athman as not only real, but in some texts claimed to be the only Reality there is.

Buddha reacted against Hinduism in its foundations. He was not interested in the domestic dispute among Hindus as to whether the Athman was actually Brahman, and man's destiny meant discovering that he and Brahman are one; or whether the Self was distinct from Brahman and the goal of human life is to finally be united with the transcendent Absolute. For Gautama the major premise of Hinduism was untrue. He spared no adjectives in denouncing what to him was the most deceitful delusion ever held by man. Why deceitful? Because it gave rise to attachment, attachment to egoism, egoism to cravings for pleasure and fame, all of which in turn leads to suffering.

The basis for Buddha's denial of true selfhood is traced by all his followers to a sacred writing entitled *Questions of King Melinda*. In this work, the master's ideas are recorded in a dialogue between the king and a Buddhist sage named Nagasena.

Nagasena opens the dialogue by asserting what he wants to prove to the king. "Your Majesty," he starts, "I am called Nagasena. However, that is just a way of counting, a term, an appelation, a convenient designation, a mere name, this Nagasena. For there is no ego here to be found." On hearing this, the king protests.

> Nagasena, if there is no ego to be found, who is it then, furnished you priests with the priestly requisites—robes, food, bedding and medicine, the reliance of the sick? Who is it makes use of the same? Who is it keeps the precepts? Who is it applies himself to meditation? Who is it destroys life? Who is it takes what is not given him? Who is it commits immorality? Who is it tells lies? In that case there is no merit; there is no demerit; there is no one who does or causes to be done meritorious or demeritorious deeds; neither good nor evil deeds can have any fruit or result.[6]

To press his point further, the king asks the preacher a series of questions (forty-five) about various parts of Nagasena's body or personality—his skin, nails, lungs, brain, sensation. "Are they not Nagasena?" Each time the Buddhist answers, "No." His Majesty is confused. He accuses the sage of speaking falsehoods. There is no Nagasena.

Gradually Nagasena leads the monarch to admit that all the terms applied to a person's limbs or faculties are just names, no less than the parts of a chariot are labels used to designate what really exists only in the mind. "In the absolute sense," he concludes, "there is no ego here to be found. And the priestess Vajira, Your Majesty, said as follows in the presence of the Blessed One (Buddha), 'Even as the word *chariot* means that members join to frame a whole, so when the groups appear to view, we use the phrase *a living being.*'"[7] All reality is merely conceptual.

This central teaching of the Buddha has never been minimized by those who are faithful to his memory. If we are to trace the source of human suffering, we must look for it in the error of giving validity to desires. In the Buddhist faith, desires are unreal on two counts: they wrongly postulate a stable universe which is really in constant flux, and a substantial Ego which is only a stream of subjective impressions naïvely called the Self.

EXTINCTION OF SUFFERING

Given the first and second Noble Truths, the third was inevitable. To be rid of suffering, one must extinguish thirst or desire.

Once again Buddhism appears as a counterpoise to Hinduism. The preoccupation of the Hindu thinkers was to dispel ignorance and thereby achieve union with or awareness of oneness with Brahman. The Hindu thrust is intellectual.

Not so in Buddhism. When Gautama urged believers to extinguish thirst, he meant it. Instead of a mental exercise of discovery as a means of final liberation, he proposed volitional effort, and instead of talking about truth and falsehood he stressed bliss and suffering, their subjective counterparts.

There is one more Noble Truth to Buddhism, the eight-step Path to Nirvana. This is only the practical implementation of what the third Truth says in principle: to achieve the goal of human destiny one must snuff out the inveterate desire all men are born with—their hankering for pleasure, for prosperity, and for existence.

The term *extinction* was well chosen. To extinguish something means to quench it, as when a person puts water on a light or fire to cause it to die out. There is the connotation of something burning which is stopped, or the idea of nullifying what is itself destructive if allowed to continue. You check a destructive process by extinguishing its progress.

This is a process, as we shall see, that is long and tedious, and not many people have the patience or strength of character to carry it through, which explains why Buddhism (at its center) is an esoteric religion that was originally meant only for the elite. It was no accident that Buddha long resisted having women as disciples. He thought they were too weak to take his teaching seriously. It was also not coincidental that his religion was meant to be monastic, with all the implications of segregation from the world and individual self-advancement apart from the madding crowd.

It is also a process that each one must work through by himself. Other human beings may help, and therefore community life is useful, but in the last analysis everyone saves himself. There is no room for grace in the Judaeo-Christian sense of divine assistance on the way to salvation, or even in the sense that Krishna in the Bhagavad Gita promised help to those who rely on him in loving devotion.

The aim of this extinction of desire is Nirvana, a term that has entered the vocabulary of all nations and yet is little understood—no doubt because Buddha could never be persuaded to explain it. Yet some understanding of Nirvana is necessary if contemporary Buddhism is to be intelligible to those who are not Buddhists. Our guide in the analysis will be Buddha and his interpreters since the word first came into use some five centuries before the time of Jesus of Nazareth.

Nirvana, as the spiritual destiny of Buddhism is the Sanskrit for the more accurate Pali word, *Nibbana*, and literally means "blowing away," as one would extinguish a lamp.

Throughout life, all of Buddha's sermons, exhortations, and counselings had only one theme, Nirvana. Yet the important question for him was not, "What is Nirvana?" but, "How is Nirvana attained?" His mission, he said, was not to explain theoretically what Nirvana means, but to witness for the Nirvana which he personally experienced when the light dawned on him under the bodhi tree. His towering urge to communicate a method did not include the wish, if he had the ability, to tell others what this method led to. Let them find out for themselves as he did, that a man who has achieved Nirvana "is like a deer living in a forest, who might lie down on a heap of snares, but is not caught by them."

Some clarification of what Nirvana means is necessary if we are to distinguish among the numerous schools of Buddhist thought and, above all, between the two great divisions of Buddhist faith, the older and more orthodox Hinayana, and the later but more popular Mahayana.

At the outset should be mentioned that all Buddhists agree on two stages of Nirvana, which correspond to the double meaning of the word itself. *Nirvana* denotes becoming cold, as in the case of one who has cooled his passions, and also denotes blowing out, as when a man puts out a flame.

Among Buddha's sermons was one on fire, in which he taught that the whole world was inflamed by the fires of greed, lust, hatred, and ignorance, and that only in Nirvana were these fires extinguished irrevocably.

Elsewhere, however, he referred to two kinds of Nirvana, one with a residue and another without a residue. The first type meant the condition attained by a living saint (*arhat*) in whom the five aggregates (*skandhas*) were still present, that is, he still had a material body, feelings, perception, predispositions, and consciousness; but the desires that bind him to existence had been snuffed out.

To illustrate this first kind of Nirvana, the story was told of the Buddha that on one occasion he was asked if he had seen some beautiful women pass by. Whereupon the master replied that he had not, but on further reflection he admitted that just a few moments ago he had heard some skeletons rattling along the road.

It was this state of enlightenment that Buddha attained here and now in his present state of life, when at thirty-five he discovered the secret of escape from reincarnation.

The second type is more often called Parinirvana, which occurs when a person dies and that, presumably, Buddha entered into when at the age of eighty he passed out of this world.

All the evidence indicates that the original interpretation of Parinirvana was to identify it with total annihilation. Buddhist sacred writings in the Pali tradition of southeast Asia leave no room for doubt. A human being is conceived as a conglomeration of physical and psychical elements that keep changing every moment. Ordinary people never touch this stream of life before death. When they die, their *karma* (past deeds) and unquenched desires project them into another organism, and they start over again.

But the perfect saint or Buddha has exhausted his karma by having quenched his desires. There is no more cause for further rebirth. Two statements about Buddha are quoted by all who favor this kind of Nirvana.

49

The Blessed One passed away by that kind of passing away in which no root remains for the formation of another individual. The Blessed One has come to an end and it can not be pointed out of him that he is here or there.[8]

That bodily form of the Tathagata is abandoned, cut down at the root, made something that is not, made of a nature not to spring up again in future time.[9]

To this day a large body of Buddhists hold that the universe and all that is in it, including man, is devolving toward a final extinction. The Theravada tradition (Hinayana) that dominates in Ceylon, Laos, Burma, and Vietnam considers Nirvana some kind of nonexistence.

By the first century of the Christian era, a new tendency developed. Buddha came to be first superhumanized and then deified. More remarkable still, the Hindu *avatars* or incarnations of the god Vishnu were extended to number ten, of whom the eighth was said to be Krishna and the ninth Buddha.

At this point, Buddhism flowered into as many varieties as there had been forms of Hinduism, but principally three that affect the concept of Nirvana. Some held that Nirvana meant the attainment of a state of happiness comparable to that of Buddha. Reaching Buddhahood was the culmination of human existence. In this theory, desires are extinguished because their object is fulfilled.

Others came closer to the Upanishad notion of Brahman as the Absolute and only Reality. Nirvana for them would be the cessation of desire upon enlightenment that all but Brahman is nonentity. A man "reaches" his destiny on discovering that he had none.

Still others took Buddha as literally God, while divorcing him from the historical personage by that name. Nirvana then becomes the attainment of Buddha in a paradise he created for those who during life love and serve him. Desires come to an end because Buddha Amitabha (Infinite Light) satisfies them.

So far theory. Yet Buddhism is eminently practical, and the real genius of Buddha consisted in the method he mapped out for achieving Nirvana. It was the eightfold Path. If Gautama had done nothing else but left posterity this technique for conquering pain, his contribution would have been monumental. He made the method part of a religion, and, as a consequence, reshaped the faith of more than half the world.

THE EIGHTFOLD PATH

Now that we have come to the essence of Buddhism, it is necessary to insert some qualifications. While all Buddhists in the world today subscribe to the eightfold Path as found in Buddha's writings, they explain the Magga (Way) differently and, on this difference, rests a balanced estimate of living Buddhism.

We begin with the sacred text in which Buddha himself is preaching the Path. Tradition places it in his first sermon at Benares.

> The Exalted One said: "What, bhikkhus, is the Aryan (Noble) Truth concerning the Way that leads to the Cessation of Ill? This is the Aryan Eight-Fold Path, namely, right view, right aspiration, right speech, right doing, right livelihood, right effort, right mindfulness, right rapture."[10]

Transmitting numerous subdivisions and lesser schools of thought, present-day Buddhism has two main forms: the Hinayana which derives from the Pali scriptures and is closest to what Buddha originally taught, and Mahayana which follows the Sanskrit tradition and has certainly changed the orientation of Buddha's legacy.

The two names are symbolic. Hinayana literally means "the lesser vehicle," implying that only a chosen few are able to follow it. Characteristic of Buddhism in southern and southeastern Asia, it is also called Theravada or "school of the elders." Mahayana· stands for the opposite. As "the larger vehicle" it appeals to the teeming millions and not only to ascetic monks. As the dominant religion in China and Japan, it has permeated every facet of Sino-Japanese life and culture.

Our attempt here is first to give the brief statement of Buddha himself on each of the eight stages toward Nirvana, followed immediately by an explanation of each successive stage according to the two main forms of Buddhist theology. It will correspond, very approximately, to comparing Catholic and Protestant interpretations of something like the Eight Beatitudes.

Buddha prefixed the word "Right" to each step, *Samma* in Pali. By this he meant to indicate that it was the "proper" or "assured" way of reaching Nirvana.

Right understanding

The master opened his discourse by asking "What, bhikkhus, is right view (*ditthi*)?" He answered by saying it was the right kind of understanding: "Knowledge about suffering, knowledge about the cause of suffering, knowledge about the cessation of suffering, knowledge about the way that leads to the extinction of suffering."[11]

In plain terms, the first step in Buddhist methodology is to have faith as an assent of the mind to what Buddha taught. His doctrine was to be normative and his teachings incontestable. What makes them dogmas is their unquestioned acceptance by anyone who calls himself a Buddhist; what makes them right is their infallible power to extinguish human desires and thus liberate from the "wheel of existence."

Orthodox Buddhism (Hinayana) considers this knowledge self-appropriated. Anyone can come by the insight if only he takes the trouble, much as Buddha did in his day. Popular Buddhism begins with the postulate that man is not self-sufficient. Where Buddha is deified, it is said to be inconceivable that the Compassionate One could be so indifferent to the needs of his people as to not come to their aid. Right understanding, on these premises, is partly if not entirely a gift from above.

Right-mindedness

Buddha realized that faith was not enough. It had to be sustained by directing the mind to thinking in the right way. He used the unexpected term "aspiration" to describe what this meant. Right-mindedness, then, is "the aspiration toward renunciation, the aspiration toward benevolence, the aspiration toward kindness."[12]

Basically, the logic of the second step is that acceptance of Buddha's teaching needs to be kept alive by reflecting on what he taught. Ever the practical man, however, Buddha was not satisfied with speculative thinking. It had to be put into practice by creating what can best be described as an attitude of mind that would prompt a man to overcome himself by doing the opposite of what he was naturally prone to do. In Buddha's terms, right-mindedness meant to preserve one's thoughts "free from lust, from ill will and from cruelty." Cultivating the attitude of renunciation of pleasure, of benevolence and kindness would counteract the negative triad.

Nowhere else is orthodox Buddhism more radically different from its popular derivate than in explaining the second stage of the eightfold Path.

Whatever the orthodox may have been at one time, they are now essentially a monastic order whose principal task in life is self-denial and meditation. They, therefore, explain this second step as mainly the object of reflection and the gradual suffocation of all natural passion.

Mahayana Buddhism, on the contrary, takes the master at his word and urges the people to practice renunciation, indeed, but in the exercise of charity rather than self-discipline.

The praise of charity among Mahayanists begins inside a man's mind. Commentators in this tradition are explicit on how this should be done.

> First deeply reflect on the likeness which exists between yourself and others. "Since all have the same pains and the same joys as I have, I should care for them as I care for myself." The body, despite the differences between its various members, is looked after as a single thing; it should be the same with the world in which different beings have their joys and sorrows in common.
>
> Reflecting on the fact that you are yourself full of faults and that others are brimming over with good qualities, you will endeavor to throw off your own personality and adopt that of others.
>
> You are interested in your various members as parts of your body; why not in men as parts of humanity? The person who wants to save himself must practice the great secret: put himself in the place of others.[13]

Coming from a recent Buddhist spiritual writer, there is no way of telling how much of these sentiments is original Mahayana. Nevertheless it illustrates the chasm that separates the two forms of the religion; both preoccupied with self-release, but one is concerned with speculation and asceticism while the other sees in charity the means of salvation.

Right speech

Buddha's psychology is consistent. He has the disciple start with thinking the right kind of thoughts, and now tells him to practice the right kind of speech. Specifically, he says it consists in, "abstaining from lying, slander, abuse and idle talk."

The more rigid forms of Buddhist orthodoxy take this passage at face value. Right speech means just that, avoid telling the untruth or harming anyone with the tongue.

But the popular religion goes much further. Not only should a man abstain from committing injustice against others by hurting them in words; but he should talk kindly to and about them even though they have no claim on his charity. "He speaks such words as are gentle, soothing to the ear, loving, going to the heart, courteous and pleasing, and agreeable to many."[14]

It is in this context that Mahayana Buddhists in China and Japan found their justification for engaging in the "apostolate" of teaching. If speaking kind words is praiseworthy and leads to Nirvana, how much more meritorious is using the same faculty of speech to instruct others. The Sanskrit canon of the Buddhist Bible quotes the Buddha to that effect. He is speaking to a monk by the name of Subhuti.

> The Lord Buddha continued: "Subhuti, if any disciple heaped together the seven treasures forming an elevation as high as Mount Sumeru and as many Mount Sumerus as there are in three thousand great universes, and bestowed them in charity, his merits would be less than what would accrue to the disciple that simply observed and studied this Scripture and in the kindness of his heart explained it to others. The latter disciple would accumulate greater blessing and merit in comparison of a hundred to one, yes, of a hundred thousand myriads to one. Nothing can be compared with it."[15]

Backtracking for a moment, this quotation throws considerable light on the opposite tradition, the Theravada people. When they read such passages in their Pali Bible they conclude that the highest form of charity is not actual giving of material goods or relieving of physical misery. Let lesser mortals do that, if they choose. Meditation and self-conquest endow a person with extraordinary wisdom, based on Buddha's revelation. To communicate this wisdom to others through education is far more noble and, according to the Buddha, far more effective for teacher and pupil in reaching the Nirvanic goal. Over the centuries, Buddhist monasteries have been centers of learning, and the reason was this precept of the master.

Right action

Buddha continues on the same faculty level as before, where the right kind of thoughts lead to the right kind of talk. The next step is to assert that correct speech somehow leads to the right sort of action. The actual text in which the precept occurs is not inspiring. To do the right thing, he tells his monks, is to "abstain from taking life, from taking what is not given, from carnal indulgence." In so many words, he is urging people not to kill, not to steal and not to give in to sexual excess.

At every point in the Nirvanic process, the conduct prescribed may have more than one degree of perfection. Accordingly Right Action may be practiced more or less perfectly. The less perfect form, in the words of Buddha, consists in "abstaining from killing, from stealing, and from unlawful sexual intercourse." On a higher plane, though, not only are these crimes avoided externally but a man detests them from within.

> The abhorrence of the practice of this three-fold wrong action, the abstaining, withholding, refraining therefrom—the mind being holy, being turned away from the world and conjoined with the path, the holy path being pursued—this is called the Ultramundane Right Action, which is not of the world.[16]

Another term for "ultramundane" might be "supernatural," in the sense that Buddha thought only of internal dispositions as truly effective of release from future incarnations. The good order of any society would prohibit murder, robbery, and sexual perversity. It was the interior abhorrence of these wrongdoings that alone had salvific value.

Correspondingly, these good actions might mean nothing more than the practice of elementary justice, or at least avoiding elementary injustice. Hinayana generally settles for that and nothing more. Not so the Mahayanists who constitute the majority of world Buddhists, especially in China.

Buddhist charity, as it is called, fits into the scheme of salvation as an expression of the fourth stage on the road to extinction of desire. Buddha's favorite term for this charity is "loving-kindness," which, he teaches, must come from the heart.

> None of the means employed to acquire religious merit, O monks, has a sixteenth part of the value of loving-kindness. Loving-kindness, which is freedom of heart, absorbs them all; it glows, it shines, it blazes forth.
>
> And in the same way, O monks, as the light of all the stars has not a sixteenth part of the value of moonlight, but the moonlight absorbs and glows and shines and blazes forth; in the

same way, O monks, none of the means employed to acquire religious merit has a sixteenth part of the value of loving-kindness.[17]

So the panegyric goes on; stars compared with moon, moon with sun—in order to bring out the glowing superiority of charity over all other means of reaching Nirvana.

The Buddhist penchant for the number four, or its multiples, has devised four planes of charity, each higher than the preceding. It begins with *ahimsa* (not harming), grows into *maitri* (loving-kindness), finds expression in *dana* (giving), and reaches perfection in *karuna* (compassion). Each stage has abundant literature to illustrate its presence and qualities, and especially to exhort the monks and laity to put it into practice.

Before we leave this little known feature of Buddhism, a word must be said about the models for the practice of charity that have entered the religion of Buddha. They are known as *bodhisattvas* and rank in importance with the angels and saints in Judaeo-Christianity.

The name means "a *bodhi* being," or "one whose whole nature is permeated with *bodhi* (enlightenment)" and, as such, appears in the ancient writings. It meant anyone who was on the point of entering on the supreme incarnation as a Buddha, but stopped at the bodhisattva stage out of compassion for a suffering humanity. In his love and pity, he preferred to remain in a position where he could help others, and therefore postponed his elevation to the full rank of a Buddha.

Bodhisattvas are believed to live in a semicelestial state, while periodically coming down to earth in one of many incarnations, often in answer to prayer or in fulfillment of a promise made during their mortal sojourn among men.

If bodhisattvas are a peculiar creation of Mahayana Buddhism, they are also its most distinctive feature. They shifted the whole center of gravity in a large part of Buddhist doctrine from concentration on self to the opposite extreme. The word is "extreme," because the strange tales told about bodhisattva charity are too extravagant to be taken literally. There is the story, among hundreds, of a bodhisattva monk whose compassion let a licentious woman seduce him; of a father who voluntarily gave his two children to a Brahmin as slaves; of a man who took pity on a starving tigress and let her devour him; of a husband who freely surrendered his wife for the asking; of the bodhisattva who turned himself into a hare, was roasted, and thus gave food to a starving Brahmin.

Accustomed to this kind of extravaganza, the average Buddhist believer took refuge in symbolism. He correctly assumed that only a vague sort of generosity was signified by all the imagery, and the very exponents of superhuman charity confirmed the assumption.

This touches on both the greatest strength and the greatest weakness in popular Buddhist piety. The strength came from Buddha's shifting the emphasis from mind to will, and from speculation to morality. He changed what had been Hindu philosophy into an authentic religion. The weakness lay in so stressing the purpose and intention that the action a man performs was often reduced to a meaningless phrase. One of the most respected Buddhist scholars held that "the thought of sacrificing all one possesses—even the fruit of one's sacrifice—to all things, is the perfection of charity. Charity is therefore entirely of the mind."[18] So that every human action, even the most pleasant and insignificant—like eating or going to bed, washing one's hands or sitting down—gathers immense Nirvanic value provided the motive is to benefit "all things." Not the actions themselves, but the desire to put them into effect constitutes virtue.

This notion of charity as love minus the observance of law has been severely taken to task by the Buddhists themselves, with critics from the Hinayana and Mahayana camps. It also explains why, in China, Buddhism could not have survived without the strong support of Confucian ethics which provided a saving balance to this "morality of mere intention." Without objective principles, love without law becomes decadent situation ethics.

Right livelihood

There is not much help in the actual words of Gautama on the next stage of his eightfold Path. "The Aryan disciple," he declared, "having put away wrong livelihood, supports himself by the right livelihood."[19] Even when he elsewhere comments further on this step, he merely repeats himself.

Some light is shed on the matter when Buddha explains that a man practices the correct form of livelihood when he follows the right mode of understanding, lives with an attentive mind, and exercises the proper kind of effort. Since understanding is fundamental to the whole process and effort with attention is one step removed from Nirvana—right living is a synthesis of all the conditions necessary to reach one's destiny.

Concretely this would include the whole gamut of a person's life, which in Buddhist language meant living a monastic (or quasi-monastic) life. Buddha made monasticism an inseparable part of his creed, and the *Triratna*, or Three Jewels, which Gautama prescribed on all his followers were: "I believe in the Buddha, in Dharma (law) and Sangha (monastic order)." As originally conceived, the function of Buddhist monasticism was to provide an orderly communal living for its members and to teach the principles and practice of Buddhism to others.

In the twenty-five hundred years since Buddha's death, the religion he founded has undergone numerous changes. Yet the monastic feature remains. Several thousand monasteries in both traditions, Hinayana and Mahayana, testify to the enduring faith in formal monastic living for those who are physically and psychologically able to follow the strict Sangha regime. But every Buddhist is expected to practice the spirit if not the letter of monasticism no matter what his position or career.

For the laity this implies a certain regularity in their daily routine, a pattern of chores done at a given hour, a rhythmic sequence of rising and retiring, and (above all) a monastic indifference to food and drink and the comforts of life which only those who know the poverty of the Orient can understand.

The name Vimalakirti, a disciple of Buddha, is a household word in Buddhist circles of a layman who achieved Nirvana by his right living without even entering a monastery. His memory has been kept alive as the paragon of sanctity. "Though he is but a simple layman," states the official hagiography, "yet observing the pure monastic discipline; though living at home, yet never desirous of anything; though possessing a wife and children, always exercising pure virtues; though surrounded by his family, holding aloof from worldly pleasures."[20] So the eulogy tells his praises, stressing that faithful Buddhists live disciplined lives whether in the monastery or in the world.

Right effort

As the Buddha approached nearer the goal of extinguished desires, he became more eloquent on the conditions needed to reach the goal. His analysis of Right Effort is detailed.

What, bhikkhus, is right effort? Herein a brother makes effort to bring forth acts of the will to prevent evil and bad states from arising. To this end he stirs up energy, he grips and forces his mind. He does the same to put away evil and bad states that may have arisen within him. He does the same to have good states arise that have not yet risen. He does the same that good states which have arisen may persist, may not grow blurred, may multiply, grow abundant, develop and come to perfection.[21]

In this short paragraph we have a summary of Buddhism's main contribution to religious psychology. Buddha's claim to fame rests mainly on the fact that he isolated the role of the will as the ultimate source of morality. Given the premises of the Buddhist faith, a man's reaching Nirvana is not some vague design of the gods but the fruit of personal volitional effort.

Moreover, when Buddha came to identify what this free will of man is capable of doing, he specified its power over the mind. If a man wants to, he can master the most interior and elusive faculty of his nature, the wild intellect that needs constant attention and that resists taming.

In Buddhist literature the mind is usually likened to a monkey, jumping hither and thither, and unable to dwell for more than a moment on any one point. The purpose of right effort is to bring the mind to remain centered on thoughts that by Buddhist standards are good and to keep it off thoughts that are bad.

This volitional power over the mind is sovereign. Buddha assumes the believer is already convinced that certain trains of thought are harmful because they divert a man from the single aim on which he should focus: how to be rid of desires. Based on this conviction, the will is duly motivated to exert its influence and actually bend the intellect in the right direction, namely toward the extinction of every appetitive drive that a person experiences.

He further assumes that what needs mastery is the states of mind that keep arising unbidden. He might have called them moods. The result is a four-ply control of the intellectual imagination by the ever alert free will. The images arising in the mental fancy may be either bad or good, that is, they may suggest either giving in to desires or resisting them; and the images may be only anticipated or they may already be in the fancy. From every angle the autonomous will has the upper hand if a man cares to use it. There is no such thing, in Buddhist morality, as good or bad actions which are independent of man's freedom. Their goodness or badness, of course, originates from whether they conform to the Buddha's ethical norms; but a man is held responsible for not attaining Nirvana because he failed to use the right volitional effort in directing his creative mental faculty on which every other movement of a human being depends.

Nor is this all. In other sacred texts, Buddha adds some valuable advice on how the will is to gain mastery over the mind. Take the case of evil thoughts; how should the disciple deal with them?

> If, while regarding a certain object, there arises, on account of it, in the disciple evil and demeritorious thoughts connected with greed, anger and delusion, then the disciple (1) should, by means of this object, gain another and wholesome object. Or (2) he should reflect on the misery of these thoughts: "Unwholesome truly are these thoughts! Blameable are these thoughts! Of painful result are these thoughts!" Or (3) he should pay no attention to these thoughts. Or (4) he should consider the compounded nature of these thoughts [their fleeting character]. Or (5) with teeth clenched and tongue pressed against the gums, he should with his mind restrain, suppress and root out these thoughts; and in doing so these evil and demeritorious thoughts of greed, anger and delusion will dissolve and disappear, and the mind will inwardly become settled and calm, composed and concentrated.[22]

I doubt if there is anything in the sacred writings of any religion that portrays more graphically the sovereignty of the will in struggling to overcome unwelcome mental images that faith tells the believer are contrary to his spiritual interests.

Before leaving this sixth stage en route to Nirvana, it may be useful to recall that Buddha elsewhere spoke of right effort as the cultivation of good habits or, more accurately, the cultivation of one basic habit: having good thoughts on the mind. The first step is to avoid bad ideas from entering consciousness; the second is to overcome them once they arise; the third step is to develop good ideas; and the last step is to maintain them after they arise. Consistent effort produces results, since every deliberate action, because it is repeatable, tends to become a habit.

Right attentiveness

Provided the will has done its task, the next step is comparatively easy. Buddha calls it right mindfulness, which stands for the almost untranslatable Sanskrit word *smriti*. In classic Hinduism, *smriti* is equivalent to sacred tradition as *sruti* corresponds to sacred scripture. For a Buddhist, the right kind of mind is a form of internal tradition.

In one of his sermons Buddha indicates in what this right mindfulness consists. It is not, as some commentators claim, merely or mainly strict attentiveness to the familiar quadrad of Buddhist theology: the body and its feelings, or the mind and its cerebration. The emphasis here as everywhere in the Path should be on the adjective "right."

Certainly attention must be made to these items, otherwise nothing happens. The point at issue, however, is that while being attentive the mind thinks about each of them correctly. In Buddha's words, talking about the body, "a brother continues so to look upon the body that he remains ardent, self-possessed and mindful, having overcome the hankering and the dejection common in the world."[23] What, then, is the right kind of attention he should give the body? Such as leaves him emotionally unmoved, in complete self-possession because (otherwise than his weaker brother) he is neither attracted nor repelled by what he beholds. So, too, of the other three commodities—feelings, mind, and ideas.

There is something else implicit in this doctrine. Why did Buddha place so much stress on will effort to overcome bad ideas and cultivate good ones; or again of resisting bad mindfulness and fostering its opposite? He assumed, without stating, that man of himself is ambivalent. There are two kinds of thoughts that rise to consciousness without bidding or even provocation. Spontaneously and left to himself, man's mind is the arena of two conflicting sets of concepts: those conducive to his Nirvanic consummation and those preventing him from reaching it.

Buddha never tried to explain why bad ideas should arise at all, or why all of them are not good. Neither did he speculate on the further question about man's nature, once he had described him as a walking battlefield. What cannot be questioned is that he took man to be a living paradox. All the while that his every instinct clamors for expression, faith tells him that giving in to this thirst is to condemn himself to another birth and another round of urges that cannot be fulfilled. Nothing but the will, enlightened as his had been, can cut the Gordian knot.

Right concentration

This brings us to the final stage, beyond which Nirvana lies. In this case the Pali and Sanskrit words are the same, and they have entered the language of all nations. *Samadhi* is a respected term in English, too, for the state of perfect concentration. In its original derivation, *samadhi* meant fixation of the mind on a single object, or more literally "one-pointedness of mind." Some would translate it "rapture," to bring out what Buddha surely intended, that anyone who struggles so earnestly up this point will finally be relieved of further effort. He will, by then, be taken out of himself in ecstatic rapture and oblivious felicity.

Once more we meet the number of four, which is the number of grades through which the faithful Buddhist passes on the verge of Nirvana. Buddha called them *jhanas*, which most authors translate as "trances." This is quite correct, except that a person in a trance does not normally know what he is doing, even though his faculties may be functioning. They are rather hypnotic states in which the subject is so preoccupied that he is insensible to external surroundings.

Buddha's own description of the process is classic, since it was purportedly based on his own experience. It is the high point of Buddhist theology and the end point of its eschatology.

> Detached from sensual objects, detached from demeritorious things, the disciple enters into the first trance. This trance is accompanied by verbal thought and deliberation; it is born of solitude and is full of joy and ease.
>
> Suppressing thought and deliberation, the disciple enters into and abides in the second trance. This trance is self-evoked, born of concentration, full of joy and ease, in that . . . the mind grows calm and sure, dwelling on high.
>
> Disenchanted with joy, the disciple abides calmly contemplative while, mindful and self-possessed, he feels in his body that ease of which the nobler Ones say, "Happy lives the man of equanimity and attentive mind." Thus he enters the third trance.
>
> Finally, after giving up all pleasure and pain, and through the disappearance of happiness and grief, he enters into and

abides in the fourth trance. This is the trance of utter purity of mindfulness and equanimity, where neither joy is felt nor any ill.[24]

Buddha held on to his principles to the end. A moment before the disciple enters Nirvana he is still besieged by cravings for happiness and shrinking from pain. But only for a moment, because there sweeps over him like an ocean wave the ecstasy of perfect poise and tranquillity. He is free.

CHRISTIAN APPRAISAL

What can Buddhism teach the Christian? Once again, we are not saying that Christianity is ignorant of what Buddhism knows or that Christian revelation is somehow defective and needs shoring up from Buddhist sources.

A better way of looking at the two religions is not to compare them at all but rather say that there are insights in the Buddhist faith which may not be absent in Christianity but may be desperately lacking in Christians. Much as we saw when talking about Hinduism, so here we assume that God's truth is essentially one, no matter where found or among whom it is professed. Add to this the fact that Buddhists have been the object of God's enlightening grace as far back as the time of Isaiah. We can therefore look into their religion profitably without fear of compromising what we also (or already) believe but maybe not with the same intensity or not with the same extraordinary practicality.

The problem of evil

Few themes in Western thought are more extensively treated than the problem of evil. It has become the mainstay of schools of philosophy and the subject of every form of art. In the religion of the Hebrews it is synthesized in the Book of Job, and for Christians it is symbolized in the cross.

Judaeo-Christianity parted company with the non-Christian religions of the West in assigning a cause to human suffering, and in giving pain a meaning that the most dramatic insights of Sophocles and Plato could never have found. One of the great "ifs" of history is the unwritten story of mankind if the message of Christ had been built on the Buddhist Orient instead of the Graeco-Roman culture of the West.

It would have been a different story, if for no other reason, at least, because Buddhism has such a strong sense of human misery and is so intent on relieving its cause.

Buddha began with the startling affirmation that all human life is suffering. He identified the two and therefore never made the mistake of trying to palliate or alleviate what he believed was intrinsic to human nature, whenever and wherever people live.

He might have remained a Hindu savant who theorized on the spectacle of an anguished humanity or lapsed into pessimism and become a Schopenhauer centuries before his time. He did neither. He took the prevalent religion of his day and changed its orientation. Hindus were great pundits; they reveled in speculation. He would preach a religion that did something.

What he proposed doing was revolutionary. He saw a Hinduism that said nothing so clearly as the inevitability of things. The Hindu vocabulary was filled with terms that stood for determinism and inexorable fate. They spoke of *dharma* as the great law of the universe by which even the gods were bound; of *karma* as the actions that people perform, from the smallest gesture like inadvertently stepping on a worm to their solemn rites of worship—all tied in with grave consequences that no one might escape; of *samsara* as the endless prolongation of life in leaving and reentering the womb; of *varna* as the caste system into which everyone is born and to whose duties he is bound to submit at the risk of rebirth in another and worse life after the present one.

Buddha reacted against this Brahmin Manichaeism. He was as ready as the most devout Hindu to admit that man's lot on earth was a sad one, but he was not ready to leave the situation to fate or, for that matter, to the tender mercies of any god.

He left the explanation as to *why* man suffers to those who cared to study the question; he preferred to find *how* the suffering might be removed. His discovery was something like Augustine's which he recorded in his *Confessions*. Augustine had been struggling for years with his passions and was not very successful in becoming a virtuous man. His nine years as a Manichaean were part of the Odyssey he went through, searching for an answer. The Manichees consoled him with the belief that such evil as sin was ultimately due to some force or deity outside of man. Unless or until that deity wished or was able to relieve a man of his sinfulness, there was no hope.

The day Augustine realized that he, Augustine, was the cause of his sins, and that, if he wanted to, he could be good—was the turning point in his life. It was the beginning of his conversion.

Something similar happened to Buddha, except that his concern was not with moral evil only (or mainly) but with physical and psychical evil which is pain. In common with Augustine, Buddha had trekked for years from one Hindu *guru* to another in hope of finding what he sought. They were no more help than his earlier voluptuous companions who told him to drown his sorrows in sensuality. All their remedies were placebos whose only function was either patiently to wait on Brahman to do something or dull one's sensitivity to suffering by inflicting still more excruciating pain.

Buddha found very much what Augustine discovered on a different plane. The fundamental root of suffering is man's own insatiable thirst. Quench this thirst by persistent effort and suffering will finally cease. Nirvana is the goal of the strong-willed. reason we follow to com.

On this level, Buddhism locates the problems of life where they really exist, inside a man's soul and, more specifically, in his undisciplined will. It would be stressing the obvious to say that a large part of the Western world has forgotten this fact.

Unfortunately Buddha left very little room for the supernatural in his system. Theravada disciples who claim direct lineage from his teaching are, even today, titans of self-mastery and models of indifference to what other men consider seductive allurements. They see no need for divine grace. no sup. naturalism not same sort of dualist

But Buddhism is not Buddha and the developments that took place in his doctrine are equally as important as the first impetus that he brought to the system. These developments since the time of Buddha afford another view of the Buddhist Orient from which everyone can learn.

From philosophy to religion

There is some justification for saying that what Buddha originally taught was more a philosophy than a religion. While he never denied the existence of the gods of his day, he never relied on them either. If he admitted their existence in principle, he ignored them in practice. Accordingly the Buddhism of its founder was not atheistic, as some maintain, but Pelagian (to coin a term) because it held that man's destiny is acquired by his own unaided efforts. Nirvana was due to man, any man, who worked for it.

65

The analogy now breaks down. While reacting against the Manichees, Augustine did not go to the other extreme of denying the
need for divine help. Quite the contrary, he was simultaneously dis-
illusioned with Manichaeism by admitting his own responsibility for
sin, and was enlightened about the absolute need of Christ to help
his weak human will.

Buddha had no such balanced religious career. To his dying
day he seems to have rejected any form of supernatural aid. His last
recorded words were an exhortation to the monks. "Behold now,
brethren," he warned them, "decay is inherent in all component
things! Work out your own salvation with diligence!"[25]

Soon after his death, however, things began to change. The religion he began as a Hindu sect retained the essentials of his program while also keeping the ritual worship from which Hinduism is
never separated. It was a simple matter for Buddha to become first
one of the *avatars* and then Indra and Brahman, and lastly the all-
prevailing God.

Once the people began to regard him as "all-knowing and all-
seeing, savior of gods and men (and) everlasting," it was not long
before they also invoked him to beg for assistance in their journey
along the eightfold Path.

As might be expected, the Mahayana Buddhists have done most
to both deify Buddha and look to him for divine grace. One of the
most common hymns addressed to Buddha is a series of couplets,
running to over a hundred in a modern edition. It is an unusual mixture of praise in the third person and petition in the second person.
But the basic purpose of the hymn is unmistakable.

To go to him for refuge, to praise and honor him,
To abide in his religion, that is fit for those with sense.
The only Protector, he is without faults or their residues;
The All-knowing, he has all the virtues, and that without fail.
So much merit have you gathered by your good actions
That even the dust of your feet has become a field of merit.
Without distinction all this world was bound to the
defilements,
That you might free it you were long in bondage to compassion.
To praise you takes all guilt away, to recollect you lifts up
the heart,
To seek you brings understanding, to comprehend you purity.

To approach you brings good fortune, to tend you highest
   wisdom,
To resort to you takes away fear, to honor you is propitious.
An island you are to those swept along by the flood,
   a shelter to the stricken.
A refuge to those terrified by becoming, the resource of those
   who desire release.[26]

Clearly this is no longer Pelagian self-mastery but formal
prayer. Gautama is recognized as either an *avatar*, where the deity
took on human form, or as *the* Buddha whose humanity became
united in Nirvana with Brahman the creator (and savior) of the
human race.

It is almost certain that the Bhagavad Gita of the Hindus was
deeply influenced by Mahayana devotion to Buddha. The beautiful
tributes to Krishna as object of man's affection and the destiny of
his existence are so similar to what we find in some phases of Chinese and Japanese Buddhism that the latter must have affected its
parental stem.

What this teaches a non-Buddhist is that, whereas scholars and
the litterati tend to reduce religion to philosophy, ordinary people
want religion and not philosophy. Even when they profit from the
insights or methodology of intellectuals, they instinctively ritualize
what they learn and prefer to ask for superhuman favor than depend on their own unaided strength.

From self-conquest to selflessness

Parallel with the foregoing is another phenomenon in the development of Buddhism. Orthodox texts in the Pali tradition speak at
length on the need for suppressing desire to reach Nirvana. The impression they leave is of a man fighting against himself, one part
against another, until they settle for an exhausted peace.

When Mahayana came along, it took the same basic notion of
self-conquest but changed its mode of operation. Instead of engaging in a domestic battle with himself, the Buddhist was told to practice first justice and then charity. The passages referring to justice
are almost certainly Buddha's original contribution; those dealing
with charity are certainly not.

There are some grounds for supposing a Christian influence on
Mahayana which will undoubtedly add to the meager evidence on

the point we now have, notably Christian Gnosticism and later scholarship. But it is not necessary to establish direct contact between the early Christians and the flowering of Mahayanism in the first and second centuries of the Christian era. It is enough to know that Buddhism introduced self-sacrificing charity into its doctrinal heritage somewhere between 100 B.C. and A.D. 200.

The change was substantial. Unlike anything in the Hinduism from which it sprang, Buddhism began to speak of extinguishing one's own desires by satisfying the desires of others. We have seen some of the forms which this altruism took and the bizarre lengths to which it occasionally went. What is more significant is the underlying principle at work, and its place in every religion, including Judaism and Christianity.

Mahayana introduced charity into the Buddhist eightfold Path within the Buddha's own premises. His guiding principle was that all suffering is basically unfulfilled desire. We should ignore for our present purpose the elaborate metaphysical structure that Buddha erected on this sound statement of psychology. If he were asked how he knew that pain is the result of unsatified wants, he would appeal to everyday experience. People are contented when they get what they want and unhappy when their wishes are denied.

He went on to explain that progress toward the goal of human existence is measured by the degree to which desires are suppressed. The sign or proof that the goal is being approached is the growing sense of peace and tranquillity that a man senses as he moves higher and higher on the eightfold ladder of perfection. Nirvana is nothing else than consummate perfection, when all conflict between desire and satisfaction has ceased.

In Buddha's vocabulary pain was the subjective experience of desires unfulfilled. Always within man there are wants that cannot be satisfied.

Mahayana took this idea as axiomatic, but it proceeded to expand on what the Buddha had taught. He correctly supposed that men are unhappy because they do not get (cannot get) all they desire. But he confined his methodology to decreasing what a man wants to acquire, whether for himself from nature or for himself at the expense of others. But always the focus was on cutting down on the desire of acquisition for oneself.

The genius of Mahayana was to distinguish two kinds of desires in man: one to acquire for self and the other to share with others.

Still using Buddha's norm of growth in perfection, the Mahayanists pointed out (also from experience) that while acquisitive desires are the root cause of pain, communicative desires bring joy.

They amplified the concept to show that the joy which comes from giving to others is not conditioned by how much or what a person actually shares. He may not have much to give. By the same token the pain brought on by unsatisfied acquisitive desires is not conditioned by how much a man has failed to acquire or lost. It is uniquely determined by how strongly he desired something which he did not get.

Then the capstone. Is it conceivable that altruism brings real peace and that growth in generosity is growth in Buddhahood, until finally Nirvana is attained? Not only is it conceivable, but Mahayana texts abound in which this is the only way a man can escape from the endless cycle of reincarnations.

> The person who only thinks of his own salvation harvests samsara. The person who does not distribute what he has gathered, meditates in vain; he will remain without virtue.[27]

If we look more closely at the reason for this, one explanation given is that each person is only a part of the whole human family. Selfishness consists in fostering the welfare of this single part at the expense of the whole. Conversely the charitable man recognizes himself as a fraction of this fullness, and gives generously to others because he knows that by helping them he is nurturing the greater at the expense of the less. He is benefiting humanity instead of merely serving a single human being.

> Have one passion only: the good of others. All who are unhappy, are unhappy from having sought their own happiness. All who are happy, are happy from having sought the happiness of others. You must exchange your well-being for the miseries of others.
>
> Reflecting on the fact that you are yourself full of faults and that others are brimming over with good qualities, you will endeavor to throw off your own personality and adopt that of others.
>
> You are interested in your various members as parts of your own body; why not in men as parts of humanity?
>
> The person who wants to save himself must practice the great secret: put himself in the place of others.[28]

69

Another explanation, which harks back to Buddha's principle of no-selfness, tells people to fight against unhappiness *per se*, as something evil, without thinking of it as something which persons experience.

> I must fight against the unhappiness of others as I do against my own, because it is unhappiness. There is no subject to experience the unhappiness; who then can have his own? All kinds of unhappiness without distinction are impersonal; they must be fought against as unhappiness. Why these restrictions?[29]

In other words, why limit myself to removing unhappiness in myself when others are just as unhappy, and the guiding motive for removing unhappiness should be its existence in whomsoever found. It cannot be that *I* am unhappy, since the Ego to whom I attribute unhappiness does not exist.

It is a telling commentary on Buddhism, as distinct from Christianity, that in all these efforts to help others the purpose is seldom to make them happy. That in itself is perfectly consistent with the larger aim of orthodox Buddhist eschatology: man's purpose in life —during this segment of his reincarnated existence—is rather to reduce and hopefully remove the unhappiness to which his unruly desires have led him.

Mental concentration

Whatever else is associated with Buddhism, its stress on the power of the will over the mind is commonplace and has profound psychological insights that the West is only now coming to see.

Less well known but equally important is the Buddhist emphasis on the mind as not only a function but also as object of contemplation. Not all forms of Buddhism reflect this attitude nor would the average Buddhist express the idea in just these words, but the lesson that Christians can learn is a profound one.

Zen Buddhism is sometimes denied the name of Buddhist by those who see it as a reversion to Hinduism, with its concern for intellectual discovery rather than volitional release. There is much to this charge, because the goal of Zen is not Nirvana, or extinction of desire, but *Satori*, or Enlightenment. Zen adherents defend themselves by explaining that they are more faithful to the master's teaching, since the essence of his doctrine was to attain to Buddhahood, which meant to become the Enlightened One. No doubt the Buddha also preached the path to Nirvana, but this path need not be taken literally. Each of the stages can be passed as well, and better, right within man's spirit, and quite apart from the elaborate methodology suggested by either the Hinayana or the Mahayana.

The Zen interpreters have something. They maintain that a person need not, indeed should not, go outside himself in search of the enlightenment that Buddha attained. They are iconoclasts when it comes to taking any of the standard principles of Buddhism, including the Four Noble Truths and the complicated eightfold Path. All of this may be scuttled, they say, and Buddhahood can as easily (and more effectively) be found by anyone who firmly believes that the Light he seeks is already within him—if only he looks long enough into the mind.

Others are satisfied with using the mind in search of Someone or Something which is not the mind. The Zen people prefer to use the mind all right, but in order to fix their gaze even more intently on the mind itself, since it has within its bosom, as it were, the treasure that man is looking for.

Their method differs with different schools of Zen, and the widest divergence is between the Chinese form, called *Ch'an* where Zen originated with the twenty-eighth patriarch, Bodhi-Dharma (died A.D. 520), descended by teacher-disciple heredity from Buddha himself, and its better known Japanese type, *Zazen*, which is shortened to Zen. All schools agree, however, on this principle: given the proper dispositions, enlightenment comes to every one who gives his mind a chance to reveal the riches hidden in its folds. The secret is to believe this and to act on the conviction.

Four steps are normally prescribed. The first is to train the body to endurance of muscular immobility, which is necessary as the first requisite for meditation. It may take years for a person to get used to sitting in undisturbed contemplation without having the body rebel against such enforced inactivity. Most people never get past the first step, if they even try it; they cannot shake off the prejudice of identifying action with bodily movement. They do not see that the highest form of human activity is spiritual, and therefore bodiless; it is movement of the intellectual faculties and not of legs and arms.

Step number two is the posture. It must be sitting cross-legged, with the arms folded or resting quietly on one's lap. Essential to the position is that the body express externally what the mind is seeking internally, namely perfect peace. At the same time, the posture must not be too comfortable, to induce sleep; the mind has to stay alert. It falls asleep with the body. For this reason, the monks allow themselves to be rudely struck with a bamboo pole if they dare to doze off during what should be their meditation.

The next step is the crucial one, to meditate on some statement or action of a Zen master, in order to experience in oneself what he experienced as the author of what he said or did. By Western, and certainly by Christian, standards these *Koans* on which the monk is to meditate make little sense. A few more intelligible samples illustrate the general trend.

> Yun-men was once asked: "When not a thought is stirring in one's mind, is there any error here?" "As much as Mount Sumeru."
>
> When Ming the monk overtook the fugitive Hui-neng, he wanted Hui-neng to give up the secret of Zen. Hui-neng replied, "What are your original features which you have even prior to your birth?"
>
> A monk asked, "All things are said to be reducible to the One, but where is the One to be reduced?" Chao-chou answered, "When I was in the district of Ch'ing I had a robe made that weighed seven *chin*."[30]

In the last step, the meditator is to wrestle with the *Koan* in such a way that he gradually reproduces in himself the state of consciousness achieved by those who spoke or performed what the *Koan* describes.

In itself, the *Koan* is not a logical proposition but the verbal symbol of a mental state resulting from the Zen discipline. To arrive at this mental state, the logical, reasoning mind must be literally "put to death." The very irrationality of the *Koan* is the means by which the rational intellect is progressively "destroyed." Yet terms like "put to death" and "destroyed" are unfair, say the Buddhists, to express what actually occurs. The ultimate purpose is to go beyond the limits of intellection, and these limits (they claim) can be crossed over only by exhausting oneself once and for all, by using up all the psychic powers at one's command. Logic then turns into psychology, psychology into mental effort, and mental effort into intuition. What cannot be solved on the plane of empirical consciousness is slowly but surely transferred to the deeper recesses of the mind.

Provided a man perseveres, light is sure to come, or rather a vision of startling intensity is the fruit awaiting anyone who strains his mind until he is "thoroughly drenched in perspiration" in the struggle to denude the mind of logical thought.

Once a man has come to this light, that is, experienced *Satori*, he knows it. The vision is described as savor and taste, rather than rational knowledge; it is intuitive as the realization of both object and the Reality behind it; once had, it cannot be doubted but remains fixed as incontestable truth; what is seen is positive and direct, not by way of comparison and contrast with other things; with it comes the sense of the beyond, of arrival at one's destination, that is, where the mind feels at home; it produces in the beholder a quiet feeling of perfect tranquillity, which Buddha would call Nirvana; except that *Satori*, unlike the Nirvana of orthodox Buddhism, is a momentary and abrupt experience—yet transient only in its presence, but so permanent in its effect that from then on (until the next *Satori*) everything in the world is seen from a new and inexpressible viewpoint.

As a Christian reads about Zen and talks with those who have spent years in its practice, his first impulse may be to dismiss the whole thing as autosuggestion, or systematic brainwashing, or an exercise in Oriental Quietism. This would be a mistake.

There are Zen practitioners who do induce self-hypnosis, and try to erase their minds of rational thought. Quietism is the besetting problem which those who know Zen best say must be fought against like the plague. It is possible to pacify the intellect into a kind of drugged state in which logic and reason are sterilized into inactivity. But this is not true Zen. The real Zen is intended to illuminate rather than obscure the intellect; but illuminate it by reproducing in oneself the enlightenment that someone centuries ago had experienced, and this is reexperienced now by contact with his spirit through reflection on the "jargon" he spoke or the "nonsense" he performed.

A Christian or, in fact, any believer in God must carefully distinguish between the adjective "Zen" and the substantive "Buddhism." Most Oriental Zen is built on the original premise of Buddha, that there is no enduring Ego and therefore no perduring mind. They describe the enlightenment of *Satori* as the discovery of "mindlessness," and the state of Nirvana as unconsciousness because "Buddhahood is attained when there is no mind which is to be used for the task."

On its adjectical level, then, Zen is not far removed from the monism of the Hindu Upanishads and is diametrically opposed to the mysticism of Judaeo-Christianity. The latter strives to attain contact with a personal God, and its spiritual literature speaks the language of intimacy between a child and its Father, or a spouse and its Beloved. Zen on the other hand, sees no such goal for its *Satori*. It envisions no Self in personal contact with the infinite Other. As the Hindu *Sankara* would put it, there is no dualism between the Absolute and the Ego. If the Absolute is postulated, then the Ego is illusion; and the Zen searcher finds what he is looking for, namely his own nothingness and the Allness of the Absolute.

So much for substantive Buddhism on which Zen is commonly built. But Zen itself is not Buddhism, no more than the practices of any religion are necessarily identified with its faith or valid only for that religion. If that were the case, then prayer should be outlawed by Christians because non-Christians pray!

As an adjective, Zen has much to teach anyone who is willing to learn. Its insistence on bodily asceticism to make the mind pliable for meditation is taught, in different terms, by all Christian masters of the spiritual life. The trouble is that too few take them seriously, and as a consequence are surprised when the body they fail to mortify resists their feeble efforts to use the mind for such spiritual exercises as prayer. No doubt many of the practices of the Orientals in their "cult of the mind" seem strange to people whose tendency is the opposite, the cult of the body. Yet the price that Zen is willing to pay in order to enter the secret chambers of the soul must be basically fair, or at least a higher price must be paid than many who do not understand Zen are willing to pay while they still want to pray. Cheap mysticism in any religion is spurious.

The bodily posture on which Zen places so much emphasis teaches more than meets the eye. This quiet, yet alert sitting position has been found by experience to be remarkably effective. It tends to induce a similar peaceful alertness of spirit, with which the body is closely joined. It keeps the imagination from flitting about to different objects, because distracting sense impressions are kept from arising through changing stimulation. The will effort spent in keeping relatively immobile results in improved concentration, since there seems to be a close connection between indiscriminate bodily movement and a wandering mind.

As a Christian reads the various *Koans* he is baffled by the extravagant claims that Zen disciples make for them. Is it possible that these conundrums actually produce the results they say?

Dismissing some of the claims as exaggeration, there must be a profound law of the mind at work if even a fraction of these results really take place. One part of this law seems to be that the mind is not made only or mainly for discursive thinking. It is a Western bias to define man as a rational animal. The East would define him as the "contemplating animal," or the "believing animal." The human mind may, of course, do much rational reflection and the tasks of daily life call for a great deal of reasoning—from premises to conclusions and from examples to general principles. All of this is useful and, for many people, is about the only kind of thinking they ever do.

But reason is only a tool, and limited in its value to things that pertain to the empirical world. Zen teaches that the mind has greater power than merely to reason and a higher role to play than just to draw conclusions. Its main purpose is to break through the empirical world of space and time, of sense and fancy and come into contact with whatever is beyond. By Buddhist premises this "beyond" is vague and impersonal and Zen commentators apologize for not being more clear about the "indescribable," and the "undefinable." The faith of a Christian tells him more about this world beyond the visible one than a Buddhist believes. What the Buddhist can teach the Christian is how he has penetrated through the shell of external phenomena and mysteriously touched the Reality which these phenomena encase.

Use of the *Koan* by a Zen Buddhist is more than a technique. It suggests that an otherwise unintelligible statement, or the description of an event that has little rational meaning may become the key that unlocks a trove of great riches if only a man does the right thing. The right thing, a Zen meditator would say, is to strive to unite oneself with the master who spoke those words, or who performed that action. By some strange alchemy of the human psyche, the strong persistent effort to take on his mind and relive his experience will produce the effect desired.

Zen teachers warn against using many words or even changing the words on which a person meditates. They insist that the same words be mentally repeated over and over again. If this looks like inducing a hypnotic state, they deny it. They explain that the words themselves are indeed mere sounds, but the inner sense of the words is something else. With each repetition, like the echo of a human voice, the mind enters deeper and deeper into the meaning of what the words mean. Repetition is only a device, but an indispensable one, of keeping the mind focused on what the words hiddenly signify.

Repetitive prayer is common enough outside of Buddhist circles to be taken for granted, but its value and need are not so easily seen. This idea of repeating a passage or a phrase in order to have its inner meaning sink more deeply into the soul—or appear more vividly to the mind—is a precious insight that every one who prays can profitably use.

More important, though, than the method of repetition is the goal of Zen meditation. Its object is not to understand with the reason but to be united in spirit with the one who originally spoke or did what the meditator is thinking about. Buddhist writers talk about religion as a living tradition that passes from one person to another, or better that one master who has seen the light relives in another person—maybe five hundred years later—by the simple (but difficult) method of rethinking the same thoughts which the former had experienced.

They count their great leaders, who had attained *Satori*, as we count successors in an office or the descendants in a royal line. But descent, in their language, is not based on election or natural heredity. It is founded on the mystical communication from one mind to another, and this transmission of spirit is as real—more real, in fact—than any transfer of administration or blood relationship from parent to son.

The implications of this concept are tantalizing. It suggests the importance of reflection, just plain serious reflection, on the thoughts and actions of Christ—for a Christian—if he hopes to put on the mind of Christ. There is no other way.

CONFUCIANISM

The symbol of Chinese Universism is *Tai-ki* (Primal Beginning)
and represents the essential features of Confucian thought. Inside the figure
in contrasting black and white are represented
the two conflicting forces, the light *yang* and the dark *yin* separated
from the beginning. The white dot in the dark (often blue) half
of the circle and the dark dot in the white (often red) half of the circle
signify that both forces are always near one another
and should work together harmoniously. Harmony is expressed
by the flowing curvature of the contrasting fields. Around the circle
are eight trigrams from the *Yi King* (*Book of Changes*). They consist
of continuous or strong lines (—) and of broken or weak lines (---)
in the different possible basic arrangements. Strong lines
symbolize the male force *yang*, while the weak lines stand
for the female force *yin*. Human existence consists in the give and take
of these forces, which the *Book of Changes* explains in mysterious terms
known only to the initiates.

As we shift our gaze from Hinduism and Buddhism to Confucianism, we change focus almost completely. Whereas Hinduism can be called the great "Religion of Being," and Buddhism the "Religion of Suffering," Confucianism is best described as the "Religion of Social Morality."

This is so true that some scholars, mistakenly, prefer to speak of Confucianism as a religionless system of ethics or even as a philosophy of agnostic morals. They are led to these conclusions because of the Confucian preoccupation with man's social behavior. However emphasis on one side of life does not mean exclusion of another.

If Confucius who laid the foundations of the religion that bears his name stressed ethics so heavily, it merely illustrates the limitations of any great leader. The aftermath in China, in fact, proved that his people wanted more than ethical norms to live a full-rounded life. That is why it is hard to describe Chinese religion in univocal terms. Otherwise than in India, where the dominant religion for centuries has been Hinduism, the Chinese may be said to practice a tripartite Universism, compounded of Confucianism, Buddhism, and Taoism—in that order of importance. In this sequence, Buddhism supplied the religious fervor and mysticism of the Mahayana tradition, and Taoism gave the Chinese some semblance of metaphysics and philosophy.

Although Confucianism is nominally associated only with K'ung-Fu-Tze, whom Jesuit missionaries in the sixteenth century gave the Latin name *Confucius*, the religion had one more founder. Mencius was more than a disciple of the master. He gave Confucianism a systematic form and clarified the principles on which the ethics of the storytelling Confucius were based. In China, two men are said to have been inspired; Confucius is the First, and Mencius, the Second Inspired One.

Confucianism is unique among the Oriental religions in having a definite set of writings, with their chronology and geography so specific you immediately recognize the literature as Chinese. There is nothing like it in either Hinduism or Buddhism.

Though not considered revelation, in the sense of the Vedas, Confucian scriptures are venerated with extreme respect. All are somehow identified with the memory of the great sage who was born in 551 B.C. and died in 478 B.C., in his seventy-fourth year, as a contemporary of Buddha who died shortly before in India.

The Confucian Bible, if we may so call it, runs to ten books according to the best calculation. The first six are the *King* texts, dealing in sequence with Changes, History, Songs, Rites, Annals, and Filial Piety. The last four are the *Shu* texts which contain the *Doctrine of the Mean, The Great Learning, Analects of Confucius*, and the *Book of Mencius.*

Most of these books are so filled with names of persons, places, and institutions, and so detailed in exact quotation that one can only marvel at the prodigious feat of memory which their oral transmission required. Yet all that we know about Confucius' insistence on preserving the past—even in minute matters of gesture and dress— makes it less surprising that the great discourses of Confucianism have come down to us in such complete form.

Among these writings, the *Analects of Confucius* and the *Book of Mencius* are the most valuable for giving us a concise, yet accurate, picture of the main features of a religion that is presently undergoing the severest test of its twenty-five hundred years' existence.

HISTORICAL SETTING

China in the time of Confucius was a feudal country that was divided into about a hundred small states. Over these ruled a king of the decadent Chou dynasty. But his authority was mostly nominal. About 517 B.C., Confucius came to the court of one of the lesser princes at Loyang, present Honan, to better pursue his study of the ancients.

It was at Loyang that his life was changed. Much as Buddha was suddenly enlightened in vision to begin preaching the Path to Nirvana, so Confucius found in the writings of the Duke of Chou the secret he was looking for. The duke had been the father of the first king of that country, and counselor to his son. Confucius discovered in him the principles he would spend the rest of his life expounding. Five hundred years separated Confucius from the Duke of Chou; but, that did not matter. Wisdom, he was later to say in the Analects, is not measured by time; truth has no age.

His shrewdness gained him a quick reputation. He was offered and accepted the governorship of a city in the principality of Lu. While he was administrator, so runs the chronicle, men were recognized for their faithfulness and sincerity, women for their chastity and submissiveness. Merchants dealt honestly with their customers and employers with their workmen.

Success as governor also brought him the envy of his enemies. They managed to distract the prince with wine and women, who then banished Confucius in disgrace.

For fourteen years he traveled the length and breadth of China, trying to find a ruler who would follow his advice. Finally at the age of sixty-nine the prince who had rejected him took him back, and gave him the leisure of five years for meditation and writing. When he died, he became the object of instant veneration. A temple was built in his honor, where at every station a sacrifice was to be offered. In 57 B.C. a decree enjoined the offering of sacrifices in his name at the Imperial University and the principal colleges of the empire. It should be added for the record that, except for a minority of ill-instructed Chinese, the honors paid to Confucius were never the formal worship shown to God. If some Western writers have wrongly identified this with divine veneration, it only shows how deeply ingrained had become that most characteristic of Confucian traits—respect for one's ancestors, to the point of being mistaken for religious cult.

RELIGIOUS FOUNDATIONS

As was suggested before, not everyone agrees that Confucianism has a religious foundation. Even as able a scholar as Max Weber was brought to say, no doubt quoting others, that, "In the sense of the absence of all metaphysics and almost all residues of religious anchorage, Confucianism is rationalistic to such a far-going extent that it stands at the extreme boundary of what one might possibly call a 'religious' ethic."[1] Part of the confusion arises from a too restricted view of religion, or more likely from looking for a Western concept of religion in the Orient and not finding it, to label what is there as irreligious.

Every one of the Confucian scriptures makes direct reference to the supreme power that rules the world. Three different designations are used. *Shang-Ti* is a composite term, meaning Supreme Originator, whereas *Ti* is the common name applied to ancestors. It may correctly be reduced in English as "God." Another term is *Tien*, which literally means "Heaven," or "Law," with the genitive "of God" being understood.

When Confucius spoke of *Shang-Ti*, he meant the supreme Lord of heaven, who ruled over all the ancestors of the human race. The viewpoint is significant. Implicitly it states that just as the human family on earth has its forebears, who have since died; so these forebears, who are not really dead but alive, have their "Great Ancestor" or Originator who is God.

The most famous single text, out of a hundred, that associates morality and religion occurs in the *Shu King*, which is China's oldest history. *Shu King* covers the period ranging from 2205 B.C. to 700 B.C. and was one of the principal works that Confucius rediscovered for his people.

In context, the great King Wu (twelfth century B.C.) had just conquered a tyrant rival, King Shau of Shang. Wu was first moved to fight against Shau because the latter, in Wu's words, "does not revere Providence above and inflicts calamities on the people below. Abandoned to drunkenness and reckless in lust, he has dared to exercise cruel oppression . . . Great Heaven was moved with indignation, and charged my deceased father Wan to display its terrors; but he died before the work was completed."[2]

The dissolute Shau was no match for the well-disciplined Wu. After having "presented a burnt-offering to Heaven," Wu conquered Shau and immediately began a consolidation of the whole kingdom.

His aim was to establish the country on the finest principles of morality. To this end he went personally to visit a former counselor of King Shau, the Count of Chi, who was then in prison. Chi was reputed among the best moralists in China and was a little surprised that Wu should consult him, adviser to the man he had just conquered. But this, too, was indicative of the "Wisdom of the Ancestors" to whom Confucius always appealed. Seek the truth wherever you can find it, even among your enemies—literally put into practice. Confucian ancestry belongs essentially to the mind.

What follows is known in Chinese annals as "The Great Plan." There is nothing like it in religious history outside of the Judaic tradition. It amounts to a short book in the *Shu King*. The passages here given are taken in sequence, and will be explained after the quotations.

> In the thirteenth year, the King went to inquire of the Count of Chi, and said to him: "Oh! Count of Chi. Heaven, working unseen, secures the tranquillity of the lower people, aiding them to be in harmony with their condition. I do not know how the unvarying principles of Heaven's method in doing so should be set forth in due order."
>
> The Count of Chi there upon replied: "I have heard that in old time Khwan dammed up the inundating waters, and thereby threw into disorder the arrangement of the five elements. God was consequently roused to anger, and did not give him the Great Plan with its nine divisions. Thus the unvarying principles of Heaven's method were allowed to go to ruin. Khwan was therefore kept a prisoner till his death, and his son Yu rose up and entered on the same undertaking. To him Heaven gave the Great Plan with its nine divisions, and the unvarying principles of its methods were set forth in their due order.
>
> "Of these divisions the first is called 'the five elements;' second, 'reverent attention to the five personal matters;' third, 'earnest devotion to the eight objects of government;' fourth, 'the harmonious use of the five dividers of time;' fifth, 'the establishment and use of royal perfection;' sixth, 'discriminating use of the three virtues;' seventh, 'the intelligent use of means for the examination of doubts;' eighth, 'the thoughtful use of the various verifications;' ninth, 'the persuasive use of the five

sources of happiness, and the reverent use of the six occasions of suffering.' "[3]

It is unnecessary to explore the whole mathematical range of morality outlined by the Count of Chi. The preference for numbers is typically Chinese. It also reveals something of its preciseness in discriminating among virtues, and within virtues of their numerous degrees.

But we cannot omit one more passage, where the count explains what he means by the five sources of happiness and the six occasions of suffering.

> Of the five sources of happiness: the first is long life, the second riches, the third soundness of body and serenity of mind, the fourth love of virtue, and the fifth is fulfilling to the end the will of Heaven.

> Of the six extreme evils, the first is misfortune shortening one's life, the second sickness, the third distress of mind, the fourth poverty, the fifth wickedness and the sixth weakness.[4]

By now we have enough material for a full volume commentary on Confucian morality as based on religion. We shall take up only the more salient features.

Count Chi lays the groundwork for a moral people by calling it Heaven's Method or, in paraphrase, "the Divine Plan." The initiator is the Great Ancestor who abides in the Heavens, and the method proceeds from his mind.

A classic expositor of the *Shu King* classic, Khung Ying-ta of the Thang dynasty, gives a remarkable exegesis of what orthodox Confucianism understands by the Method of Heaven.

> The people have been produced by the Supreme Heaven, and both body and soul are Heaven's gift. Men have thus the material body and the knowing mind. Heaven further assists them by helping them to harmonize their lives. The right and the wrong of their language, the correctness and errors of their conduct, their enjoyment of clothing and food, the rightness of their various movements—all these things are to be harmonized by what they are endowed with by Heaven.[5]

As traditional Confucianism views man, therefore, he has been made by Heaven, and endowed from on high with a mind to recognize the goodness and badness of things. Moreover, in some mysterious way Heaven further continues to assist him with what, in Christian language, would be called grace, that he might harmonize his life.

Harmonization is a technical term that stands for everything noble in the Chinese character. It is at once conformity with the divine plan, acceptance of God's will, submission to his dictates, and agreement with his precepts. It finds expression in the strong Confucian love for music, which the people are taught to regard as the human counterpart of the cosmic harmony in the universe. Music thus becomes man's imitation of the variety of creatures in the world, all placed in their respective spheres of action and, though all different, cooperating to a common end—as in the interplay of celestial bodies with the forces of earth. Hence the Chinese proverb, that "Music is the harmony of Heaven and earth."[6] Something akin to this harmony is made possible within man and between men, by the assistance which Heaven is said to offer people—beyond having endowed them with a thinking mind.

This Method of Heaven is manifold. It is a method because it is an orderly plan for the guidance of men personally and in society. It is also methodical in that its purpose is to insure harmony in men's lives and between men in community life. It is Heaven's Method because it comes from *Tien*, that is, Providence, who guides the destiny of mankind. It is further heavenly because the whole of man's nature comes from *Tien*, and so also man's ability to know what is right and wrong. It is finally heavenly because Heaven gives man the strength to live up to what his reason tells him he should do.

Count Chi is explicit in attributing anger to God and divine retribution for misdeeds; yet, strangely, the retribution was not visited on King Khwan for having rejected the Great Plan with its nine divisions: that was to presumably have been given him had he been faithful. He was unfaithful to the light of reason he possessed and therefore proved unworthy to receive the enlightenment from Heaven. His son Yu received the "revelation" of the Great Plan with its nine categories.

Heaven's Method is notoriously categorical. Nine classifications of more subclassifications until the head reels in bewilderment at the profusion of three kinds of virtue, five dividers of time, six occasions of suffering, and eight objects of government.

We mentioned it before, and stress the point again: Chinese morality is minute in prescriptive detail and in refinement of guilt (or virtue). What seems to be an obsession with numbers is rather a close (inseparable) correlation in the Chinese mind between heaven, which is immensurate spirit, and earth, whose most prominent feature is dimension and division into calculable parts.

Throughout the Chinese religious classics, and especially in the sayings of Confucius, the two are regularly coupled together. Heaven and earth this, and Heaven and earth that, are connected so often that some commentators have read into Confucianism what is not there—an indiscriminate animism that never rose above identifying the elements of earth with the divinities supposedly in the sky.

The correlation is there all right, but its meaning can be drawn only from the corporate body of Confucian literature. It then appears as the subtle recognition that the nearest analogue on earth to the Method decreed in Heaven is order; and order on earth can best be expressed in numbers—whether this is in the numeration of duties, or the specification of frequencies, or the harmonization that takes place in religious music and ritual.

Repeatedly in Confucian writings, and several times in the short passage we just quoted, the Method of Heaven is called a Great Plan. If it's a plan, though, what is the object planned? The objective is man's happiness, which is the ninth and final category toward which the plan inevitably leads. Or, in negative terms, its object is the avoidance of suffering which is the obverse of happiness in the same ninth category.

A closer look at the five sources of happiness is rewarding. They are evidently in ascending order of value: from a long life and riches to fulfilling to the end the will of Heaven. Why should fulfilling to the end the will of Heaven be the source of greatest happiness, unless (after the end) a man had the prospect of enjoying the fruits of his fulfillment? Eschatology could scarcely be clearer. The best assignable date for this text is before 1116 B.C.

Conversely, the six occasions of suffering correspond to the five sources of happiness; except that two ways are given for not fulfilling the will of Heaven, either through wickedness, that is, boldness in doing evil, or through weakness, that is, cowardice in failing to do good.

All that we know from contemporary sources indicates that long before Confucius, China had a sophisticated notion of reward and punishment after death. Confucius did not touch this phase of the religion. His task was to bring into the open the moral conditions on which reward and punishment would follow. In his terminology, reward was happiness (notably peace and serenity of spirit) and punishment was the opposite.

One more aspect of the religious basis of Confucian morality has to be seen. The Method of Heaven, it is said, contains "unvarying principles." Nothing could better express the unchangeable character of the divine law; unchangeable because coming from Heaven and consequently not subject to the whims of changeable moods of man.

When the Chinese sources say that Heaven's principles do not change, they mean to assert more than their independence of human caprice. As we shall see in analyzing Confucian filial piety, the unvariable nature of God's laws is the reason why they are essentially as binding a thousand years hence as they were a thousand years ago. Confucius' whole moral system was founded on the premise that Heaven's preceptive attitude toward man is a constant; certain principles of conduct are ever the same.

It is the same invariability which makes possible the transmission of laws from one generation to the next without fear that they are outmoded. It was also the reason why Confucius spoke with such confidence about the wisdom of the ancients and thought nothing of recovering the dusty manuscripts from centuries before. He honestly believed he had discovered something new!

FILIAL PIETY

In the popular mind, the most typical feature of Confucianism is its stress on the worship of one's ancestors. This will have to be severely qualified. But it does bring out a more fundamental element of Confucian morality, namely its concern for filial piety.

The practice of filial piety is the wellspring of Confucianism. Its beginnings might be traced to writings centuries before the master, who never tired of confessing that "I am a transmitter and not an originator, as one who believes in and loves the ancients."[7] Yet it was Confucius who most clearly stated the norms by which filial piety was raised to the dignity of a universal law—equally binding on parents and offspring, on ruler and the subjects under his political domain.

In Confucius' theory, the family stands at the foundation of the entire social and political order. This was no cheap platitude for him. As the family so the state, and every other social unit in the human community.

He laid the foundations well. No single topic in the Analects is treated more extensively than the duties of children toward their fathers and mothers.

He began by dividing these duties into two categories, the material or physical and the spiritual. Under the material, he listed careful attention to the bodily needs of one's parents; caring for one's own body as a legacy received from mother and father; rearing children to provide for the family continuity and perpetuating the family tree. In this connection, one of the best known sayings of Confucius was that "There are three things which are unfilial, but the most unfilial is to have no sons." China has been prodigiously faithful to this precept. Its present birth rate is literally twice that of the United States.

Under spiritual obligations, he included obedience to parental authority; respectful remonstrance with them when they fell into error; being mindful of them after death; carrying out their cherished wishes and unfulfilled plans; and winning all the success and honor that brings luster on the family name.

We get a fair taste of Confucian dialogue in one section of the Analects where the teacher is being questioned about filial piety. Each questioner brings out a new facet of the virtue.

To a question of Mang-i, as to what filial piety consisted in, the Master replied, "In not being perverse." Afterward, when Fan Ch'i was driving him, the Master informed him of the question and answer, and Fan Ch'i asked, "What was your meaning?" The Master replied, "I meant that the Rules of Propriety should always be adhered to in regard to those who brought us into the world; in ministering to them when living, in burying them when dead, and afterward in offering to them of sacrificial gifts."

To a query of Mang Wu respecting filial piety, the Master replied, "Parents ought to bear but one trouble—that of their own sickness."

To a like question put by Ysze-yu, his reply was this: "The filial piety of the present day simply means being able to support one's parents—which extends even to dogs and horses, all of which may have something to give in the way of support. If there be no reverential feeling in the matter, what is there to distinguish between the two?"

To a like question of Tsze-hia, he replied: "The manner is the difficulty. When work has to be done, if the children merely take on themselves the heavy labor; or, as regards food and drink, if they merely set these before their elders—is this to be taken as filial piety?"[8]

Among the virtues that children were to practice toward their parents, obedience was the touchstone of the rest. One of his disciples asked Confucius what was the main duty of a son. The Master answered in one word, "Obedience!"

Foundation of all virtue

In the Confucian moral system, filial piety is more than respect for one's parents or obedience to their commands. It is the mainstay of human society.

The standard treatise on filial piety is now the sixth and last of the *King* books, appropriately entitled the *Hsiao King*. In its introductory chapter, the memory of Confucius is recalled to warrant the composition of a whole volume on this one subject. But no apology was needed because the Master is quoted as saying that "Filial piety is the root of all virtue, and the stem out of which grows all moral teaching." How so?

Our bodies—to every hair and bit of skin—are received by us from our parents, and we must not presume to injure or wound them: this is the beginning of filial piety. When we have established our character by the practice of the filial course, so as to make our name famous in future ages, and thereby glorify our parents: this is the end of filial piety.

It commences with the service of parents; it proceeds to the service of the ruler; it is completed by the establishment of character.[9]

With that introduction, the author, Tsang-tze, who was a disciple of Confucius, continues through eighteen chapters to examine every aspect of this primordial virtue of the moral order. His analysis compares favorably with anything in the *Ethics* of Aristotle or the *Laws* of Plato. It is, in fact, superior to the Greeks in sublimity of moral principle and in such practical wisdom that China has lived on it for three thousand years. Greece could not have survived on Plato's idyllic *Republic* for one generation!

Since so much depends on a correct understanding of this virtue, filial piety should first be briefly analyzed before seeing how broadly the Chinese have come to apply it to the whole of man's life and to every aspect of his conduct.

Everyone who is born into the world has the innate principles of this virtue. It is the common moral denominator of the human species in every age.

With some people it rises early and develops quickly; with others it grows more slowly and may never reach maturity. It starts in infancy with the first dim signs of gratitude that a child shows to those from whom it is receiving everything—without being asked to give anything in return. Vague gratitude grows into respect and honor, generosity and love; and it shows itself by all the tokens of affection that characterize a primary response of the will to a basic fact of knowledge.

"The feeling of affection," declares the *Hsiao King*, "grows up at the parents' knees."[10] So we have stage number one in the analysis of filial piety: the exchange of affection between parent and child long before the age of reason.

"The son derives his life from his parents, and no greater gift could possibly be transmitted."[11] This is stage number two: with the dawn of reason, a child begins to realize what a gift he received (and is receiving) from his parents—the most that anyone can give.

"Hence, he who does not love his parents, but loves other men, is called a rebel against virtue."[12] Here we reach stage number three: as the conscience develops, a child should realize that no one ought to be loved more than his parents. To love any one more than them is to be a traitor to virtue.

"As the duty of nourishing those parents is exercised, the affection daily merges in awe."[13] Stage number four: as the child grows into a man, his love for mother and father (shown mainly in obedience) matures into honor and reverence that increase with the years.

"The sages proceeded from the feeling of awe to teach the duties of reverence, and from that of affliction to teach those of love. The teachings of the sages, without being severe, were successful, and their government, without being rigorous, was effective. What they proceeded from was the root of filial piety, implanted by

Heaven."[14] This is stage number five and the last. It bridges the gap between the filial piety of children toward their parents and the piety of citizens toward their rulers. They are not two virtues but one; only the object is extended beyond its original scope.

Let us take stock of things for a while before going any further. Confucian morality teaches that each person is born with the capacity for filial piety, "implanted by Heaven" or God. Its first object of exercise is the child's parents, presuming they evoke this virtue by their love and tender care. The parents never cease having the same basic relationship to their children, even with the passing of years. Children are always to respect their parents.

As a person enters the larger relationships of society and takes on the role of active citizen in the State, the rulers of government become for him new objects of filial piety—not unlike what his parents were (and remain) in his own immediate family.

On the level of government, the practice of filial piety applies not only to subjects toward their officials and finally toward the sovereign. It is just as necessary that those who govern others are themselves faithful in the practice of this virtue.

Here we reach a turning point in the Confucian moral system. There are two sides to it: one looks upon filial piety as essentially deferent and obedient, where the adjective "filial" describes how sons (or daughters) ought to behave toward those who gave them life—whether their physical life as parents or their political life as rulers in society.

The other looks upon filial piety as also deferential, but now exercised as humility and generosity not only toward parents or rulers but also toward children and subjects. On this level, not much is said (for obvious reasons) about the need for parents practicing filial piety toward their offspring; but a great deal is made of its practice by princes and kings toward their subjects.

We are now in a position to say what Confucianism understands by filial piety on every level and in whatever shape or form. It may be defined as devotion to the originators of one's being. Devotion is living dedication, and the originators of one's being are all those in any way responsible for a man's existence and welfare, beginning with *Shang-Ti*, the Supreme Ruler, and extending to every last person who contributes to the well-being of his neighbor.

When speaking of filial piety in rulers, the author of the *Hsiao King* was careful to distinguish between a ruler's piety toward his own ancestors and his piety toward the citizens of a State. Ancestral piety starts with infancy, matures in adolescence, and must keep growing through adult life—no matter how exalted a prince's position or wisdom or power. Nothing, absolutely nothing excuses a ruler from the continued practice of filial piety until his own death. The more sound this virtue is in him, the better off will be his people; and conversely, if he is wanting in piety toward his own elders (living and dead), he will be a bad ruler and tyrannize those under his domain.

A ruler's filial piety toward his subjects is not different in essence from the piety expected of him toward his ancestors. Confucius and Mencius and their disciples circle round the topic from every angle. They are at special pains to show what kind of piety the ruler ought to exercise since they know that, like prince like people, so that the more "pious" in the strictest Confucian sense are a nation's rulers, the more virtuous will be its citizens.

The superior man

Confucius seems to have coined the one term that embodies the perfect ruler. He should be *Chun-tzu,* a "superior man," whose exemplary conduct will inspire others to become "superior men" in their turn.

"Look at a man's acts," the master advised, "watch his motives; find out what pleases him. Can the man evade you?" His personality is self-revealing from the actions he performs.

> What is a superior man? He puts words into deeds first, and sorts what he says to the deed. A superior man is broad and fair; the vulgar are biased and petty.
>
> A superior man has no likes and dislikes below Heaven. He follows right, superior men cherish worth; the vulgar cherish dirt. Superior men trust in justice; the vulgar trust in favor.
>
> A superior man considers what is right; the vulgar consider what will pay. Men of old were loth to speak, lest a word they could not make good should shame them. A superior man wants to be slow to speak and quick to act.
>
> Tzu-lu asked "What is a superior man?" The Master said, "A man bent on shaping his mind." "Is that all?" asked Tzu-lu. "On shaping his mind to give happiness to the people," said the Master.

91

A superior man makes right his base. Done with courtesy, spoken with deference, rounded with truth, right makes a superior man. His unworthiness vexes him; to live unknown does not vex him. He fears lest his name should die when life is done. He is firm, not quarrelsome; a friend, not a partisan. He is consistent, not changeless.[15]

As extensive as the qualities of the superior man seem from this single recitation of his virtues, it is only a fraction of all that Confucianism conceives him to be.

Fortunately there are two qualities that keep recurring often enough to be considered indispensable. The superior man must possess *jen* and he must practice *li*. Around these two pivotal concepts revolves the whole moral system.

Etymologically, *jen* combines the character that is identified with "man" and "two," as though in English we joined the words "manly" and "friendly." Its range is all the properties of human-heartedness that the Christian West has come to associate with love —with some notable differences, however.

On one occasion, Confucius was asked by a disciple, "What is love?" He was informed: "Love is to mete five things to all below Heaven—modesty and bounty, truth, earnestness and kindness. Modesty escapes insult; bounty winds the man; truth gives men's trust; earnestness brings success; kindness is the key to men's work."[16] Few men have defined love more accurately.

Along with the possession of *jen*, the truly superior man practices *li*. Again etymologically the Chinese word *li* combines two elements that, at first, seem to be unconnected. It stands at the same time for "propriety" and for "ritual."

On the "propriety" side, it has nothing to do with etiquette or that maze of trivial details that we now call "social conventions." In the mind of Confucius and those who trusted him, *li* was the embodiment of a nation's traditions and the inherited wisdom of the past. It was the accumulation of all the great sayings of the masters and the distillation of their spirit, expressed in pithy epigrams.

Concretely the virtue of propriety affected five sets of human relationships, whose faithful exercise by the ruler would guarantee their practice by the people: between father and son, elder brother and junior brother, husband and wife, elder friend and junior friend, and ruler and subject.

Part of this sense of propriety was respect for old age in every social relationship. It was also meant to be mutual. A father should be loving, a son reverential; an older brother considerate, his younger brother respectful; husbands should be "good" to their wives, and the wives must "listen" to their husbands; an elder friend is to be understanding, younger friends should look up to their elders, rulers must be benevolent, and their subjects loyal.

On its ritual side, *li* entered the life-style of China from time immemorial. As Confucius saw it, whatever a man does in the presence of others or for others should partake of worship. It thus becomes the external embodiment of what is presumed to be the internal motivating spirit: harmony in a person's affections between orderly self-love and sincere altruism. There is to be a pattern for every human act, from the way the Emperor three times annually rendered to Heaven an account of his stewardship right down to the way a family entertains the humblest guest in their home and serves him a cup of tea.

So much for what Confucius expected of the superior man. But he also believed the superior man would acquire something mysterious, which he called *Te* (power), for which there is no substitute and, without which, civilization withers away and dies.

Te is already a possession of Heaven, and represents the moral power that *Shang-Ti* has, to get men to live orderly lives without the mechanism of compelling them to be good. *Te* is the way a good father runs his household. His integrity is the moral hold he has on their affections to persuade wife and children to do what he thinks is best for them. *Te* is the only effective means a ruler has to govern his people. Threat of punishment was the last thing Confucius recommended for ruling a country.

Observing on one occasion that the three essentials of government were economic sufficiency, military sufficiency, and the confidence of the people, he added that confidence of the people was primary. "Unless the people can trust their government, it cannot stand." This confidence is possible only where the rulers of government possess *Te*.

CONFUCIAN OPTIMISM

It should be evident by now that Confucian ethics is thoroughly optimistic. The bedrock of orthodox Confucianism is the belief that all men, by nature, are intrinsically good.

While Confucius found the principle already in the annals of his people, and his own discourses breathe the most sanguine type of optimism, it was Mencius who actually developed the familiar Chinese philosophy of undespairing hopefulness. He first laid down his thesis and then explained what this means.

Man's nature is endowed with feelings which impel it toward the good. That is why I call it good. If men do what is not good, the reason does not lie in the basic stuff of which they are constituted. All men have the feelings of sympathy, shame and dislike, reverence and respect, and recognition of right and wrong. These feelings give rise to the virtues of benevolence, righteousness, propriety and wisdom. These virtues are not infused into me from without; they are part of the essential me. Therefore, it is said, "Seek them and you will find them, neglect them and you will lose them." Men differ from one another, some by twice as much, some by five times as much, some incalculably, simply because in different degrees they are unable fully to develop their natural powers.[17]

At the outset, then, Confucianism regards man as basically good because this is natural to the mind which responds by producing good actions. The response is instinctive, much as the eyes, ears, and mouth are made for sight, hearing, and speech, and spontaneously react to their respective stimuli.

The works of Mencius are filled with dialogues and aphorisms in which he argued for the essential goodness of man. Arguing against a little known philosopher named Kao Tzu, he first quoted Kao Tzu as saying that, "Our nature is like a whirlpool: if a breach is made in the east, the water flows east; if a breach is made to the west, it flows west. As water does not discern between east and west, so man's nature does not discern between good and evil." Mencius disagreed. "Truly water does not discern between east and west," he admitted. "But does it not discern between up and down?" In the same way, "Man's nature is good, as water flows down. No man but is good, no water but flows down. Hit water and make it leap, you can send it above your forehead, and you can bring it up a hill. But is that the nature of water? It is done by force; and when a man is brought to do evil, the same is done to his nature."[18]

He never let go this concept. Man of himself and left to himself, would develop into a good person. If he is found bad, it is because he was made bad through outside influences upon him, similar to the unnatural carrying of water to a height, whereas its natural tendency is to run down.

Approaching the principle from another angle, Mencius illustrated what he meant by claiming that "all men have a mind which cannot bear to see the sufferings of others." Pity over another person's misery is typical of human goodness.

My meaning may be illustrated thus: Even nowadays, if men suddenly see a child about to fall into a well, they will without exception experience a feeling of alarm and distress. They will feel so, not as a ground on which they may gain the favor of the child's parents, nor as a ground on which they may seek the praise of their neighbors and friends, nor from disliking the reputation of having been unmoved by such a thing.

From this case we may perceive that the feeling of commiseration is essential to man, that the feeling of shame and dislike is essential to man, that the feeling of modesty and complaisance is essential to man, and that the feeling of approval and disapproval is essential to man.

The feeling of commiseration is the principle of benevolence. The feeling of shame and dislike is the principle of righteousness. The feeling of modesty and complaisance is the principle of propriety. The feeling of approval and disapproval is the principle of knowledge.

Men have these four principles just as they have their four limbs. When men, having these four principles, yet say of themselves that they cannot develop them, they play the thief with themselves, and he who says of his prince that he cannot develop them, plays the thief with his prince.

Since all men have these four principles in themselves, let them know to give them all their development and completion, and the issue will be like that of fire which has begun to burn, or that of a spring which has begun to find vent. Let them have their complete development, and they will suffice to love and protect all within the four seas. Let them be denied that development, and they will not suffice for a man to serve his parents with.[19]

This is the most concise statement in Confucian literature on what the Chinese mean when they say that man is naturally good. It still leaves several questions unanswered, for example, what is the scope of this necessary development? If a man goes bad, is it only for lack of education and care? However, the pivotal position is beyond question: virtue is as natural to man as gravity is to water or burning is natural to fire.

A great deal depends on a correct understanding of this concept for a correct appraisal of Chinese culture. The average Chinese is not a pure Confucian; he is also Buddhist and Taoist. Yet, Confucianism dominates his ethical life, and on this level we cannot probe too deeply into the cardinal principle of its morality.

For one thing, how far would Mencius go in seeing goodness—only goodness and no evil—in human nature? He would go very far.

How often it happens that we do our best to please people, and they do not reciprocate. The spontaneous reaction is to judge them harshly and conclude that they are wanting in goodness. Mencius disagrees.

> If a man loves others, and no responsive attachment is shown to him, let him turn inward and examine his own benevolence. If he is trying to rule others, and his government is unsuccessful, let him turn inward and examine his own wisdom. If he treats others politely, and they do not return his politeness, let him turn inward and examine his own feeling of respect.
>
> When we do not, by what we do, realize what we desire, we must turn inward, and examine ourselves in every point. When a man's person is correct, the whole empire will turn to him with recognition and submissiveness.[20]

The implication is clear enough. We tend to judge others rashly and charge them with lack of goodness, when we ought really to look at ourselves to see if we have evoked in others the virtues which they infallibly possess.

Immediately on making this astounding statement, Mencius added what must be the simplest formula for virtue in the Chinese language. He quoted from the *Shih King* or Book of Songs (which he called the Book of Poetry). One imperative sentence: "Be always studious to be in harmony with the ordinances of God, and you will obtain much happiness."[21]

It would seem, then, that Confucian (or Mencian) optimism is not as naïve as some would make it out to be. It does not claim that man is so inveterately good, he cannot be deviated from the course of virtue; nor so inevitably good that all he needs is encouragement and good example to bring out his virtue. But before passing judgment on others, a man should first look to himself; and his own possession of virtue, which is experienced as happiness, depends ultimately on how zealously he tries to conform himself to the ordinances of *Shang-Ti*, the Supreme Lord.

CHRISTIAN APPRAISAL

As a change from the way we dealt with Hinduism and Buddhism, in giving a Christian appraisal of Confucianism we shall cover a broader spectrum—at the risk of leaving many things unsaid. There is too much wisdom in the Chinese sages to omit any single aspect of it that deserves attention. This wisdom is being challenged by a rampant Marxism on a scale unprecedented in the history of nations. A deeper appreciation of what is at stake may also deepen our concern for the future of Asia if the heritage of the ancients, as Confucius called it, is lost to the world.

Primacy of the family

The spirit of Chinese Universism is penetrated with great respect for the family. If China had given the world nothing else, it will have more than earned its place as a benefactor of the human race by the strong, uncompromising insistence on the family as the bulwark of society.

Mencius said, "People have this common saying: 'The empire, the State, the family.' The root of the empire is in the State. The root of the State is in the family. The root of the family is in the person of its head."[22] By the empire, he meant, the whole Chinese commonwealth, by the State, he meant, the local political community to which families belonged. And by the family, he meant, the whole lineage of ancestors, from the oldest living forebear to the furthest removed of whom there was record as the progenitor of a particular clan.

Political historians have marveled at the stability of Chinese civilization for so many millennia, in spite of the vastness of territory involved and the relative absence of a strong government—such as we commonly know in the West. Besides China has always been a myriad of principalities and petty kingdoms, and so densely populated that today's estimate of seven hundred million is only a calculated guess. The relative density, compared to the rest of Asia, has been fairly constant since the time of Confucius.

Yet China has been strong, and its strength lay in its exalted notion of the family.

In the Confucian vocabulary, the family is so important because it is a reflection of the basic relationship in human existence, the origin of mankind from God. The most sacred term in Chinese is *Ti*, ancestor; where it stands for one's own father and mother, beyond them to their parents, beyond them—on and on—to the earliest ancestors of the human race terminating in *Shang-Ti*, the Supreme Father and Creator of the whole human family.

The family is also important because it is there that a child learns the primordial virtues of *jen* and *li*. No substitute for this school is conceivable in Chinese thought, and no substitute is ever offered. Either a child learns to respect others and harmonize its tastes with the needs of those with whom it lives in the family, or it does not learn these virtues at all. There is a black-and-whiteness about Confucian faith in the family as the unique way to develop character that leaves many Western commentators aghast. "What!" they exclaim. "The family is the only way to teach virtue and train people to behave themselves in society!" To which Chinese answer: "Yes, and if there is another and better way, would you tell us?"

They take this so literally that, if a child's upbringing was neglected, they would despair of its ever being raised to maturity.

Devotion to ancestors

Built into this concept of the family is the one virtue that keeps the family united, not only geographically in space but historically over the reaches of time.

Devotion to one's ancestors, we have seen, is an expression of filial piety. It is founded on the realization that all a man has he had received from others, and these others are a long, long line that goes back to the dawn of history. No matter how remote, every ancestor in that line is equally indispensable to a person living now. Whether the forebear lived five hundred or fifty years ago, as forebear, the veneration he deserves is the same.

It is next to impossible for us to visualize what this meant to the believing Chinese. His religion began with the Highest Parent, which is a good rendering of the term *Shang-Ti*. Nor did he ever lose sight of that fact. But it was practiced daily in the attitude assumed toward those who were nearest in the ancestral line and most obviously in need of respect from those whom they brought into the world.

"The duty of children to their parents is the fountain from whence all virtues spring," according to Confucius. This was not a Chinese proverb. It was the rock of Chinese civilization.

Chinese literature abounds in stories that reveal this truth. There was the woman whose aged mother-in-law was pining for fish to eat in the depth of winter. The young woman prostrated herself on the ice of a pond and bared her bosom to melt the ice so she might catch the fish which immediately swam up to the hole. There was the emperor who had all that his heart desired—power and wealth, influence and devoted people, peace at home and profitable treaties abroad. Yet, he was unhappy. His mother was displeased with all this pomp and splendor. He confessed to all who were willing to listen that he could not enjoy his possessions as long as he knew that his mother was saddened by them.

Ancestral worship after one's parents died was not, as in most other religious traditions, a single act of devotion or only a periodic expression of piety. A young Chinese was introduced to venerating his ancestors from early childhood. His parents were still alive, and maybe his grandparents, too. But many generations had already gone out of this world, and their memory was to be kept alive.

The result of this studied concern to remain in touch with those to whom a person owed his existence had the remarkable effect of keeping the past alive more than anyone except a faithful Confucianist can understand. It gave those who believed in ancestor worship a kinship with history that has no counterpart in any other culture of antiquity. As you read the Confucian classics, or even modern Chinese writing, you are struck by the ease with which its characters move across the centuries as though they were talking about yesterday. On one page of Mencius, sages will be quoted from ages apart, with no hint that it made any difference how many dynasties separated them.

Value of sound education

With so much emphasis on the family and filial piety, it is natural to expect Confucianism also to stress the value of education.

There is nothing comparable to it, in size and scope, even in the Golden Age of Athens or of ancient Rome.

The education that Confucius and his disciples prized so highly was not academic instruction in philosophy or mathematics, though they respected these. It was the schooling that children received at home under the parental roof and on which their whole future would depend.

We can be very explicit here. In the story of Chinese civilization, two men were the axis around which it revolved for over twenty-five hundred years. Confucius was the "prophet," to use a borrowed term, and Mencius was the philosopher. Between them Confucianism became the religious culture we are still studying in the present century.

But this culture did not arise without challenge, and would not have survived without education.

Confucius had discovered the secret of China's greatness in the past, and he synthesized the principles on which this greatness would depend in the future. In the course of time, his teachings were called into question, and his ideas were turned to scorn. "Simpleton" and "dreamer" were the mildest names by which his enemies tried to bring his doctrine into disrepute, and they succeeded on a large scale.

His notions of man's basic goodness, of the need for strong family ties, of loving kindness toward others that comes from the experience of kindness at home, of loyalty to civil authority at the sacrifice of self-interest, and of patience with one's parents and devotion to them even beyond the grave—these were not abstruse concepts. They were presented in plain, everyday language and illustrated with scores of anecdotes.

Those who disagreed with him were doing harm among the people by casting doubt on the value of what he had taught.

It was at this crucial point that Mencius entered to save Confucianism for posterity. Mencius received his training from the disciples of Tzu Ssu, the grandson of Confucius. He saw how imperative it was to combat the "heretical" teachings that had become rampant by his day. Two in particular threatened the future of Confucianism and, so Mencius believed, of Chinese civilization. They were Taoism and Mohism—the first being then propounded by a certain Yang Chu and the second by Mih Teih. That was about 300 B.C. It is not a coincidence that Marxist intellectuals in China today have chosen these two men as archcritics of Confucianism. In true Confucian fashion, they are going back to the sages of the past to rebuild, as they say, a new China of the future. Mencius anticipated their arguments. His words read like a prophetic commentary of what would one day come to pass.

Mencius began by pointing to the cycle of prosperity and decadence that had befallen China in the preceding centuries. Just before Confucius came on the scene "the world fell into decay, and principles faded away. Perverse conversation and oppressive deeds waxed rife again." Then the great master preached and persuaded and things improved for awhile. Now the cycle starts over again.

> Once more, sage emperors cease to arise, and the princes of the States give rein to their lusts. Unemployed scholars indulge in unreasonable discussions. The words of Yang Chu and Mih Teih fill the empire. If you listen to people's discourses throughout it, you will find that they have adopted the views of either Yang or Mih.
>
> Now Yang's principle is—"each man for himself," which does not acknowledge the claims of the sovereign. Mih's principle is—"to love all equally," which does not acknowledge the peculiar affection due to a father. But to acknowledge neither king nor father is to be in the state of a beast.
>
> If the principles of Yang and Mih are not stopped, and the principles of Confucius not set forth, crooked words will bewitch the people, and choke love and right.
>
> When love and right are choked, beasts are led to eat men, and men will eat each other. I am afraid, therefore. I defend the way of bygone holy men, withstand Yang and Mih, stop the rise of crooked speakers, and banish wanton words. Working in man's hearts, they hurt his daily order of life; working in his daily order of life, they hurt his conduct. When a holy man arises again, he will not change my words.[23]

Mencius took issue with Yang, who propounded Taoism, because the religion he defended was fundamentally selfish. He opposed Mih, who taught Mohism, because Mohism failed to distinguish between the special love due to one's parents and the general affection owed to all human beings.

Both Taoism and Mohism have been adopted by Chinese Marxism, and are being used to undermine the teachings of the Master.

Confucianism in conflict

Taoism is better known than Mohism. It means etymologically the "Way" (*Tao*) and historically seems to have preceded Confucianism. Its best known expositor, Lao-Tze, apparently a contemporary of Confucius, wrote the *Tao Teh Ching* (The Classic of the Way and Virtue) and thus gave posterity the nearest thing to a Bible of the Taoist faith.

Central to Lao-Tze's classic is the idea of *Tao*, which he invested with a meaning altogether foreign to Confucianism. Where Confucius would understand *Tao* as the "way" or "method" assigned by God and ordered to be followed by all mankind in accordance with the will of Heaven, Lao-Tze made *Tao* into a symbol for the ineffable first principle of being, at once eternal, all-present, which guides the destinies of men and rules even over the gods.

> Tao is all-pervading, and its use is inexhaustible.
> Fathomless, like the fountain-head of all things,
> Its sharp edges rounded off, its tangles untied,
> Its light tempered, its turmoil submerged.
> Yet crystal-clear like the water it seems to remain.
> I do not know whose Son it is,
> An image of what existed before God.[24]

Although great beyond compare, *Tao* is not really transcendent. It is at the same time primordial matter, formative principle, the self-existing, self-acting, homogeneous, omnipresent, boundless and inscrutable, the Real One, beside which the "many" are phenomenal and unreal.

All of this sounds strangely familiar. It is Oriental monism in Chinese form and strongly impatient with the activist virtues of Confucius and his followers. "The ancients," according to Lao-Tze, "who knew how to follow the *Tao* aimed not to enlighten the people, but to keep them ignorant." If there is a conflict among citizens, the reason is that they had been taught too much. "Those who seek to rule a country by knowledge are the nation's curse. Those who seek not to rule a country by knowledge are the nation's blessing."[25]

If that was contrary to what Confucius and Mencius believed, it was so intended. Taoism had no great respect for man's inherently good nature, and less still confidence that education would help any. Living in accordance with nature was its maxim, and "let things be as they are" was its motto.

There have been Taoists who rose above their own philosophy and who found in Confucianism the necessary balance for the vague naturalism that Lao-Tze had taught. But they were the exception. Certainly Yang Chu, whom Mencius took to task, was no friend of what Confucius stood for and openly hostile to his ideals. Yang was an individualist who was unwilling "to pluck out a single hair even if it might have benefited the whole world." Personal advantage and self-protection, "to live as long as possible," were the main tenets of his school.

Two millennia after Yang Chu, Chinese Communists have rediscovered him. They are finecombing the documentary sources to quote every phrase that this rebellious egoist reportedly ever said. His egoism is not mentioned, but only his "progressiveness in reflecting the desire of the freemen of his time" to escape from the shell of antiquarian piety created by Confucius and his school.

The same with Mohism. It was quite different from Taoism in acknowledging the existence of *Shang-Ti*, the Supreme Ancestor on whom depends the moral law. Like Taoism it has coexisted with Confucianism since the time of its founding by Mo-tzu or Mih Teih (468 B.C.-390 B.C.).

But where Confucius was a realist who recognized the need for implementing the moral law and not merely thinking about it, Mohism painted such an idyllic picture of what society should be that— to this day—it is a synonym for Utopian impracticality.

Mo-tzu started with a safe premise. He painted a dark picture of the calamities in the world: enmity between States, thievery between citizens, injustice among people, disobedience of parents, disloyalty to rulers, discord among relatives. He then asked, "Whence did these calamities arise?"—and answered, "They arise out of a want of mutual love."

All very true. And "how can we have the condition altered?" His reply would be fine except for its unrealism, in the absence of practical means and, worse still, in its exclusion of the hierarchy of love and program of education in love postulated by Confucius.

> What is the way of universal love and mutual aid? It is to regard the state of others as one's own, the houses of others as one's own, the persons of others as one's self.
>
> When feudal lords love one another there will be no more war; when heads of houses love one another there will be no

mutual usurpation; when individuals love one another there will be no more mutual injury. When ruler and ruled love each other they will be gracious and loyal; when father and son love each other they will be affectionate and filial; when elder and younger brothers love each other they will be harmonious.

When all the people in the world love one another, then the strong will not overpower the weak, the many will not oppress the few, the wealthy will not mock the poor, the honored will not disdain the humble, and the cunning will not deceive the simple. And it is all due to mutual love that calamities, strifes, complaints, and hatreds are prevented from arising. Therefore the benevolent exalt it.[26]

Mencius' criticism of this kind of panegyric of "mutual love" was its unrealism. Of course strife will cease and wars will end when men love one another. But the point is: how do you get people to love one another? Confucius' answer was to capitalize on the deepest, ingrained human instinct of filial respect, cultivate this instinct by a strong family life, and sustain it by keeping love for one's ancestors foremost in the people's minds.

As with Yang Chu, so with Mo-tzu, Chinese Communists have been using him to discredit Confucianism in the eyes of the masses. His starry idealism sounds like an ancient prelude to Marx' classless society, where everybody will love everybody else, and all conflict between capital and labor will cease.

There was another side to Mo-tzu that Marxist intellectuals have not been slow to recognize: his passion for economic progress and impatience with religion and ritual. As Mo-tzu foresaw the perfect State, there would be no squandering of wealth nor of precious labor time which means wealth. Time-consuming and expensive rituals, ceremonies with long passages of music, and the like, were to be pared down to a minimum. It was not that these things were bad in themselves, but they took too much time and were useless in promoting business and the increase of wealth. He likewise condemned the economic waste of the funerals so beloved of the Confucians. Burial rites and mourning periods should be shortened and simplified. They were, in his words, nothing but the pious embroideries of culture. Minimize them and get on with the real business of life. Even feast days and recreation should be reduced and, if possible, outlawed as a waste of time.

In the fourth century before the Christian era, these sentiments provoked the wrath of Confucian leaders who accused him of sacrificing culture and religion for the sake of economic gain. His philosophy never prevailed and his ideas remained unknown, except when they found a temporary champion who urged the Chinese to break the shackles which bound them to Confucianism.

Western observers feel that, perhaps, Mo-tzu is finally coming into his own, after the long eclipse by a religion that placed piety before prosperity. But Chinese writers who are not Marxists are not so sure.

Christians have much to learn from all of this. They are mainly familiar with European Communism, with its long history of opposition to the Christian religion, Orthodox, Catholic, and Protestant. Some had begun to wonder if it was perhaps Christianity, and not religion as such, to which Marxism was really opposed. If only the churches removed their abuses and Christians were more faithful to their principles, Communism would lose its motivation and the free world could breathe freely again.

The rise of Chinese Communism proved how mistaken was this notion and how wrong it is to think of Marxism as merely a reaction against the unchristian conduct of people in the West. It is an ideology hostile to every religion, and uncompromising in its struggle to replace faith in a spiritual world with faith in this-worldly values alone. "Marxism is materialism," wrote Lenin. "As such, it is as relentlessly hostile to religion as the materialism of the Encyclopedists of the eighteenth century or the materialism of Feuerbach."[27]

The progress of Marxism in China showed how literally this was to be taken. Leaders of the future People's Republic knew that if Communism was to succeed in that country, Confucianism had to be rooted out. All they needed was a method, which they found in the centuries-old conflict with Taoism and Mohism.

They waged a systematic campaign of propaganda of attrition, lasting thirty years. They slowly convinced their own intellectuals to reject the past traditions of their nation and build a New China, after the ruins of a discredited Confucianism had been cleared away.

Their motto was: "Destroy the past! Create a new future!" The past was Confucian faith in *Shang-Ti* and its reverence for the "wisdom of the ancients." The future was to be faith in dialectical materialism. China's Red masters see their main task as a massive reeducation in this new creed.

Mao Tse-tung made this very clear, when he said "I hated Confucius from the age of eight." And in *China's New Democracy* he claimed that "emphasis on honoring Confucius and the reading of the classics, along with advocacy of the old rules of propriety (*li*) and education and philosophy are part of that semi-feudal culture" which must be overthrown. "The struggle between the old and new cultures is to the death."[28]

How many Christians in Europe or America believe that something of the same Marxist spirit of enmity pervades the revolutionary movements in the West? How few are able to see that Christianity, like Confucianism, evokes the same animosity in those who deny their common belief in the heavenly Ancestor of the human race?

ISLAM

The symbol of Islam is the *Shahadah*, or profession of faith,
which every Moslem recites several times daily: "There is no God but Allah,
and Mohammed is his prophet." Enclosed in a circle, it contains
all the essentials of the Moslem religion, that there is only one God,
the unique Creator of heaven and earth, and that Mohammed
is the last of the great prophets to proclaim the existence
of Allah. This is the authentic symbol of Islam as a religion.
The more familiar figure of the crescent and star is political
in origin and meaning. It dates from the horoscope of Sultan
Osman I (1288-1326), and is now featured on the flags
of several Moslem countries.

Although we classify Islam as a non-Christian religion, along with Hinduism, Buddhism, and Confucianism, the designation must be explained.

Oriental religions properly so-called are non-Christian in the privative sense. They were founded by persons who lived centuries before the time of Christ, and their development over the centuries has taken place independently of Christianity. Where Christian ideas have, on occasion, penetrated into Oriental beliefs or practices, the entrance has been sporadic, oblique, and incidental.

Not so with Islam. Its founder lived in the seventh century of the Christian era. His religion, as described in the Koran, shows constant and essential dependence on the life and work of Jesus of Nazareth. In the more than a thousand years since then, Islam has been conscious of Christianity as of no other religious tradition in the world. Its conflicts with Christianity have been neither few nor unimportant. Its studied awareness of the beliefs of Christians, and its rejection of what they stand for, is built into the fabric of the Koran and has been defended in a vast literature that has no counterpart in the religious world.

If Islam is to be called non-Christian, the term is more than privative. It is part of the history of the religion in that Christianity has been excluded as a legitimate rival. Yet, while excluding Christianity, it includes Christ and much of his teaching and shows a respect for the Son of Mary that is one of the paradoxes of Islam— as it is also the problem it poses for those who accept Jesus Christ and profess to be Christians.

If there were reasons for studying other religions outside the ambit of Christianity, there are overwhelming reasons for knowing as much as possible about Islam. Like Christianity, it stems from a Judaic ancestry and has much in common with Judaism. The three traditions offer much in contrast with one another, though all three acknowledge Abraham as the father of all the faithful.

Islam, along with Judaeo-Christianity, is the third great monotheistic religion of the world. Its adherents number about five hundred million, more than any single group of monotheists outside of Roman Catholicism. Its presence in the Orient is big and formidable, and it stands as the most powerful obstacle to organized Marxism in southern and southeastern Asia.

The resurgent nations in Africa are finding in Islam a powerful protector and the promise of religious unity which has a strong attraction to people who, until recently, were a conglomeration of suspicious and warring tribes. Islam offers them a religion which is not, so the argument goes, connected with the despised colonial powers of the West; and it does not teach the patient submissiveness which, for too long, has kept the Africans virtual slaves of their Christian masters.

In countries with militant Negro minorities, the people are told to turn to Islam and away from the Gospel, which so far has brought them only misery and the folly of the cross. The Black Moslems are a symbol of this violent reaction.

In the Near East a storm is brewing that may erupt into a world conflagration. To those who know Islam, it is a confrontation that has been long in the making. To be exact, it goes back to the Battle of Badr (624), when the enemies of Mohammed were first roundly defeated and where the Jews were, once and for all, ostracized by Mohammed for refusing to accept him as their prophet.

HISTORICAL SETTING

Islam cannot be understood without first knowing something of its historical beginning. The whole period of any significance covered not more than twenty years, from A.D. 610-612, when Mohammed emerged in Mecca at the age of forty, as the messenger of a new revelation, to the time of his death in Medina at the age of sixty-three, in A.D. 632.

As far as scholarship is able to tell, the Semitic people who formed the permanent population of Arabia before the time of Mohammed were native Arabian animists, Jews, and both orthodox and Nestorian Christians.

Idolatry was combined with elements of biblical tradition to give the native Arabs their religion. Derived from a primitive form of nature worship, it consisted largely in the veneration of heavenly bodies. Though they seemed to have believed in one God, the early Arab found little trouble combining his weak monotheism with adoration of the fixed stars and planets, or at least with offering sacrifice to the spirits who were believed to dwell in these stellar bodies. They gave the title "goddesses" or "daughters of God" not only to these intelligences but to their images as well.

Estimates differ on the number of Jews and Christians in pre-Islamic Arabia. Most likely they were not numerous, except in the larger cities along the Mediterranean coast. They were certainly not dominant in the bevy of small towns and nomadic villages that were the mainstay of the territory where Mohammed lived and propagated his religion.

What Mohammed saw around him was not pleasant. Sharp business practices, corruption among the Arab chiefs, neglect of things religious, and immorality that made the coastal towns along the Red Sea proverbial haunts of the lowest dregs of humanity. The father of Mohammed died before his son was born, and the mother died when Mohammed was ten. He was brought up in the homes of several relatives in succession, and his early propensity to reflection and prayer only further separated him from the already estranged environment in which he was reared.

Mohammed's first message to the worldly Meccans was only too plain: they were living in sin and, unless they repented, the hand of God's justice would visit them. Almost from the beginning he also saw himself as an instrument of God's vengeance. He was the new Jeremiah, but wielding a sword.

Ten years of preaching were in vain. Mecca was not interested in this visionary and paid no attention to him until he made some converts, mostly among the slaves and foreigners. When the converts grew, opposition also began, and Mohammed was forced to flee Mecca in the fall of 622. This flight from Mecca to Medina, with a handful of followers, is the year "one" in Moslem history. It is known as the *hijrah* (departure), and has since become the most solemn feast day in the Islamic calendar.

All the while, Mohammed was writing his Koran. But at this point there is a radical transition. In fact, chapters in the Koran are variously (though not uniformly) designated as "Written at Mecca," or "Written at Medina."

It became Mohammed's consuming passion to establish Islam as the divinely authorized religion of Arabia. From a mystic he first became preacher; and from preacher he became military leader. In a series of successful battles at Badr, Medina, and Hunajn, Mohammed conquered those who opposed him. The people of Medina were overwhelmed by superior numbers and zeal; the citizens of Mecca begged for mercy. From Medina, in 631, the prophet issued his definite norms which excluded idolaters from the pilgrimage to Mecca which had become entirely Islamized. In 632 (the year of his death) over forty thousand persons made the pilgrimage with him, as a symbol of his sweeping success and to pledge their allegiance to Mohammed.

His mission was finished: paganism had been crushed, the new faith was solidly established, and a young generation of ardent followers was ready to carry his message to the far reaches of Asia and northern Africa.

He left as the main legacy to his followers the Bible of Islam, called the Koran because it was to be recited. It is autobiographical and consists of the revelations which Mohammed claimed to have received from God through the mediation of the angel Gabriel.

Even today, Islam is the Koran. No deviation from its doctrine is permitted and acceptance of its teaching is unequivocal. What the Koran teaches, therefore, is what Moslems believe—more so than can be said of any other religion. In the absence of a hierarchical church or magisterium within Islam, and in the presence of its worship of the dictated text as the inspired word of God—the Koran has for thirteen hundred years spoken with an authority that is only approximated but never equaled by anything in Christianity.

Our analysis of Islam will be based on the Koran, with only such excursions outside the sacred text as may be necessary to better understand its meaning.

There is a logic in Islam that has only to be pointed out to be recognized. It can be stated in four terms, each of which follows necessarily on the preceding, and the four together constitute all the essentials of the Moslem faith. God and spirits, messengers and Moslems are so closely related that, unless each one is given its due measure of importance, the whole structure of Islam as a theologically coherent system would disintegrate.

Islam begins with the affirmation of one personal God, creator of heaven and earth, and sovereign master of the man's destiny.

Below God, yet above men, are created spirits of varying grandeur and dignity. We might call them angels. Their role is mainly to act as mediators between God and the human race. It was the angel Gabriel who served this crucial role as spokesman for God in favor of Mohammed. Except for Gabriel, there would have been no divine revelation to the prophet and consequently no Islam.

Between the angelic spirits and ordinary men are certain chosen persons, call them prophets, who are divinely appointed to receive communication from on high and pass it on to their fellowmen. Mohammed was such a prophet and, in fact, the greatest in the history of God's communication with men.

Finally that which Mohammed believed he had received from God was the revelation whose acceptance meant submission, that is, Islam, of God's will as manifested to his messenger Mohammed.

On each of these four levels, Islam has distinctive teachings and a doctrinal stance that marks it off unqualifyingly from all other religions: from any form of polytheism, from Judaism, and from Christianity. Always self-conscious, Islam has no doubt about its identity and its writers are absolutely clear where their faith stands and why it should be accepted as the final and decisive religion of the human race.

CONCEPT OF GOD

The fundamental doctrine of Islam is that there is only one God. Mohammed never wavered on that doctrine from the earliest days at Mecca to his last dictated words in the Koran. One single passage has been quoted to the contrary; it was occasioned when he was momentarily tempted to compromise with the Quariash tribe by acknowledging the existence of other beings as intercessors with Allah.

For the most part, Mohammed developed his notion of a single personal deity in opposition to polytheism of his own Arab people. Historically, then, Moslem monotheism started as a reaction to the prevalent worship of many gods in pre-Islamic Arabia.

We may divide the Koran into two unequal parts, the earlier Meccan composition and the later done at Medina; the first part presents an uncompromising monotheism against the background of the idolatry, as Mohammed denounced it, of the pagans in mid-western Arabia; the second part shows a monotheism which Mohammed pitted against what he thought was the belief in three gods among the Christians of his day. This distinction is quite useful to explain those many passages in which Mohammed condemned those who "assign partners to God." The unpardonable crime was to derogate from the unique attribute of Allah as creator of the world; in the work of creation, no one could be a companion to the Lord.

Characteristic of Allah is his power to create. False gods have created nothing; and, by this norm, the truth is to be distinguished from error.

> He unto whom belongs the sovereignty of the heavens and the earth, He has chosen no son nor has He any partner in the sovereignty. He has created everything and has meted out for it a measure.
>
> Yet they choose beside Him other gods who create nothing but are themselves created. They have no power to hurt nor to profit for themselves; they possess neither death nor life, nor the power to raise from the dead.
>
> Those who disbelieve this say: "This is nothing but a lie that he has invented, and other people have helped him with it, so that they have produced a slander and a lie."[1]

God's creative power did not end with bringing the world into being. He continues his providential care of the universe, with special care for mankind.

> Lo! Your Lord is Allah who created the heavens and the earth in six days. Then He established Himself upon the throne, directing all things. There is no intercessor (with Him) save after His permission. That is Allah your Lord. So worship Him.

Unto Him is the return of all of you. It is a promise of Allah in truth. Lo! He produces creation, then reproduces it, that He may reward those who believe and do good works with equity. As for those who disbelieve, theirs will be a boiling drink, and painful doom because they disbelieved.[2]

Like the prophets of the Old Testament, Mohammed asked the unbelievers to show him anyone else than Allah who qualifies as God: "Show me any part of the earth that they have created, or have they a share in the heavens?"[3] Again, "Those whom you call upon apart from Allah will not create a fly, even if they all joined together to do it."[4] There simply cannot be a god other than Allah, for then "each god would go off with what he had created, and set himself up against the others."[5] Thus the perfect harmony in the physical forces of nature, conspiring to the benefit of man, is evidence of the one Creator to all who are willing to think.

Your God is one God. There is no god save Him, the beneficent, the merciful.

Lo! In the creation of the heavens and the earth, and the difference of night and day, and the ships which run upon the sea with that which is of use to men, and the water which Allah sends down from the sky, thereby reviving the earth and dispersing all kinds of beasts therein, and in the ordinance of the winds, and the clouds obedient between heaven and earth—these are the signs of Allah's sovereignty for people who have sense.

Yet of mankind are some who take unto themselves objects of worship which they set as rivals to Allah, loving them with a love like that which is due to Allah only.

Oh, that those who do evil had but known, on the day when they behold the doom, that power belongs wholly to Allah, and that Allah is severe in punishment.[6]

When Islam comes to describe the false gods, its approach varies. The dominant attitude is that they are nothing at all. Mohammed calls them al-batil, "the vain thing."[7] People take their own desires as gods.[8] "What you worship apart from Allah are only names which your fathers invented."[9]

On the last day, polytheists will be asked where are their gods.[10] They will call on them but no one will answer.[11]

Elsewhere in the Koran, the false gods are given a certain degree of real existence. In one passage they are said to be *jinn*, that is, creatures like men but made out of fire instead of earth.[12] Or idolaters are accused of adoring the rebellious Satan instead of Allah.[13] Surprisingly, on the day of judgment, the false gods will repudiate any responsibility for the worship paid them by men. The latter chose to venerate gods to suit their own pleasure; they did so without instruction from anyone.[14]

Since everything men possess has come to them from Allah, they are to acknowledge his goodness and, in doing so, fulfill the basic precept of religion which is gratitude. Failure to show gratitude is *kufr*, a term that now simply means "unbelief" in Moslem theology.

The name that has come to be used for the religion founded by Mohammed, Islam, did not appear until relatively late in Mohammed's career, certainly after he had gone to Medina. Essentially it means "surrender," by which Mohammed understood three things especially: with the mind a recognition of Allah's supreme majesty and uniqueness as Lord; with the mind, too, the realization of complete dependence on God; and finally with the will (and the whole man) responding to those two beliefs in the precise ways specified by God.

There is also evidence of some development within the Koran of the concept of God. Allah becomes more and more obviously transcendent as the Surahs go on, with a gradual hardening of the divine attributes. He appears more gracious and merciful at the beginning, and more arbitrary toward the end of the Koran. One explanation is that Mohammed's struggle for acceptance and the opposition he met from those who refused to accept his message was reflected in the image of God which he projected in the twenty years of his preaching.

God is designated by two names in Islam, the more familiar Allah and the less well-known ar-Rahman. Almost certainly Allah was a contraction for the two terms, *al'Ilah* = the God, to distinguish him from all others and spurious deities. Each tribe among the Arabs in Mohammed's day might refer to its own god; hence the need for some unique identification.

Ar-Rahman is most likely a borrowing from the Semitic language and may be traced to the stress Mohammed placed (until later on) on God's mercy, that is, *rahman*. The term had been widely used by the Christians before Mohammed's time as a name of endearment, and in contrast to the notion of God as the Lord of justice and vengeance.

In the subsequent history of Islam, the religion has oscillated between these two approaches to the divinity: as maker of the universe to whom obedience is due because he is master of creation. He is therefore to be feared and worshiped as Allah. But as the beneficent One who knows man's weakness and sustains man in his trials, he is also to be loved as ar-Rahman.

CREATED SPIRITS

Mohammed did not leave his religion there. Having pictured Allah as sovereign ruler of the world, he saw in this world three kinds of intelligent beings, men and women who are born by natural procreation, *jinn* who are like men except that their bodies are igneous and not strictly corporeal, and angels (*mal'ikah*) who are spiritual powers and without bodily form.

One stage above mankind are the *jinn*, whom Mohammed identifies as preternatural beings that may be either good or bad, depending on their own choice. As among men, so among the *jinn* there are believers and infidels. Like unbelieving men, the rebellious *jinn* will be judged and finally condemned to hell. Rebellious *jinn* are called *shaitans*, corresponding to the English "satans." They lead men astray, oppose the prophets, and try to overhear what is discussed in heaven but are driven off by shooting stars. They teach men sorcery and are assigned to unbelieving men and women as mates.

Like human beings, the *jinn* are organized into societies and nations, and they have their leaders in *jinn* communities. The Koran is filled with references to these midway creatures, some good and others wicked, but all just as responsible to Allah as the men and women toward whom they serve as more than human but less than angelic instruments of Providence.

The angels are in a class by themselves. They are subordinate and created beings, whom God appointed his messengers and mediators to mankind. Select passages from different parts of the Koran illustrate the general tone in Moslem angelology, which stands as the keystone of the Islamic faith.

Praise be to Allah, the Creator of the heavens and the earth, who appoints the angels messengers having two, three and four wings. He multiplies in creation what He wills. Lo! Allah is able to do all things.[15]

Those who bear the Throne and all round about it, hymn the praises of their Lord and believe in Him and ask forgiveness for those who believe, saying, "Our Lord! You comprehend all things in mercy and knowledge. Therefore forgive those who repent and follow your way. Ward off from them the punishment of hell."[16]

Lo! There are above you guardians, generous and recording, who know all that you do.[17]

The function of the angels is so similar to what we know of Jewish, especially Rabbinic angelology, that the borrowing is certain and extensive. Angelology has always been an integral part of orthodox Judaism, and the same—with emphasis—is true of orthodox Islam.

While their normal role in Jewish belief is to act as messengers of God, this becomes so prominent in Islam that on it depends the whole Moslem religion. As Mohammed understood the human situation, men are not (of themselves) capable of knowing the true God nor, much less, the proper way of worshiping him. They must be informed of God's nature and told about his will, and the informants are the angels of God.

Among these the most prominent is the angel Gabriel, who was sent by Allah to his servant Mohammed. At strategic places in the Koran, Mohammed recalls the fact that he was chosen to receive the communication from heaven, and that it was no less than Gabriel who spoke in the name of God.

Say, O Muhammad, to mankind: Who is an enemy to Gabriel! For it is he who revealed this Scripture to your heart by Allah's leave, confirming that which was revealed before it, and guidance and glad tidings to believers.[18]

This is in truth the word of an honored messenger, mighty, established in the presence of the Lord of the Throne, one to be obeyed, and trustworthy.[19]

At the opposite side to Gabriel, who is the link between Allah and Mohammed, is *Iblis*. He is the leader of the evil spirits and the only one whose fall from divine friendship is detailed in the Koran.

Remember, when your Lord said to the angels: "Lo! I am creating a mortal out of potter's clay of black mud altered. So, when I have made him and have breathed into him of my spirit, do you fall down, prostrating yourselves unto him."

So the angels fell prostrate, all of them together. Save Iblis. He refused to be among the prostrate.

The Lord said: "O Iblis! What ails you that you are not among the prostrate?"

He said: "Why should I prostrate myself unto a mortal whom you have created out of potter's clay of black mud altered?"

The Lord said: "Then go forth from hence, for truly you are an outcast. And lo! The curse shall be upon you till the Day of Judgment."

He said: "My Lord! Because you have sent me astray, I shall certainly adorn the path of error for them in the earth, and shall mislead them every one. Save such of them as are your perfectly devoted servants."

The Lord said: "This is a right course incumbent upon me. As for my servants, you have no power over any of them except such of the arrogant as follow you. And lo! For all such, hell will be the promised place."[20]

Between these two revelations, the one of Gabriel communicating Allah's message to Mohammed and the other of *Iblis*, permitted by Allah to lead most of mankind into error, lies the essential theme of Islam. The implied epistemology is that religious truth is unattainable except by revelation.

God's prophet is spokesman for divine truth. His archenemy is the evil spirit whose "mission" until the end of time is to seduce people from accepting the Moslem revelation. Those who listen to Gabriel, through the lips of Mohammed, will be saved. Those who are deluded by *Iblis* into rejecting Gabriel's communication are promised hell.

If Islam is not more often seen in this light, the reason cannot be that its teaching is not clear enough in the Koran. It may be that the subject of angels and demons is less relevant to the modern mind, and, consequently, even the cardinal principles of a religion may be obscured if they are judged from the viewpoint of sense empiricism. But Mohammed lived in the world of the invisible. For him angels and *jinn*, Gabriel and *Iblis*, were the most real persons in the world, after the invisible Allah himself.

THE PROPHETS AND MOHAMMED

In the Islamic sequence of divine communication, revelation comes from Allah. It is directly given to the angels. They pass it on to human beings specially chosen for the task.

These human intermediaries are sometimes called prophets, more often messengers, and sometimes apostles. If the inhabitants of the earth had been angels, angels would have been sent to them.[21] But since they are men, men who eat and drink, who have wives and children, they are God's ambassadors to their own kind.[22]

On this crucial point, the Koran is not fully consistent. In many passages, certainly those in the early stages of his career, Mohammed writes of the prophets almost casually. They were men like himself, to whom "suggestions" were made by God and an invitation that they share these "suggestions" with others.[23] They came of the people to whom they were sent and used their language. They wrought no signs, and worked no miracles, except rarely by permission of Allah. They were concerned only with the proclamation and delivery of the message with which they were charged. They had no authority over their people or responsibility for their unbelief.

As Mohammed's mission moved on, he saw himself accepted by some but rejected by others. Moreover, as he came more into contact (and conflict) with the Jews and Christians whom he was persuading to accept Islam, the role of the prophet also changed.

From the time he went to Medina and saw himself growing in leadership, Mohammed began to proclaim an ever higher status for the *nabiy*, the prophet of Allah. The *nabiy* is sent to be obeyed.[24] He is given the Book that he may judge among the people.[25] To be given the Book is the prerogative of the prophet, which no one may usurp.[26] Along with the right to judge, he also receives the power of jurisdiction over those to whom he is sent.[27] He is a witness over his people.[28] Though not explicitly stated, it is also implied that a *nabiy* may be allowed by Allah to intercede for those to whom he is commissioned and, in this sense, become simultaneously priest and prophet.

Altogether the Koran mentions twenty-eight prophets of the Lord; of these, four are Arabian personages, eighteen are Old Testament figures, three belong to the New Testament, and two are identified by epithets without further description.

The oldest of the prophets was Adam, followed by Noah and Abraham. The New Testament *nabiy* were Zechariah (husband of

Elizabeth), John the Baptist, and Jesus. The last and greatest of the prophets was Mohammed.

All the prophets preached basically the same doctrine, namely the oneness of Allah and the retribution awaiting those who reject the message preached in his name. Yet there was also an evolution in the content of the prophetic communication, in rising crescendo from Adam through Abraham to Mohammed. Each major stage of development is marked by the production of an epoch-making book, of which there have been four in the history of mankind. There will be no others.

To Moses was given by divine inspiration the *Tawrah*, the Jewish *Torah* or Law, corresponding to the Pentateuch. David was the human author of the *Zabur*, identified in the Koran with the Psalms. Jesus was the bearer of the third great written revelation, the *Injil* or Evangel, which is the Gospel of the Christians. Lastly, Mohammed received from Allah the doctrine which was to be set down in the *Qur'an* or Recital of Islam.

All four scriptures were intended to be written revelations, and all alike are to be accepted and believed by the people. Each has a message that confirms what preceded and predicted what was to follow. Thus David confirmed Abraham, and Jesus the preceding two. Mohammed received the final revelation, since no prophet sent from God will ever follow him. He cleared up all uncertainties and is the repository of perfect Truth.

Mohammed attached himself personally to the family of Abraham. The patriarch is described in the Koran as the founder of the first monotheistic religion, from which all had more or less strayed since his day. Mohammed's task was to restore the faith of Abraham among the people.

Once he made this correlation between himself and Abraham, Mohammed made Islam the religion of the chosen people of God. The prophetic office, he explained, belongs by right to the descendants of Abraham. In the Abrahamic line were Moses and David and Jesus. In the same line was Mohammed. Comparable, therefore, to the role of the Jews as the *gens electa* of Yahweh, whose prophetic function was to communicate to the Gentiles the wisdom of the Lord; and comparable to the mission of the Christians, told by Jesus to go and preach the gospel to all nations—the followers of Mohammed were commissioned to do the same. Their divine mandate is solemn and specific.

> All that is in the heavens and all that is in the earth glorifies Allah, the sovereign Lord, the Holy One, the mighty, the wise.
>
> He it is who has sent among the unlettered ones a messenger of their own, to recite unto them His revelations and to make them grow, and to teach the Scriptures and Wisdom, though heretofore they were in manifest error.[29]

So much for the providential role of Mohammed, who was sent by Allah to the Arabians of his day to preach the true faith to a people sunk in the darkness of idolatry.

Those who have received the Moslem faith are then bidden to communicate it to others. Much as Mohammed was God's prophet to Moslem, they, in turn, are to be prophets to other people. Even as he preached and propagated by military arms, they are to follow his example.

There are two classic passages in the Koran which prescribe what has become known as *jihad,* the Holy War. They direct the use of the sword for the extension and not merely the preservation of Islam.

> When the Sacred Months (of truce) are over, kill those who ascribe partners to God, wheresoever you find them. Seize them, encompass them, and ambush them. Then if they repent and observe the prayer, and pay the alms, let them go their way.
>
> Fight against those who do not believe in Allah, who do not prohibit what God and His prophet have forbidden, and who refuse allegiance to the True Faith—until they pay the tribute readily after being brought low.[30]

Moslem scholars recognize the clear injunction of the Holy War in the Koran but insist that, even so, it is not an article of faith based on scripture (the Koran) alone. Its unquestionable prescriptive character comes from the *Hadith* or sayings of Mohammed, which constitute Islamic tradition.

According to the *Hadith,* the Holy War is a binding institution in Islam as a communal and not an individual obligation. The incentive for *jihad* lies in its twofold benefit: legitimate booty for this life and martyrdom with its immediate promise of a blissful eternity hereafter for those killed in battle. They become the *shahada,* martyrs of Allah if they die in fighting for the promotion of Islam.

The exercise of *jihad* was the immediate responsibility of the Moslem *imam* or religious leader, and of the caliph, when the powers of the office were still in his hands. They were divinely sanctioned to wage war on the unbelievers in the regions bordering on Islam (*dar al-Islam*). The yearly raids against the Byzantines soon after Mohammed's death, and later the Turkish incursions into Asia Minor were sanctioned by the *jihad*. It was the *jihad* that prompted the invasion of India in the tenth and eleventh centuries, and the same zeal to spread the doctrine of the Koran which ended in the creation of such modern Islamic countries as Pakistan and Egypt, Indonesia and the Sudan.

Through the *jihad*, every faithful Moslem entered into the prophetic office of Mohammed and shared in the risks and prospective rewards promised to the founder of Islam. He had seen the vision and passed it on to others in the jeopardy of his life; they were partakers in this vision and were to expose their lives to danger in the same cause.

THE MOSLEM BELIEVER

All that we said so far is preliminary to the main question, and the fourth stage in our analysis of Islam: What is a Moslem?

This question is neither speculative nor academic. Many times in the history of Islam it was literally a matter of life and death, in a way that no Hindu or Buddhist would ever be called upon to answer. It is part of the strength of the religion founded by Mohammed that he made it very clear who is a true follower of Allah and who is not.

A simple definition of a Moslem would be that he is one who believes. Islam is, before everything else, a religion of faith. The faith it demands of its adherents is undiluted acceptance of one God, sovereign Lord of the universe and absolute Master of creation.

But this would not be enough. A Moslem not only believes in the God who revealed himself through Gabriel to Mohammed, he also gives public testimony to his faith. Two statements in the Koran synthesize what this means.

> Lo! The religion with Allah is *al-Islam* (the Surrender) to His will and guidance.[31]
> He has named you *Muslimun* (those who submit) . . . of old time and in this Scripture that the messenger may be a

witness against you, and that you may be witnesses against mankind.[32]

When a Moslem is said to believe, the implication is that this costs him something. The price demanded is self-surrender. Why self-surrender? It is because Islamic theology says that man's natural tendency is to believe in the gods of his own making, who are always the projections of his own Ego.

Left to his own devices, the pattern of man's religion is the same. He creates reflections of his own desires and calls them deities. They become idols, therefore, because they are the images conjured up by human fancy as though they were real; though nothing but subjective hopes and fears, they are invested with objectivity and worshiped as though they were divine.

Concretely the surrender of the Ego which is Islam requires the acceptance of Allah's will and guidance instead of self-will and self-reliance in the conduct of one's life.

The two words, *will* and *guidance* of Allah are not a poetical repetition. They stand for two different concepts in the Moslem religion. To do the will of Allah is to keep his commandments. It may be called fidelity to God's manifested intention toward the human race. It is basically uniform for all men and requires obedience to the divine precepts.

To accept the guidance of Allah, on the other hand, is to submit to his providence. It may be called resignation to God's special designs on each individual person. It is consequently different for every one, and requires conformity to the divine plan which mysteriously includes demands on one person that no one else has to make.

This idea of complete surrender to God's providence in the least detail of daily life is eloquently expressed by a modern Egyptian Moslem.

A Muslim should believe in his heart, and confess with his tongue, that the most exalted God hath decreed all things: so that nothing can happen in the world, whether it respects the conditions and operations of things, or good or evil, or obedience or disobedience, or sickness or health, or riches or poverty, or life or death, which is not contained in the written tablet of the decrees of God.[33]

As a Moslem sees it, there is no such thing as chance in the divine vocabulary. With Allah, you can never say that anything "happens." Nothing ever happens; it is always decreed. And to emphasize the eternity of this decree, it is said to have been always "contained in the written tablet" as predetermined by the Almighty. This includes those most difficult things to accept as coming from God, the "evil" or "disobedience" to the divine will committed by other men when their evil crosses my path and I pay for their disobedience.

A Moslem may seem to be fatalistic when it comes to putting up with pain, and Western writers have often painted him that way. But a more honest appraisal would be to say he is (when faithful to his religion) incredibly resigned to the divine will. The warrant for what may seem like irrational patience is the promise of Allah, first made to Mohammed and then to all Moslems.

> We shall try you with fear and hunger, and loss of property and life and blessings. Therefore, O Prophet, give good tidings to those who are patient.
> When misfortunes befall them, they should say: "Verily we belong to God, and to Him we shall verily return." On such as these, blessings and mercy will descend from their Lord. They are the followers of the right path.[34]

Moslem history is filled with stories of refined cruelty suffered for years with marvelous endurance. It also helps to explain the reluctance of Moslem societies to change cultural patterns or to relieve what Christians would consider objects of social welfare and of corporal works of mercy.

That is one side of a Moslem's faith: his resignation to the will and guidance of Allah.

The other side is the duty imposed on him to testify to what he believes. There is a strange expression in the Koran referring to this duty; in practicing it, a Moslem is declared to be witnessing against mankind. Why *against* mankind?

The reason is plain from the whole spirit of Islam. Mankind is naturally prone to idolatry. Whenever a man professes to believe in only one God and is willing to submit to God's will, instead of feeding his own desires, he publicly witnesses against the selfishness of the world. At the heart of Islam is this sense of an Other whose will, and not man's own, should be the norm of human existence.

The manner of giving this witness is common knowledge. There are five main "Pillars of Islam" or fundamental duties by which a Moslem gives testimony to what he believes.

We can transmit three of these duties with only a brief comment. They do not touch on the constants of the faith. A Moslem is expected to give alms, paid in the form of a tax, the *Zakah*. He is to fast during the month of Ramadan in memory of the time that Mohammed received the Koran from the angel Gabriel. Fasting (*Sawm*) is ordered in the Koran as a practice that went back before Islam was founded. "O you who believe," the precept reads, "there is prescribed for you the fast, as it was prescribed for those before you, that you may ward off evil."[35] The reference to "those before you" was to the Jews who fasted on various occasions, notably on the Day of Atonement, but especially to the Eastern Christians who in pre-Islamic Arabia fasted on at least thirty-six days in the year. A Moslem is also told to make a pilgrimage or *Hajj* to the sacred monuments of Mecca at least once in a lifetime, if he is physically able to do so and can afford it. The pilgrimage occurs during the days from the seventh to the tenth of *dhu-'l'Hijah*, at which time thousands of believers converge on the city and live in encampments as far as the eye can reach.

But the *Zakah, Sawm,* and *Hajj* are occasional testimonies of the faith, and neither so basic nor typical as the daily Moslem worship. It is usually treated as two different expressions of belief, although in practice they are regularly combined. Nothing in Islam is more fundamental than the verbal recitation of the Creed, the *Shahadah*, and the public performance of ritual prayer, the *Salah*. Those who are faithful to these two customs are Moslems; anyone else is not.

Islam requires its followers to give repeated witness to their belief in the one true God. *Al-Shahadah* means "bearing witness," and consists of two professions in one. First is the statement, "I bear witness that there is no god whatsoever but God (*Ashadu anna la ilaha illa 'l'Lah*)" followed by "and that Muhammed is the messenger of God (*wa anna Muhammadan rasulu 'l-Lah*)."

It is common doctrine that anyone becomes a Moslem by pronouncing this phrase because he believes it. To say the *Shahadah*, according to Islamic jurisprudence, is to profess the faith of Mohammed and enter the Moslem fold.

The *Shahadah* are the first words spoken in the ears of a newborn child, and the last on the lips of the dying. The *mujahid,*   125 fighter for Islam in the holy war, becomes a *shahid* (witness), or martyr for the faith precisely because during life he had pronounced the sacred phrase. No words are more often spoken than these. Twenty times a day would be minimal, and a hundred times a day would not be excessive. They are the principal message of the *muezzin* as he summons the faithful to prayer from the top of a minaret.

If the *Shahadah* is the basic Moslem Creed, the *Salah* is the fundamental Moslem rite. To say that *Salah* literally means "ritual prayer" is not to say much because in Islam this is *the* ritual prayer and the substance of Moslem liturgy.

Five times a day, at dawn, midday, midafternoon, sunset, and nightfall, the muezzin mounts the balcony of narrow minarets throughout the world of Islam and intones in melancholy tones and resounding voice a formula that has been heard now for thirteen centuries. He cries out: "God is great (four times). I bear witness that there is no god but God (twice). I bear witness that Muhammad is the messenger of God (twice). Come to prayer (twice). Come to contentment (twice). There is no god but God." During the first call at dawn, the muezzin reminds the faithful that "prayer is better than sleep."

City dwellers normally gather together in mosques for *Salah*, although the believer may perform the prayer ritual wherever he finds himself at the time. The only time he is obliged to pray with his fellow Moslems is at the noon service on Friday, the Moslem Sabbath, which is not a day of rest. Mohammed made the Friday *Salah* binding on all the faithful.

> O you who believe! When the call is heard for the day of congregation, hasten unto remembrance of Allah and leave your trading. That is better for you, if you did but know.
>
> And when the prayer is ended, then disperse in the land and seek of Allah's bounty; and remember Allah much, that you may be successful.[36]

Every mosque has a semicircular alcove called the *mihrab* that indicates the direction in which prayer should be said. It must always be toward Mecca. When Moslems pray, they are to turn toward the Mecca of Mohammed, recall the history of their people, and see themselves as part of thousands of concentric circles of believers around the world—all praying with their faces toward the sacred Ka'ba Stone, which symbolizes the conversion from paganism to Islam.

In the mosque, the faithful stand in straight lines facing Mecca, and all behind their *imam* or leader whose back is to the worshipers. This posture has been unchanged for more than a thousand years, and based on what is believed to have been the custom in Mohammed's time.

The daily *Salah* must be done five times, no more and no less, with the times specified in five words that a Moslem child learns at his mother's knee: *subh* (when the sky is filled with light but before the actual sunrise), *zuhr* (right after midday), *asr* (sometime between three and five in the afternoon), *maghrib* (after sunset but before actual darkness), and *isha* (any hour of night).

Also specified is the duty of performing the *Salah* in the state of legal purity or ceremonial cleanliness, *taharah*.

> O you who believe! Draw not near unto prayer when you are drunk, until you know what you are saying, nor when you are polluted, except when journeying on the road, until you have bathed. But if you are ill, or on a journey, or one who of you comes from the closet, or you have touched a woman, and you do not find water, then go to high clean sand and rub your faces and your hands with it.[37]

A Moslem must be absolutely free from every defilement, great or small, when he prays. Purity of body implies purity of spirit; cleanness of dress and place implies sacredness of action. However, except for the ablutions required by the Koran, no other restrictions exist, since there are no priests, or sacrifices, or absolutions to prepare a Moslem for full participation in the Moslem liturgy. Islam has no hierarchy.

The ablutions are of two kinds, a general form (*ghusl*) and a more limited kind (*wudu*). *Ghusl* is required after such major defilements as marital intercourse; *wudu* must be performed after minor defilements like simple contact with the opposite sex.

Even the minor purification is quite elaborate. Legally pure water must be used. First the worshiper bathes his face, then the hands and forearms up to the elbows; next the right hand passes over his head, followed by the washing of his feet. Everything must be done in that order. Clothes must also be perfectly clean; otherwise the efficacy of the prayer is lost.

Not only must the Moslem be purified, but the spot where he prays has to be undefiled. To make sure of this, he will carry with him a "prayer rug," on which he kneels and there forms a *templum* or immediate sanctuary where he takes up his position facing Mecca.

The *Salah* ritual is most detailed. It begins with the Moslem standing upright, repeating the call to prayer (*iqama*), and putting into words his intention to undertake the required number of bows. Unless this intention is made, the prayer is invalid. Then he raises his hands to the level of the shoulders, while pronouncing the *takbir* (magnification), by which he indicates that for the duration of the prayer he wants to be dissociated from all earthly affairs. Any word or gesture foreign to the ritual cancels the prayer, since such distractions are believed to interrupt the worshiper's union with God.

There are eight principal postures to be assumed during ritual prayer, to be performed in a set sequence: (1) from a standing position, the left hand is placed in the right; (2) the upper part of the body is inclined forward from the hips; (3) erect posture; (4) prostration on the ground, as the posture of greatest surrender to God; (5) while kneeling, the worshiper stretches his hand in front of him and touches the ground with his brow at the base of the nose; (6) body is raised on the base of the heels while still in a kneeling position and the hands stretched along the thighs; (7) second complete prostration; (8) back to the sitting position, followed by turning one's head first over the right and then over the left shoulder.

At each of these positions, appropriate prayers are recited, notably the first chapter of the Koran, the famous Fatihah (Opening).

> Praise be to Allah, Lord of the worlds, the Beneficent, the Merciful.
>
> Owner of the Day of Judgment. You alone we worship; You alone we ask for help.
>
> Show us the straight path, the path of those whom You have favored; not the path of those who earn Your anger nor of those who go astray.[38]

From the opening gesture and recitation of the Fatihah to the second prostration is called a full *rakah* (cycle). Every period of prayer has a number of prescribed *rakahs*: four each for midday, midafternoon, and night; and two apiece for dawn and sunset.

The ritual in the mosque on Friday is mandatory whenever feasible and at least forty have assembled. It is conducted by the *imam*, who may come from any walk of life, since there is no priest-hood in Islam. His sermon to the people is the highpoint of the weekly liturgy, supplemented by the invocation of God's blessing on the congregation. For most Moslems, this is the only time they worship together. Their main ritual practice is the intensely detailed *Salah* performed five times a day.

Moslems who comment on their ritual prayer bring out the two elements which they find most prominent: discipline and obedience. The orderly requirements of the *Salah*, specifying which hand should be lifted and how high, at what time and in what direction, is disciplinary in the extreme. The conformity to a set pattern of words, proclaiming God's majesty and man's dependence on him, induces a spirit of internal obedience to the divine will that only those who practice Islam can understand.

CHRISTIAN APPRAISAL

It is comparatively easy for Christians to speak about Islam, once they come to know it, because of the kinship between Chris-tianity and the religion founded by Mohammed.

The two religions are very different, as we shall see, and Mo-hammed never doubted that the revelations he received were to supersede the faith of the followers of the Nazarene. In fact, from Mohammed's viewpoint, Islam is antithetical to the Christianity he had seen in Arabia.

But they also have much in common, and it is here that Islam reflects certain features of basic monotheism that are also present in the Christian religion but are brought out with startling clarity in Islam.

God transcendent and immanent

Everything else in Islam pales into insignificance compared with the stress placed on God's unique transcendence. The worst crime in Islamic theology is ascribing partners to God by attribut-ing divine qualities to anyone or anything else.

The orthodox Moslem conceives of God as absolutely one; he has no sharers in the divinity. He is singular; there is no one like him. He is uniform, having no contrary. He is separate, having no equal. He is ancient, having no first. He is eternal, having no begin-ning. He is everlasting, having no end. He is ever-existing, never having not been. He is perpetual and constant, with neither interruption nor change. He is the Alpha and the Omega, the Manifest and the Hidden. He is the truly Real.

All of this is familiar enough in Judaeo-Christianity, even when the words used are a bit unfamiliar. What is less commonly known, perhaps because of biased interpreters of Islam, is that Allah who is so completely above man and the visible world is also near to man and mysteriously approachable to those who call upon him in faith.

Authentic monotheism, such as prevails in Islam, comfortably spans what some Western writers keep insisting are disparate qualities in God. He is Creator, but he is also Beneficent; he is almighty, but he is also merciful. The Koran plays these two lights on the image of Allah in almost every surah and never tires repeating that, while God is so high he is also very near.

Better than any amount of theorizing, is an example of this combination of God's allness and nearness as found in the classic prayer of Ali, Mohammed's son-in-law.

> My Lord, the Eternal, the Ever-existing, the Cherisher, the True Sovereign whose mercy and might overshadow the universe; the Regulator of the universe, and Light of the creation.
>
> Thou art the adored, my Lord; Thou art the Master, the Loving, the Forgiving; Thou bestowest power and might on whom Thou pleasest; him whom Thou hast exalted none can lower; and him whom Thou hast lowered none can exalt.
>
> Thou my Lord, art the Eternal, the Creator of all, All-wise Sovereign Mighty; Thy knowledge knows everything; Thy beneficence is all-pervading; Thy forgiveness and mercy are all-embracing.
>
> O my Lord, Thou art the Helper of the afflicted, the Believer of all distress, the Consoler of the broken-hearted. Thou art present everywhere to help Thy servants. Thou knowest all secrets, all thoughts, art present in every assembly, Fulfiller of all our needs, Bestower of all blessings. Thou art the Friend of the poor and bereaved; my Lord, Thou art my fortress, a Castle for all who seek Thy help. Thou art the Refuge of the weak, the Helper of the pure and true.
>
> O my Lord, Thou art the Creator, I am only created; Thou art my Sovereign, I am only Thy servant; Thou art the Helper, I am the beseecher.

I am groping in the dark; I seek Thy knowledge and love. Bestow, my Lord, all Thy knowledge and love and mercy. Forgive my sins, O my Lord, and let me approach Thee, my Lord.[39]

These sentiments are typical of a large segment of Islam. They are not commonly associated with the religion of the Koran. Yet they reveal something profound about all religion, and not only Islam, in maintaining the twofold perspective of God who stands above man and of God who dwells within man. He stands above man because he is man's only Creator. He therefore transcends what he created by all the implications of the symbolic preposition, "above." Compared with man, Allah is Master, Sovereign, Mighty, Lord, Creator, King, Dominator, Irresistible, Supreme—all Koranic attributes of Allah.

At the same time, he abides in man by all the connotations of man's need of God and trust in his goodness and willingness to come to man's aid. Nothing is nearer than a God who hears the voice of one crying to him for assistance; nor the same God when he promptly comes to rescue one of his creatures who prays to him for help. The dialectic of God's goodness and of man's desperate want is also Koranic: Helper and afflicted, Knower and secrets, Fulfiller and needs, Friend and the poor, Refuge and weakness— are part of the faith of Islam and a lesson to anyone who is tempted to make God so great that he becomes distant, or so transcendent that men forget to invoke his provident care.

Christ in Islam

The Koran gives a greater number of honorable titles to Jesus than to any other figure of the past. He is a "sign," a "mercy," a "witness," and an "example." Mohammed calls him by his proper name Jesus, by the titles Messiah (Christ) and Son of Mary, and by the names Messenger, Prophet, Servant, Word, and Spirit of God.

There are two accounts of the annunciation and the birth of Jesus in the Koran, which also speaks of his teaching and healings, his death and exaltation. Three surahs of the Koran are named after references to Jesus; he is further mentioned in another hundred verses. He is always spoken of with reverence; there is not a breath of criticism of Jesus in the Bible of Islam.

The proper name of Jesus in the Koran is 'Isa, which is used in the personal sense without explanation. A classic Moslem commen-

tator suggested that 'Isa was an arabized form of Ishu, corresponding to the Syriac Yeshu which is derived from the Hebrew Yeshua,
meaning "one who saves."

A careful reading of the Koran shows that it honors Jesus, and
Islam has done the same. Mutual misunderstandings between Christians and Moslems have led sometimes to the depreciation of Jesus
or the Gospel, but Moslems generally have distinguished between
Jesus and his followers. To this day, when the name of Jesus is mentioned, the pious Moslem will say, " 'Isa, on whom be peace." This
is likely derived from the Koran, which attributes to Jesus the statement, "Peace is upon me the day of my birth, and the day of my
death, and the day of my being raised alive."[40]

By far the most common title for Jesus in the Koran is Son of
Mary (*Ibn Maryam*). This metronymic occurs twenty-three times in
the Koran, which is all the more surprising since "Son of Mary"
occurs only once in the New Testament.

A typical instance is the double account of the birth of Jesus.
The angels announce to Mary the coming of a word from God,
"whose name is the Messiah, Jesus, Son of Mary."[41] Then again,
"the Son of Mary and his mother" are said to have been chosen by
God as a sign, for Jesus gave what Mohammed calls "evidences" or
"proofs" of God. "The Son of Mary is used as a parable" against the
polytheists, for he came with Wisdom, to make differences clear and
to show piety toward God.[42]

The title Son of Mary is so remarkable, it should be more
closely examined by Christians. Some Moslem exegetes claim that,
while *Ibn Maryam* is treated as a name, yet it was first used by the
angels in speaking to Mary to call attention to the fact that Jesus
would be born without a father. They explain that children are generally called after the father, and not the mother, except where the
father is not known.

Mary, the mother of Jesus, is said to have conceived her son
without carnal intercourse. According to Mohammed, quoting Allah,
"Mary . . . guarded her chastity. So we breathed into her some of
our Spirit and made her and her son a token for all peoples."[43] Several times in the Koran, she is defended against those who attack
her virginity. The Jews who spoke against her were guilty of
"a mighty slander."[44] She was a "faithful woman."[45] When she
brought her baby home and was suspected of improper behavior,
the child himself justified his mother by saying, "I am the servant of

God."[46] On two other occasions she is praised for having kept her purity, and twice more she protests that she is a virgin when the birth of Jesus was foretold.

Over the centuries the purity of Mary has been highly regarded in Islam. One of the ancient biographers of Mohammed spoke of "Mary the virgin, the good, the pure." The greatest Moslem woman mystic, Rabi'a, was called "a second spotless Mary." Present-day, orthodox Islam considers Mary sinless, in comparison with all the prophets. One basis in the Koran for Mary's sinlessness is the prayer of her mother, "I seek refuge with Thee for her and her progeny from Satan the stoned."[47] It is part of Islamic tradition, traced to Mohammed, that no child of Adam is born without a demon touching him at the moment of birth. The one whom the demon touches gives out a cry, which is why all infants cry shortly after birth. There have been no exceptions except Mary and her son.

The Koran describes Jesus as a great healer of the sick. Some of his miracles are mentioned in summary form and others given in more detail. What is most unusual about this fact is that Mohammed himself never claimed to work miracles and appealed to none performed in his own name. The Koran is the prophet's only miracle.

All the miracles narrated by Mohammed of Christ were produced in order to convince those who doubted his mission. More than once the Koran states that Jesus healed the blind and the lepers and even raised the dead to life. As Moslem commentators came into closer contact with Christian writings, they assimilated more of the New Testament narratives and, as a result, incorporated more of the teachings and works of Jesus of Nazareth into their own tradition. They began to look for parallels between the Koran and the Gospels. One of the best known is the Koranic story about the miraculous table.

The apostles said, "O, Jesus, Son of Mary, is your Lord able to send down to us a table from heaven?" He replied, "Show piety toward God, if you are believers." They said, "Our desire is that we may eat from it and our hearts be at peace, that we may know that you have spoken truthfully to us and that to it we may be among the witnesses." Jesus, Son of Mary, said, "O God our Lord, send down to us a table from heaven, to be to us a festival, to the first and to the last of us, and a sign from You, and do You provide for us, for You are the best of providers." God said, "Verily I am going to send it down to you; so if any of you afterwards disbelieve, I shall assuredly punish them as I punish no one else of all the world."[48]

Some Moslem writers compare this episode with the gospel story of the Last Supper, others with the Feeding of the Five Thousand, and still others see it as a graphic exposition of the Lord's Prayer, especially of the invocation, "Give us this day our daily bread." All recognize it as evangelical.

As might be expected, Moslems who do not believe in the supernatural react the same way toward the miracles of Christ as their rationalist counterparts in the Christian West. They either deny that miracles are possible, or they question the validity of the miracle narratives. But most Moslems have made the signs worked by Jesus part of their own religion and have no difficulty reconciling them with the power and the mercy of Allah.

Although the Koran quotes the Son of Mary many times, the passages are not remarkable, mainly because they center around only one theme: the role of Christ as sign-worker to prove his mission from the Lord.

One text is different, however, because it has become the keystone of the Moslem faith. It occurs early in the Koran.

> Jesus, Son of Mary, said, "O children of Israel, I am God's messenger to you, confirming the Torah which was before me, and announcing the good tidings of the messenger who will come after me, bearing the name Ahmad."[49]

The Koranic version has a parallel text, recorded by Ubayy b. Ka'b, Mohammed's secretary. The two variants should be taken together.

> O children of Israel, I am God's messenger to you, and I announce to you a prophet whose community will be the last community and by which God will put the seal on the prophets and messengers.[50]

Besides the two variants, which have both entered Islamic thought, is a statement by Ibn-Ishaq (died A.D. 768), whose *Life of the Apostle* is the standard biography of Mohammed. He makes no direct reference to the Koran but from another angle touches on the same idea of Jesus foretelling the coming of Mohammed.

Among the things which have reached me about what Jesus the Son of Mary stated in the Gospel . . . is extracted from what John the Apostle set down for them: "When the Comforter has come whom God will send to you from the Lord's presence, and the spirit of truth which will have gone forth from the Lord's presence, he shall bear witness of me and you also, because you have been with me from the beginning. I have spoken to you about this that you should not be in doubt." The Munahhemana (God bless and preserve him) in Syriac is Muhammad; in Greek he is the paraclete.[51]

All three claims that Jesus foretold the coming of Mohammed have since become part of the Moslem tradition: that Mohammed was the Ahmad predicted as the prophet of good tidings, that is, another Gospel; that Mohammed is the final and greatest of the prophets; and that he is the paraclete or comforter of whom Jesus spoke at the Last Supper.

It is at this crucial point that Islam and Christianity differ on the essentials of their respective faiths. Islam believes that Mohammed, no less than Christ, was a true prophet.

Woven into the Koran as a Christological theme and since become the cornerstone of Islam is the dogma that God could not have had a son and therefore that Jesus could not be one with Allah. "Jesus in Allah's eyes is in the same position as Adam," wrote Mohammed. "He created him of dust and then said to him, 'Be,' and he is." This was revealed by Gabriel, and "whosoever disputes with you concerning him (Jesus), we will summon our sons, and your sons, and our women and your women, and we will humbly and solemnly invoke the curse of Allah upon those who lie."[52] In one eloquent passage, Mohammed consigns all Trinitarian Christians to eternal doom.

They surely disbelieve who say, "Behold, Allah is the Messiah, Son of Mary." The Messiah himself said, "Children of Israel, worship Allah, my Lord and your God." Whoever ascribes partners unto Allah, for him Allah has forbidden Paradise. His abode is the Fire. For evildoers there will be no relief.

They surely disbelieve who say, "Behold, Allah is the third of three," when there is no god save the One God. If they desist not from so saying, a painful doom will fall on those who disbelieve.

> The Messiah, Son of Mary, was no other than a messenger. Many were the messengers that passed away before him. See how God makes His signs clear to them (Christians); yet see how they are deluded away from the truth.[53]

No Moslem who professes to accept the Koran questions these judgments about Jesus and his followers. Christ is for him only a great teacher and the precursor of Mohammed.

Yet a Christian should not generalize. Islam is not a uniform creed and those who profess it are as varied as only thirteen centuries of commentary and criticism and, above all, contact with Christianity, could diversify what has never been a creedal religion.

There are hundreds of sects in Islam, and these in turn are broken into more subdivisions. Each has its own attitude toward Jesus and its own estimate of Christianity.

At one extreme are Moslem Deists, who profess Islam as a cultural tradition and vaguely subscribe to the Koran as "revealed" to the prophet. Their verdict on Christ is the most uncompromising. Jesus was made into a God by the fervent imagination of his followers and the ambition of bishops and priests.

> With all his (Jesus') dreams and aspirations, his mind was absolutely exempt from these pretensions which have been fixed on him by his overzealous followers. He never claimed to be a "complement of God" or to be a "hypostasis of the Divinity."
>
> The New Testament itself, with its incubation of a century, leaves the revered figure clothed in a mist. And each day the old idea of "an Aeon born in the bosom of eternity," gathers force until the Council of Nicea gives it a shape and consistency, and formulates it into a dogma.[54]

Most Moslems, however, are not Deists. They believe in the supernatural and they think of the Son of Mary, not indeed as divine, but as extraordinarily holy. Depending on their knowledge of Christianity, they are less prone to dismiss the Christian faith in Christ's divinity as a threat to God's unicity.

For the believing Moslem, the focus of the problem is the dreaded fear that, by making Christ divine, Christians are giving partners to Allah. They are guilty of the crime of *shirk* which Mohammed condemned as equal in gravity to paganism. In the degree that Moslems come to recognize what Christians really believe, that they do not worship three (or even two) gods, their attitude changes. To get this recognition, however, has been difficult in the extreme.

What complicates the issue is the plain fact that Christians differ from the Jews in their acceptance of Jesus, and that they further differ among themselves on the same question. Present-day scholars in Islam favor this as the reason why Mohammed bypassed Jesus and Moses to choose Abraham as the founder of the true religion. In seventh-century Arabia, as today, there are some Jews and Christians who do not quarrel over their differences; but the majority are intransigent dogmatists. Hence the same judgment that Mohammed made then, his followers make now.

> This religious dissociation of Abraham . . . from the main body of Jews and Christians was an inevitable consequence of two strands among the Jews and Christians. The Qur'an continuously praises the one strand, and condemns the other, e. g., "From among them (i.i. the People of the Book) there is an upright group but most of them perpetrate misdeeds" (Surah 5:66).

> They were asked to live up to the *Torah* and the *Evangel* (5:68), but, like the proprietors of all organized religious traditions, Jews and Christians quarrelled among themselves and each claimed that the keys of salvation were firmly in their exclusive grasp: "The Jews say the Christians have nothing to stand on and the Christians say the Jews have nothing to stand on, and they both read the Book" (2:113). "Neither the Jews nor the Christians will ever be pleased with you until you follow their faith. Say: Guidance is the guidance of God" (2:120).[55]

The inevitable result of this state of affairs in Mohammed's time, say the Moslems, was for the Koran to proclaim that Abraham was neither a Jew nor a Christian, and that those with most claim to him were those who really followed him. Once he had "dismissed the pretensions of those who claimed proprietary rights over truth and divine guidance," Mohammed proceeded to erect his own understanding of religion.[56] But he added the warning that what happened to the Jews and Christians would also befall the Moslems, "If you turn your back on this mission." Should this happen, "God will replace you with another people, who will not be like you," even as he had done to the disciples of Moses and Jesus of Nazareth.[57]

The one redeeming feature of this verdict on Christians (and Jews) is that a growing number of Moslems are more than ever concerned to change the course of history. They appeal to two texts in the Koran that justify a more irenic approach to the ancient problem of how Islam is to see itself in comparison with Judaism and Christianity.

In the first passage, Mohammed declares that "Those who have believed, including the Jews and the Christians, . . . Whosoever believe in God and the Last Day and act righteously, they shall have their requital from their Lord and shall neither fear nor grieve."[58] Here the Jews and Christians are placed on the same footing and given equal prospects of salvation.

In the other text, Christians are individually compared with the Jews and placed next to Moslems as having a chance to be saved.

> You shall find that the most relentless enemies of Believers are the Jews . . . while the nearest to Believers in friendship are those people who say they are Christians. This is because among them are God-fearing men and monks and because they are not proud. When they listen to the revelations sent down to the Prophet, you see their eyes flowing with tears because of the Truth they have recognized in it.[59]

Why this sharp distinction between Jews and Christians? Moslems see themselves as quasi-Christians because they accept the Son of Mary as the Messiah foretold by the prophets. If professed Christians show that they are amenable to Moslems—in their strong allegiance to one true God, Moslems will be more tolerant of Christians —in their loyalty to the Son of God.

Status of women in Islam

Few areas of Moslem belief need to be better understood by Christians than the status of women in Islam.

The problem is not superficial. It has deep historical rootage and touches on the vitals of the two faiths, of Christianity with its raising of the dignity of women to new heights and of Islam which is thought to have done the opposite.

Women figure a great deal in the Koran, but most of it is legislation on dealing with their conduct, marital relations, and what some have generalized as "keeping women in their place" by making them inferior to men.

The most frequently cited evidence for the low estate of women in Islam is the laws governing freedom to marry, divorce, and polygamy, and the duty of women not to be seen in public. Each of these seems to conflict with the Christian attitude and should be carefully reappraised.

Women do not enjoy the right to marry whom they please. By Islamic law, marriage is a civil contract. The bridegroom concludes the contract with the legal guardian (*wali*) of the bride. The *wali* is the nearest male relative, in the order of succession. He can give his ward in marriage even against her will if she is a minor, but when she comes of age she has the right to rescind the contract. Yet, according to some customs, she may be forced to accept anyone, no matter what her age, if the one giving her away in marriage is her father or grandfather.

Divorce in Islam favors the husband almost exclusively. The Koran gives him the right to repudiate his wife. No intervention of any judicial authority is necessary, nor any assignment of reasons or justification; only a "certificate of divorce" need be given to the wife. After a first repudiation the wife may not remarry for at least three months, during which time she may be taken back without a further contract. The same holds after a second repudiation. But the third repudiation is irrevocable, unless the woman has meanwhile married and been divorced by another man. An ancient custom allows a triple repudiation to be made at one and the same time, with corresponding effects on its irrevocability.

A woman's right to divorce her husband is highly restricted. She cannot repudiate him by mere declaration. One possibility is to insert a clause in the marriage contract, offering to return the dowry in case she decides to dissolve the marriage. If he accepts the dowry, she is granted a divorce. Many Moslem women nowadays protect themselves by stipulating precise conditions which the husband must fulfill; if he fails, they can sue him for breach of promise and hope for an annulment of the marriage.

More partial still is the practice of polygamy. The express permission in the Koran allows up to four wives simultaneously for the average Moslem. High officials, like Caliphs and Sultans, are permitted to have nine wives—after the example of Mohammed who had nine according to one tradition and fourteen according to another. "Marry of the women who seem good to you, two, or three, or four," was the prophet's injunction.[60]

Since slave concubines are directly sanctioned in the Koran, concubinage is credited with divine approval.[61] The same with temporary marriage, which many have extracted from an ambivalent passage to the effect that "Allah would make the burden light for you, for man was created weak."[62]

Parallel with these liberties given to men and liabilities imposed on women is an unusual concern to have women not appear in public, that they always "lower their gaze" and "not display their beauty" except to their husbands, fathers, and a restricted clientele of male relatives and friends. Covering their faces with a veil was the most practical way of fulfilling this prescription.

According to strict orthodox Islam, the husband has exceptional power over his wife. He may forbid her to leave the house. If she does so against his wishes, he may then and there divorce her. He may restrict access to her relatives. A disobedient wife is liable to correction by the husband, not excluding corporal punishment.

With the right of divorce on demand and (in practice) to concubinage, a woman's position is notably affected when she becomes pregnant. Always in the husband's mind is the question of whose child this is. Islamic custom recognizes the duration of pregnancy from six months to two years. This implies that the husband has up to two years from the dissolution of a marriage to acknowledge the child as his own. His refusal to do so is equivalent to declaring the child illegitimate, unless the wife has remarried in the meantime.

On the face of it, the wife's right to maintenance looks like a concession, but in reality it can be used against her by the husband. The amount is usually substantial and enough to pay for food, clothing, and lodging, that is, a separate house or at least a separate room which can be locked. The trouble is that the husband has the right to suspend maintenance for all sorts of reasons: if she is disobedient, if she leaves the house unauthorized, if she refuses marital intercourse, if she contracts a debt that makes her liable to punishment, if she goes any great distance without her husband, if she converts to another religion than Islam. So detailed are the conditions that make her liable to lose maintenance and so completely is the husband sole judge of his wife's guilt—that, in effect, what seems to be a benefit to married women may become the source of their greatest anxiety. Moslem law, for instance, says that a wife may be deprived of her maintenance if she is found "guilty" of kissing her stepson. Her motives are immediately under suspicion.

The foregoing recital of limitations under which Moslem women have lived for centuries is necessary if we are to appreciate another side of the picture: the improvement in the status of women in Islam, as compared with what they had been before Mohammed and in contrast to their condition up to modern times. Both sets of contrasts are necessary to get a balanced perspective of what is undoubtedly the most common ground of invidious comparison between Islam and Christianity.

No doubt Moslem women, even now, do not enjoy the freedom of their Western sisters when it comes to the choice of a partner in marriage; but, all the evidence points to a marked improvement over what had been the situation in pre-Islamic Arabia. The purchase of brides seems to have been commonly practiced. Moreover, it was not until the nineteenth century that the Hindus were effectively restrained (by English law) from widespread child marriages. Indian girls of six and seven were married to boys by their respective parents; and another Hindu custom required the widow to commit suicide on her husband's funeral pyre—though she may never have lived with him as his wife.

Anyone familiar with practices in the Near East before Mohammed must admit that he went a long way to giving women some liberty in whom they would marry. At least they could try to persuade their fathers not to marry them off to someone they disliked.

Divorce in the Orient, including Arabia, is an historical institution and Mohammed did not try to change what he considered unchangeable. Under ancient Jewish law, a husband could divorce his wife for any cause whatsoever. It was enough that he did not like her. There were no checks to an arbitrary use of his power. Women were not allowed to demand a divorce from their husbands, no matter what the complaints may have been. Later on one school of Hebrew jurists, the Shammaites, somewhat modified the custom of divorce; but orthodox Jews, followed Hillel, upheld the law in its primitive arbitrariness. The Hillelite doctrine prevailed among the Jewish tribes in Arabia in the time of Mohammed, and repudiation of wives was as common among them as among the "pagan" Arabs.

As Moslem historians view the matter, the Arabs in Mohammed's day recognized no rule of humanity or justice in the treatment of their wives. Mohammed looked upon the custom of divorce with extreme disapproval, and regarded its practice as calculated to undermine the foundations of society. He often declared that nothing pleased God more than the emancipation of slaves, and nothing displeased him more than divorce. It was impossible, Moslems say, under the existing conditions of society to abolish the custom entirely. He was to mold the mind of an uncultured and semibarbarous community to a higher development so that in the fullness of time his spiritual lessons might blossom in the hearts of mankind.

The reforms of divorce by Mohammed marked a new departure in the history of Eastern legislation. He restrained the husband's right to divorce his wife; he gave women the right of separation on reasonable grounds. Toward the end of his life he went so far as to forbid divorce without the intervention of arbiters or a judge. He pronounced "*talak* (repudiation) to be the most detestable before God of all permitted things," because it was a constant threat to marital happiness and interfered with the upbringing of children.

In the same way, much has happened in the thirteen hundred years since Mohammed to indicate that his true spirit is gradually coming into its own, and that divorce is becoming less and less acceptable in Islam.

An eminent body of Moslem jurists now regard *talak* coming from the husband alone as completely opposed to the mind of Mohammed, except in such grave cases as proved infidelity. The Hanafis, the Mailikis, the Shafe'is, and most of the Shiahs allow *talak*, but they maintain that it cannot be used without justifiable and proven reasons.

In Pakistan and elsewhere, Moslem writers condemn easy divorce proceedings in scathing terms. Arguing from the Koran, they point out that many conditions must be fulfilled before divorce should be granted. First with softness ("admonish them") and hardness ("beat them") a reconciliation should be sought. Next, after the report of a third party ("then send a judge from his people and a judge from her people") an objective verdict must be passed to see whether some compromise can be found ("if they wish for reconciliation"), or a divorce remains the only solution left.[63]

So, too, with polygamy. Moslems are especially offended when they read that Mohammed is said to have either adopted or legalized polygamy. Fewer Western commentators still suppose that the prophet introduced plural marriages; but they tend to believe that he legalized it among the masses.

Actually the reforms effected by Mohammed reflect a marked improvement in the position of women in the matter of polygamy.

Among the ancient Arabs there existed, besides the system of plurality of wives, the custom of entering into conditional as well as temporary contracts of marriage. A woman was considered a mere chattel. She formed an integral part of the estate of her husband or her father; and the widows of a man descended to his son or sons by right of inheritance, as any other portion of patrimony. Hence the frequent unions between stepsons and stepmothers which were strictly forbidden by Islam and came to be branded as *Nikah ul-Mekt* (shameful and odious marriages).

The pre-Islamic Arabs had so little respect for women that they often destroyed, by burying alive, many of their newly born girls. This offensive custom was especially prevalent among the tribes of Koreish and Kindah, whom Mohammed denounced in burning language. He forbade the practice under severe penalties, along with the custom of sacrificing their offspring to the gods.

As one reads the Koran, while it sanctions polygamy, the attitude is one of guarded restraint and concern to reduce its prevalence by hedging it with numerous and difficult conditions. The passage which permits the practice is not generally seen in context. First Mohammed says, "You may marry two, or three or four wives." But immediately he adds, "And if you fear that you cannot do justice to so many, then marry only one."[64]

Moslem exegetes point out the great importance of the word "justice" (*'adl*) in the Koranic teachings. The term *'adl* means not merely equality of treatment in the matter of lodging, clothing, and other domestic necessities, but also (as far as possible) complete equity in love, affection, and esteem.

Under the influence of monogamous Christian cultures, the best minds in Islam are seriously talking about monogamy as objectively and in principle preferable to polygamy; they are suggesting that Moslems rethink what for too long has been (they claim) mistakenly identified with the name of Mohammed. The reference to Mutawakkil is to one of the early successors of Mohammed who shaped the Moslem tradition along fundamentalist lines.

> As absolute justice in matters of feeling is impossible (between husband and wives), the Koranic prescription amounted in reality to a prohibition. This view was propounded as early as the third century of the Hegira. In the reign of al-Mamun, the first Mutazilite doctors taught that the developed Koranic

143

laws inculcated monogamy. And though the cruel persecution of the mad bigot, Mutawakkil, prevented the general diffusion of their teachings, the conviction is gradually forcing itself on all sides, in all advanced Moslem communities, that polygamy is as much opposed to the teachings of Mohammed as it is to the general progress of civilized society and true culture.[65]

These are not isolated sentiments but the growing attitude of Moslem leaders, notably those who have come to know and admire the Christian position on monogamy. They are frankly saying that "the verses in the Qur'an relating to polygamy refer specifically to the war-orphans, girls and widows. This means that polygamy was allowed only for abnormal times, specially during a period of war to solve an urgent social problem."[66]

Comparable development is taking place in the matter of women's seclusion and noninvolvement in society. Sympathetic writers first of all explain that Westerners should not judge others by themselves. Some form of female isolation is practiced throughout Asia.

Not unlike the reinterpretation of polygamy, Moslem scholars are successfully urging that seclusion of women is no essential part of the Koranic creed. They argue that the Koran never formally taught that women should be segregated or that they should go about in public with faces veiled. Such restrictions as Mohammed set down were called for by the times. It would be a mistake, however, they conclude to perpetuate the custom.

If the trend toward giving women more equality with men and a higher status in society is widespread in Moslem societies, the motivating forces behind this trend are varied and impossible to reduce to a single dominant cause. Two main attitudes have been at work for generations: psychological and cultural pressure from non-Moslem society, and religious ideals native to Islam.

The cultural pressures are enormous, with women in so many countries enjoying such freedom as they have never before experienced in history. Moslem women have been affected by this fact and in one country after another they are seeking (and getting) more rights guaranteed by law, similar to those possessed by women in Europe and America. Education and employment, acceptance in the professions, and removal of restrictions because of their sex— are part of the opening pattern in Turkey and Pakistan, in Egypt and Indonesia.

But more fundamental is the religious inspiration which sees in women the symbol of a nation's ideals. The role of Mary, the mother of Jesus, has never been more prominent in Islamic literature than today—among those who realize the importance of raising the dignity of woman in human society.

They are not so ready to accept the Western standard of woman's equality with men as a norm for them to follow. Much that passes in the West for feminine rights, they believe, is exploitation of the female sex and Moslems want none of it.

Even Muhammad Iqbal, the Father of Pakistan and the most daring modernist the Muslim world has produced, issued a wholesale rejection of Western social ethics on the status of women. In his eyes, the Western woman is not looking to Maryam, the mother of Isha, as her model. Woman has been made to love, and only on that basis should she speak of emancipation. To illustrate what he means, he pictures a Westernized feminist addressing a gathering of Eastern women. The four lines are a commentary that Western Christianity can take to heart.

> Ladies! Mothers! Sisters!
> How long shall you live as beloveds?
> Belovedness is sheer privation;
> It is sufferance of oppression and tyranny.[67]

The implication is only too obvious. As Moslems are recovering their vision of woman as the ideal of human love, they want something more than Western promoters of a feminine mystique have to offer. But all the while a struggle is going on in Islam. On the one hand, there is a strong reaction "against Western society, wherein the central point is the figure of the woman and her relationship with the family." At the same time, "modern institutions, the most important of them being the universities and their co-educational system, continue to forge ahead producing the opposite results."[68] Some believe this poses the gravest single crisis for Islam in the future: how to develop a balanced concept of woman's dignity, founded on spiritual principles, without giving in to what passes for dignity in the secularized Western world?

Christians have a serious responsibility in this crisis: to help Moslems distinguish between the gospel teaching on womanhood and the conduct of unworthy Christians. Much of this teaching is already part of the Koran. It is unlikely, however, that Moslems will recognize this unless the *Nasara* (followers of Jesus of Nazareth) cooperate in the discovery. The Moslem veneration for Mary is the key to a closer cooperation with Christians. When Mohammed entered Mecca in triumph, he gave orders to destroy the idols of Ka'ba and its paintings of prophets and angels. But when his followers began to wash away the paintings with water from the Zamzam well, he put his hands over a picture of Mary with Jesus at her side and said, "Wash out all except what is below my hands." This is still the faith of Islam, as also of authentic Christianity: that Mary is the greatest of women and, after 'Isa her son, the model of holiness for the human race.

THE CHURCH'S MISSION

It should be abundantly clear by now that the Western world has much to learn about the East, and that increased knowledge will inevitably lead to improved relations between what are still two halves of the human family.

Yet even as we were looking at the great religious cultures of the Orient, we could not, as Christians, help asking ourselves the difficult question of our reaction to all of this. Reaction is the right word, because it implies doing something and not merely reading or thinking about it.

If Hinduism and Buddhism, Confucianism and Islam have so many profound insights into man's nature and relationship with the ultimate source of his being—what have Christians to offer the non-Christian world? Should Christians presume to set themselves as judges of the human race and continue what they have been trying to do for centuries, convert the "heathen" masses to the Gospel of Jesus Christ?

This question extends far beyond the confines of Afro-Asia. It touches on the basic issue of evangelization wherever Christians come into vital contact with those who have not heard the teachings of the One whom his followers consider the unique Savior of mankind.

Anyone familiar with the Christian missions knows that this was never a purely speculative problem. But it is urgently practical now.

As new nations in Asia and Africa come into being, they become impatient with the paternalism of the Western world. They tend to exclude, along with colonial policy, also the religious influences which for so long have been identified with the Christian people of the West.

The real pressure, however, to take a stand comes from inside the ranks of believing Christians. There are two extremes currently vying with each other for reappraising the role of Christianity in its missionary outreach to those who are outside the Christian fold.

One attitude is more familiar. It postulates that there is nothing substantial in the "mythology and paganism" of the Orient on which to build the Church of Christ; that the few strands of truth or goodness found in Eastern religions are too insignificant to be taken seriously. The only feasible approach is to erase whatever the Orientals believe and start over again with preaching to them Christ and his unique message of salvation.

Karl Barth accurately voiced this position when he branded all non-Christian religions as foes of Christendom. A true Christian's response must be an intolerant No! "Does Christendom know," he asked, "how near to her lies the temptation, by a slight betrayal of her proper business, to escape such an imminent conflict with those alien religions? Does she know that this must not happen? We can only ask: Does she know that under no circumstances must she howl with the wolves?" There must be no suggestion of incorporating anything from outside the Gospels into the pure religion of Christ. "Christendom must advance right into the midst of these religions whatever their names may be, and let come what will, deliver her message of the one God and of His compassion for men forlorn, without yielding by a hairbreath to their demons."[1]

At the other extreme are those who see nothing but good in the Vedas and its adherents; for whom Buddha preached a doctrine not unlike that of Jesus of Nazareth. Some, like Arnold Toynbee, tell

Christians "to purge our Christianity of the traditional Christian belief that Christianity is unique."[2] They see so much similarity between the Upanishads and St. John, Confucius and Christ, and so
little difference between the ideals of Buddhist and Christian charity that they wish to settle for a missionless Christianity. They would
blot out the name of St. Paul from Christian history and find it impossible to forgive him for insisting that "there is no other Name
under heaven" by which men are to be saved.

There is no easy way of steering a middle course between these
extremes, except on paper and in theory. In practice, Christianity
seems to be faced with the option of hard-line evangelism or compromising syncretism. If some critics say that the Church's missionary enterprise formerly was too evangelistic and too little conscious
of the good in "paganism," the situation today is just the reverse.
Missiologists are now challenged to defend any kind of serious
preaching of the Gospel among non-Christian peoples, and some
theologians (generally in Europe) are suggesting a complete re-
assessment, if not reversal, of the Matthaean injunction to "make
disciples of all nations."

It is not quite correct to say that a balanced compromise is
needed between seeing nothing and seeing only good in the religious cultures outside Christianity. In a sense, both positions are
wrong, and you do not find the truth somewhere in the middle.

Missionaries in past centuries were theologically right when
they went to such exquisite pains to bring the Good News to a
world that had scarcely heard the name of Christ. Their concern
for the salvation of the millions "groping in darkness and the
shadow of death" was based on some formidable teaching of the
New Testament. They were not naïve enthusiasts when, like Fran-
cis Xavier, they begged their fellow Christians to cooperate in the
grand project of snatching countless souls from the power of the
Evil One and entrusting them to Christ.

If some nowadays do not write in these terms, the reason cannot be that the perspective of the Church's mission has changed, or
that suddenly the logic of St. Paul's letter to the Romans that "faith
comes by hearing" has lost its meaning.

Christians today, no less than in the time of Paul or Xavier,
have the mandate of their Founder to share with others the treasures of divine revelation which they had received from their forebears, and which Christ wants them to communicate.

Certainly it is possible to take such a narrow view of revelation as practically to exclude from God's salvific providence everyone except those who have actually heard the preaching of the Gospel. On this premise, however, it would be hard to explain how God seriously "wants all men to be saved" and yet not provide millions of people with the means of salvation—if the *only* source of faith was the actual hearing of the message of Christ.

But revelation can be understood in a wider and more cosmic sense. When Christians say that the public revelation of God to mankind closed with the apostolic age, this implies that from the dawn of history he had been manifesting himself "in various different ways." All nations, therefore, have at some time or another and in one form or another come into contact with the revealed Word of God. Those who lived in the centuries between Adam and Abraham were not left to their own devices and deprived of all access to God's revealed truth; those outside the Jewish tradition before the time of Christ also received some communication from on high to make their salvation possible; and those since the time of Christ who are not Christians because they have never heard of the Savior cannot have been left with no means of salvific faith.

Viewed in this light the whole perspective changes. The presence of deep religious values among the non-Christians (and their cultures) is explainable as a share (though faint and fragmentary) in the riches of historical revelation, building on the native wisdom of the human mind, and elevated by grace to the supernatural order.

The revelation in most cases may be attributed to divine communications that preceded by centuries the call of Abraham and the beginnings of Judaism. In other cases, the migration of the ancient Jews accounts for some astounding remnants of the Mosaic faith in the farthest reaches of Africa. In still other instances the penetration of the gospel message, though distorted and often minimal, has been so widespread that no part of the world is untouched by Christianity.

A good example of how the Christian spirit has "invaded" the interior of Asia is the remarkable stone tablet recently discovered at Sian-fu in China, dating from A.D. 781. Carved dragons and a cross adorn its summit, and its main shaft of ten feet is completely covered with Chinese characters. They tell the story of how Nestorian monks came from the Near East and converted thousands of people. As a tribute to the faith which they embraced, their emperor erected this tablet. In English translation, it runs to eleven pages in duodecimo. Its opening lines are typical of the whole monument.

> Behold the unchangeably True and Invisible, who existed through all eternity without origin; the far-seeing perfect Intelligence, whose mysterious existence is everlasting. Operating on primordial substance, He created the universe, being more excellent than all holy intelligences, inasmuch as He is the source of all that is honorable. This is our eternal true Lord God, triune and mysterious in substance.[3]

Similar evidence of Christian ideas entering non-Christian cultures may be found in Japan and India, where present-day Shinto and Hinduism have been affected. It is impossible to read a single article by Mahatma Gandhi in his periodical *Harijan* without sensing how much this Hindu and Jain had imbibed of the Gospels he loved so well, or how incalculable must be his influence on all future generations of Hindus who venerate him as a prophet.

For anyone who knows the religions of Asia and Africa it is not difficult to defend them against the charge of being no more than pagan mythology joined to empty speculation. They contain too much wisdom and their adherents give too many signs of virtue to deny the presence of God or question the workings of his grace.

On the other hand, knowledge of these religious cultures will also protect one from indulging in such panegyrics as make Hinduism a latent Christianity which needs no evangelization but only "actuation of a Christian faith already present." It should also prevent such extravagances as the suggestion that African polygamy is an equal ethic with Christian monogamy, and therefore "converts" to Christianity should not be required to cohabit with only one wife. The Greeks and Romans, not Christ, taught monogamy![4]

Part of the zeal to advance the Gospel of Christ among the Gentiles is the knowledge that these people need Christ; that he can offer them wisdom and principles of life which promise peace and happiness even in this world and not only in the world to come.

It is easy to get a different impression from reading the foregoing pages on the major non-Christian religions of the world. Certainly many writers on Hinduism and Islam are willing to leave their readers with the idea that Christianity has little, if anything, to give the nations of Asia and Africa.

Some would say that to even mention, let alone dwell on, the limitations and inconsistencies of non-Christian cultures is to undercut future dialogue with them. You also hear of "giving up the siege mentality" among Christians who are more ready to consign the "pagans" to eternal doom than surrender one iota of what they consider the "core of adamant in our Christian faith" that is not any single person's private property to barter or to buy or to sell.

Yet the better a person understands the religions of the non-Christian world, the more aware he becomes of its limitations and of the abyss which separates the cultures that have known and followed Christ from those that are still mainly strangers to his name.

Every level of personal and social living, and every phase of human civilization offers a study in contrast between people who have and those who have not been directly influenced by the person and teachings of the One whom Christians call the Savior.

To ignore these differences or gloss over them is to be unscientific in the basic sense of bypassing objective evidence in favor of doctrinaire theory.

At this point the reader may wonder if he has not been misled. Are all the fine things said about Hinduism and Islam true, and are the great intuitions of Buddha and Confucius valid? If they are, can it also be that these same religions are inadequate and that sometimes their teachings are wrong?

No one has a right to pass such judgment unless he believes that his own religion, objectively and ontologically, is normative for all other religious systems of mankind. There are nominal Christians who refuse to make this judgment because, as they say, it is not clear to them that Christianity is so absolutely certain of its premises or that Christians have any sure way of knowing what is religiously true or false.

They go back to the famous controversy in the fourth century between the Christian bishop, Ambrose, and the pagan senator, Symmachus, to drive home their views on the relation of Christianity to other religions.

Symmachus opposed the removal from the senate house of the image of the Roman goddess Victoria, which Ambrose insisted upon as a sign of the triumph of Christianity in the Roman Empire. The senator argued that "it is not possible that a mystery so great [as religion] should be accessible by one road alone." Christian syncretists reprove Christianity for never answering Symmachus. They side with the senator against Ambrose and state their position in the most ambiguous terms: "We cannot harden our hearts against Symmachus without hardening them against Christ."[5]

But Symmachus' abstract concept of religion as a "mystery" to which many different roads may lead, presupposes a thoroughly unchristian approach to man's relation with God. Christianity does, indeed, speak of mystery, but only after having accepted a revelation. Only because Christians are first assured that God has shown himself in the person of Jesus Christ, do they comfortably accept mysteries which transcend the human mind and, no doubt, have much in common with God's communication with the rest of mankind. Yet all the while Christians know they are not groping in the dark; that the revelation they received in Christ is more than the poetic inspiration of a Homer or the philosophic insight of Plato. The Christ in whom they believe was no mere human genius and the wisdom he taught was more than mystic speculation. He identified himself as *the* Truth and his followers—if they really believe in him—consider themselves (humbly but confidently) judges of other men's religions. They are sure that whatever truth there is outside of Christianity is at once evidence of Christ's presence in the world which he redeemed and is credible if it agrees with what he revealed.

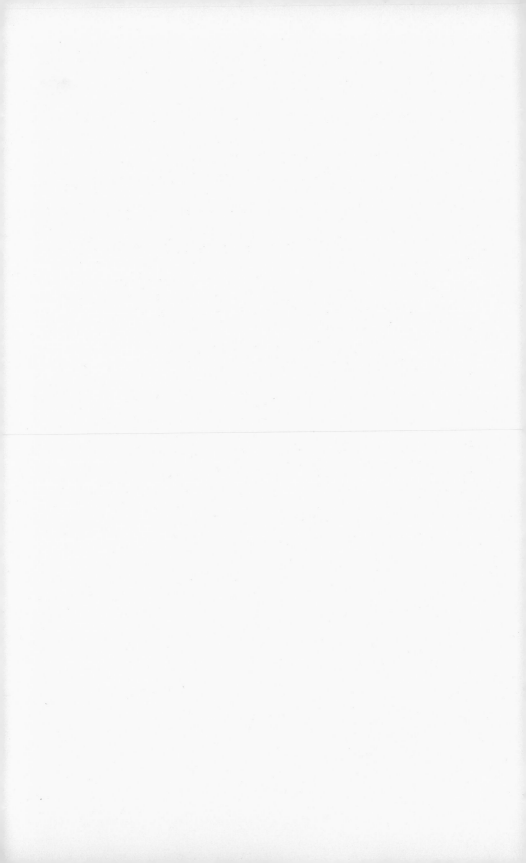

HISTORICAL OUTLINES

TOPICS FOR DISCUSSION AND
QUESTIONS FOR EXAMINATION

GLOSSARY OF TERMS

SELECT BIBLIOGRAPHY

REFERENCES

INDEX

HISTORICAL OUTLINES

HINDUISM

2000 B.C.	Immigration of the Aryans to India.
1500-600 B.C.	Vedic Period: Development and dissemination of the *Rig Veda, Sama Veda, Yajur Veda,* and *Atharva Veda.*
1000-800 B.C.	Priestly Period: Composition of the ritual literature, the *Brahmanas.*
800-600 B.C.	Philosophic Period: The *Upanishads* (14) as speculative commentaries on the Vedas.
600 B.C.-A.D. 300	Period of Reaction: Rise of Buddhism and Jainism against the caste system. Composition of the three main epics of Hinduism: *Bhagavad Gita, Ramayana,* and *Mahabharata.* Origins of the six main philosophical systems (*Darsanas*), namely: *Nyaka, Vaisesika, Samkya, Yoga, Mimamsa,* and *Vedanta.*
A.D. 300-1200	Pauranic Period: Sectarian writings (*Puranas*) favoring one of three favorite deities, that is, *Vishnu* (6), *Brahma* (6), and *Siva* (6). Also development of the *Tantras,* that is, theological treatises of the sects.

157

A.D. 750-800 — Sankara, a Brahmin scholar, introduces *Advaitavada* (nondualistic illusionary monism) to restore Vedanta form of Hinduism.

A.D. 1137 — Death of Ramanuja, restorer of anthropomorphic theistic Hinduism.

A.D. 1199-1278 — Madhava (Anandatirtha), a Brahmin scholar, opposes Sankara monism. Teaches modified dualism between God and the world.

A.D. 1200-1857 — Moslem Period: Entrance of Islam has deep influence on Hinduism, in the direction of monotheism.

A.D. 1469-1538 — Guru Nanak, Hindu convert to Islam, begins Sikhism.

A.D. 1857 — Sepoy revolt led to abolition of the East India Company and transfer of Indian rule to the English crown.

A.D. 1836-1886 — Ramakrishna, Hindu ascetic, advocates syncretism of all religions. Hinduism introduced to the West.

A.D. 1869-1948 — Mohandas Karamchand Gandhi, Hindu and Jain, labors for Indian independence.

A.D. 1950 — India becomes Sovereign Republic, guarantees freedom of religion, but Hinduism given special recognition.

BUDDHISM

567 B.C. — Birth of Buddha at Kapilavastu in the Himalayas.

531 B.C. — Buddha is enlightened near Uruvela, on the banks of the Neranjara River.
Buddha preached his first sermon to five disciples at Sarnath, near Benares.

487 B.C. — Death of Buddha at Kusinara, probably the modern city of Kasia.

272-232 B.C. — Reign of Emperor Asoka, greatest patron of Buddhism in India.

246 B.C. — Buddhism brought to Ceylon by Mahinda.

200 B.C. — Beginnings of schism; origins of later Mahayana by the Monk Mahadeva.

80 B.C. — Pali scriptures of Hinayana written down. Also first composition of Mahayana Sutras (sermons).

A.D. 25-60	Buddhism spreads to China.
A.D. 78-103	Reign of King Kanishka in North India. Highpoint of Indian Buddhism. Decisive schism between Hinayana and Mahayana. Earliest collection of Mahayana writings under Kanishka.
A.D. 220	Annam (Vietnam) converted to Hinayana Buddhism.
A.D. 372	Buddhism enters Korea.
A.D. 438-452	Buddhism spreads to Burma, Java, and Sumatra.
A.D. 552	Buddhism takes root in Japan.
A.D. 651	First Buddhist temple in Tibet.
A.D. 900	Islam supersedes Buddhism in Central Asia. Koan system of Zen Buddhism inaugurated.
A.D. 1191	Eisai brings Zen from China to Japan.
A.D. 1260-1294	Kublai Khan favors Buddhism.
A.D. 1340	Laos converted to Buddhism.
A.D. 1360	Buddhism becomes official religion of Siam.
A.D. 1480	Hinduism supersedes Buddhism in Java and Islam in Sumatra.
A.D. 1577	Final conversion of Mongols to Buddhism.
A.D. 1642	Fifth Dalai Lama becomes priest-king of Tibet.
A.D. 1769	Nepal turns to Hinduism.
A.D. 1849	Confucian persecution reduces Buddhism in Korea.
A.D. 1852-1868	Chinese and Japanese immigrants bring Buddhism into Hawaii.
A.D. 1897	Establishment of the Women's Buddhist Association.
A.D. 1899	Buddhism organized by Japanese Americans in the U.S.A.
A.D. 1900	Establishment of the Young Men's Buddhist Association.
A.D. 1928	Rama VII (King of Thailand) authorizes the *Buddhamamaka* oath, adapted from Catholic confirmation, to be taken by students going abroad.
A.D. 1939	Religious Bodies Act orders a merger of Buddhist sects in Japan.
A.D. 1942	Buddhist Churches of America founded to succeed the Buddhist Mission of North America (1914).
A.D. 1943	Buddhist Society founded for the English-speaking world.
A.D. 1949	Organized Buddhism begins to wane under Communist domination in China.
A.D. 1951-1959	Communist extermination of Buddhism in Tibet.
A.D. 1954-1956	World Buddhist Council at Rangoon in Burma.

CONFUCIANISM

551 B.C.	Confucius (K'ung-Fu-Tze) born in the Chinese province of Lu (now Shantung).
517 B.C.	Confucius discovered the wisdom of the ancients, especially of the Duke of Chou (from the eleventh century B.C.).
478 B.C.	Confucius died in Lu, three years after the death of his favorite disciple, Yen Hui.
475-221 B.C.	Period of the Contending States—Confucian school progresses but protracted war made Confucianism impracticable.
342-291 B.C.	Mandarin Meng-tze (Mencius), Chinese sage, whose *Book of Mencius* is a classic commentary on Confucius.
221-141 B.C.	Confucianism eclipsed under the Ch'in and early Han emperors.
141-87 B.C.	Reign of Han Wu Ti, great patron of Confucianism, notably its three principles that: (1) the wise should have dominant role in government, (2) wisdom comes from study under a qualified teacher, (3) the ancient books approved by Confucius are normative for China.
106-35 B.C.	Period of imperial edicts dealing with training of scholars along Confucian lines.
A.D. 37	Earliest evidence of a regular cult of Confucius. Sacrifices, like those common to ancestors, ordered by Kuang Wu in honor of Confucius in A.D. 29.
A.D. 37-220	Development of the state cult of Confucius through imperial encouragement.
A.D. 443-497	Chang Yung, court official and scholar, teaches that Confucianism, Taoism, and Buddhism are essentially the same. Differences due only to historical expression.
A.D. 605	Edict by Emperor Yang Ti, reestablishing Confucianism in the schools.
A.D. 741	Emperor Hsuan Tsung favored Taoism over Confucianism. Lao Tzu becomes competitor of Confucius in China.
A.D. 1130-1200	Chu Hsi, scholar and cofounder with Ch'eng Yi (1033-1107) of Neo-Confucianism by incorporating with Buddhism and Taoism.
A.D. 1280-1368	Mongol emperors bring Confucian culture into contact with Europe.
A.D. 1368-1643	Ming dynasty: China gradually a closed country, with Confucius studied and honored above other sages.

A.D. 1644-1912	Manchu dynasty encouraged veneration of Confucius, but Confucianism more and more challenged by Western ideas.
A.D. 1912	Sun Yat-sen, provisional president of the new Chinese Republic. Connection ended between civil-service examinations (Confucian inspired) and government educational system.
A.D. 1918-1922	Under President Hsu Shih-ch'ang, Confucianism held compatible with new order.
A.D. 1948	Establishment of Republic of China, under Chiang Kai-shek, favorable to Confucian principles.
A.D. 1949	Founding of the People's Republic of China, under Communist rule. Confucius regarded as a major obstacle to the spread of Marxism.

ISLAM

A.D. 570	Mohammed, son of Abd Allah, born of the Quraysh tribe at Mecca, now capital of Hejaz, Saudi Arabia.
A.D. 610	Mohammed begins his prophetic career.
A.D. 622	*Hijra* (flight) of Mohammed, from Mecca to Medina. Marks beginning of Moslem era. Formula is $G = H + 622 - H$ *over* 33, where G is the year in the Gregorian and H is the Moslem calendar.
A.D. 632	Mohammed died at Medina on Monday, June 8, leaving nine wives (four legal and five honorary), no sons but several daughters. Favorite daughter, Fatima.
A.D. 632-634	Abu Bakr, successor of Mohammed, begins caliphate.
A.D. 644-656	Caliphate of Uthman (Othman) who compiled the canonical text of the Koran. Chaldea, Assyria, Iranian territory conquered by Moslems.
A.D. 670-767	Rise of theological sects and first stage of development of law.
A.D. 768	Death of Muhammad ibn Ishaq, earliest compiler of the *Hadith* (actions and sayings of Mohammed). *Hadith* are second to the Koran in Islam.
A.D. 922	Mansur al-Hallaj, Sufi mystic, crucified at Baghdad on charges of claiming to be Allah.
A.D. 980-1037	Avicenna (Ibn Sina), Arab philosopher whose interpretation of Aristotle influenced Aquinas. Taught that God alone is necessary being; the world is contingent.

161

A.D. 1058-1111	Al Ghazali, Arab theologian ranked with Augustine in religious insight. Venerated in Islam as saint. Preserved Islam from rationalism. Taught prayer, love of Allah, and fear from hell. Influenced writings of Aquinas.
A.D. 1071-1270	Crusades undertaken by Christians to recover the Holy Land from Islam. Eight crusades: 1096-1099, 1147-1149, 1188-1192, 1202-1204, 1217-1221, 1228-1229, 1248-1254, 1270. The effect on Islam was to reunite the Near and Middle East Moslems in Sunnite (traditional) orthodoxy.
A.D. 1126-1198	Averroes (Ibn Rushd), Cordova philosopher whose theory of monopsychism (only one intellect for mankind) evoked reactions throughout Christian Europe, for example, Albertus Magnus and Aquinas.
A.D. 660-1922	Islam established by military conquest in series of caliphates: Omayyad Caliphate, center at Damascus (660-750). European progress checked at Tours (732). Abbaside Caliphate (Baghdad) from 750 to 1258. Spanish Caliphate at Cordova (755-1236). Moorish Caliphate at Granada (1238-1492), last Moslem empire in Europe. Fatimite Caliphate (910-1171), ruled Egypt and North Africa. Ottoman Caliphate, began with Turkish rule in 1299. Constantinople taken in 1453 and Egypt in 1517. Principal Moslem power in the world until 1922, when Sultan (Mohammed VI) deposed by Turkish National Assembly.
A.D. 1947	Pakistan became sovereign nation. Its constitution states that "the principles of democracy, freedom, equality, tolerance and social justice, as enunciated by Islam, should be fully observed."
A.D. 1954	Pan-Islamic Conferences, to be held annually at Mecca, organized by Egypt, Saudi Arabia, and Pakistan.

TOPICS FOR DISCUSSION
AND
QUESTIONS FOR EXAMINATION

HINDUISM

Topics for discussion or further study

1 According to Mahatma Gandhi, "If I were to define the Hindu creed, I would simply say, a search after truth through non-violent means"
2 The difference between the *avatars* of Hinduism and the Incarnation of Christianity
3 Hinduism as a philosophy compared with Hinduism as a religion
4 The caste system as a form of religious fatalism
5 Social implications of the Hindu attitude toward the visible world as *maya* or illusion
6 Some popular misconceptions about Hinduism
7 Why Hinduism has remained practically confined to India over the centuries
8 Attitude of present-day Hindus toward Christianity
9 *Bhakti* devotion compared with the Christian love of God
10 Belief in reincarnation in Hinduism and faith in the resurrection in Christianity—differences and similarities

Questions for examination

I ESSAY FORM

1 Briefly describe each of the four Vedas.
2 How do the Upanishads differ from the Vedas?
3 Early Hinduism was very mythological. Explain.
4 Each of the four main castes is said to derive from one of the parts of Primal Being. Why is this significant?
5 Distinguish the following: Brahman, Brahmin, and Brahma.
6 What are the essentials of the Hindu belief in reincarnation?
7 Analyze the theme of the *Bhagavad Gita*.
8 Describe the *bhakti* method of reaching Brahman.
9 The Upanishads are both monistic and monotheistic. Explain.
10 How does the Christian idea of salvation differ from the Hindu concept of *moksha*?
11 What can we learn from the Hindu stress on Being?
12 Discuss the value of the Hindu search for truth.
13 What problems are raised by the close relationship between Athman (Self) and Brahman (the Absolute)?
14 Comment on Krishna's description of God in the *Bhagavad Gita*.
15 How do the moral virtues recommended in the *Bhagavad Gita* compare with the norms of Christian morality?

II MULTIPLE CHOICE

In each of the following groups, select the letter of the item that does *not* belong.

1 A name for God: (a) Brahman, (b) Deva, (c) *maya*, (d) Krishna
2 Sacred writing of the Hindus: (a) *bhakti*, (b) Bhagavad Gita, (c) Vedas, (d) Upanishads
3 The Hindu Absolute: (a) Athman, (b) Brahman, (c) Krishna, (d) Arjuna
4 Hindu castes: (a) Sudras, (b) Pariahs, (c) Brahmins, (d) Vaishyas
5 A personal deity is recognized in: (a) monotheism, (b) polytheism, (c) monism, (d) henotheism

III COMPLETION TEST

Write in the space provided the words or phrases that best complete each statement.

1 The name for the language, ..., and for the religion, ..., both derive from the name for the country, India.
2 Hindus call the descent of one of their gods to earth ....
3 The most popular Hindu scriptures are the ...., the most philosophical are the ....
4 The highest Hindu caste is the ...., the lowest is the ....
5 Every believing Hindu hopes to escape *samsara*, which means ....; the escape is known as ....

IV MATCHING TEST

Write in the space provided at the right the number of the statement that best fits each item on the left.

1 The Hindu Absolute .... Rama
2 Reincarnation .... *Bhagavad*
3 Brahman as Lord .... Rig Veda
4 Unknown god .... Henotheism
5 World as illusion .... *Ka*
6 One chief deity among many .... *Om*
7 Incarnation of Vishnu .... Athman
8 Principal original sacred book .... Kshatriya
9 Solemn invocation of Brahman .... *Mahabharata*
10 The immortal Self .... *Maya*
11 Brahman as God .... Siva
12 God of earth and sky .... Deva
13 Himalayan deity .... Vishnu
14 Source of Bhagavad Gita .... *Samsara*
15 Second highest caste .... Brahman

BUDDHISM

Topics for discussion or further study

1 The meaning of suffering in Buddhism
2 Why Buddha left Hinduism to start a new religion of his own
3 Historicity of the tales about Buddha's life and activities
4 Symbolism of the Buddhist Wheel of the Law
5 Comparison of the Buddhist Four Noble Truths with the three theological virtues of Christianity
6 The popular misconception that Buddhism is not theistic
7 Role of the free will in Buddhist morality
8 Significance of Buddha's rejection of the Hindu caste system
9 Value of Zen for people who are not Buddhists
10 Similarity and difference between the Buddhist Nirvana and heaven in the Christian scriptures

Questions for examination

I ESSAY FORM

1 Why was Buddha dissatisfied with Hinduism?
2 How do you account for the fact that Buddhism, unlike Hinduism, spread throughout Asia?

165

3 What importance should be given to the long period (over four centuries) from Buddha's death to the writing of Buddhist scriptures?
4 In what countries is Hinayana Buddhism most prevalent? Mahayana Buddhism?
5 Briefly explain each of the several names by which Buddha is known.
6 Trace the various stages in Buddha's original process by which he became the "Enlightened One."
7 According to Buddha, clinging to existence is suffering. Explain.
8 Comment on each of the three thirsts which, according to Buddha, cause suffering.
9 Why should cessation of desire bring an end to suffering?
10 Give an equivalent term, or synonym, for each of the eight steps in Buddha's Path to Nirvana.
11 How would you describe Nirvana, as Buddha himself understood it?
12 Briefly list the different types of suffering which Buddhism classifies.
13 Classic Buddhism maintains that everything is in the process of becoming. Comment.
14 How do the two main forms of Buddhism, Hinayana and Mahayana, differ in their basic attitude toward man and his destiny?
15 What are the essentials of Zen practice, as distinguished from Zen as a religion?

II MULTIPLE CHOICE

In each of the following groups, select the letter of the item that does *not* belong.
1 Buddha had been a: (a) *guru*, (b) Hindu, (c) Brahmin, (d) Sannyasi
2 Hinayana Buddhism is most prevalent in: (a) Ceylon, (b) Vietnam, (c) Burma, (d) China
3 Reincarnation means: (a) *samsara*, (b) metempsychosis, (c) wheel of existence, (d) *bodhi*
4 Egolessness in Buddhism affirms: (a) no permanent self, (b) *anatta*, (c) no existence, (d) no distinct personality
5 Regarding Nirvana, Buddha's main preoccupation was to: (a) define what Nirvana means, (b) explain how Nirvana is attained, (c) help people avoid reincarnation, (d) teach his followers the eightfold Path

III COMPLETION TEST

Write in the space provided the words or phrases that best complete each statement.
1 In the pre-Christian era, the most influential patron of Buddhism in .... was ....
2 According to .... Buddhism, ... is attained by concentrated meditation on the ....
3 The original Buddhist scriptures of .... were written in ...., about the year ....; whereas the Mahayana sacred writings were written in ....

4 Three principal theories of Nirvana hold that it means attaining beatitude like ...., extinguishing desire through absorption in .... as taught by the ...., or reaching .... which satisfies all desires.

5 Hinayana Buddhism is also called the .... vehicle, or ...., that is, school of the elders.

6 In Christian terms, Buddha's right understanding corresponds to possessing the ....; whereas right action corresponds to ....

7 In the practice of right action, Buddhism assumes there are .... of perfection; higher than external conduct is ....; and higher than justice is the practice of ....

8 The technical names for each of the four planes of charity are ...., ..., ..., and ....

9 Three terms referring to enlightenment, most commonly found in Buddhist literature, pertain to a condition, historical personage, and class of individuals, namely ...., ..., and ....

10 The three articles of the Buddhist creed state that, "I believe in the ...., in ...., and ...."

11 Buddha's claim to fame in religious .... is the fact that he clarified the function of man's .... in the practice of ....

12 Buddha held that what should mainly be mastered by the .... are .... that arise unbidden in the human ....

13 In Buddhist morality, people are responsible for not reaching .... because they had not exercised sufficient .... power in controlling their ...., on which all other human faculties depend.

14 The .... and Sanskrit words for right concentration are the same, namely .... which may be translated as .... or ...., and is the last stage before ....

15 It is very likely that .... devotion to Buddha influenced the Hindu concept of devotion or ...., as found in the .... Correspondingly it is likely that .... influenced Mahayana .... in its strong emphasis on ....

IV MATCHING TEST

Write in the space provided at the right the number of the statement that best fits each item on the left.

1 Model of Buddhist laymen	....	*Ch'an*
2 Buddhist monk	....	*Sankara*
3 Practice of noninjury	....	*Dharma Chakra*
4 Cycle of cosmic reincarnation	....	Sakya-Muni
5 Goal of Zen enlightenment	....	Bhikkhu
6 Hindu spiritual guide	....	*Nibbana*
7 In dialogue with King Melinda	....	*Arhat*
8 Original Zen Buddhism	....	Karma
9 Taught nondualist illusionary monism	....	*Ahimsa*
10 Siddhartha Gautama	....	*Smriti*
11 Human acts having retribution	....	*Satori*

12 Right mindfulness	....	*Guru*
13 Buddhist eschatology	....	*Kalpa*
14 Saintly ascetic	....	Vimalakirti
15 Wheel of the Law	....	Nagasena

CONFUCIANISM

Topics for discussion and further study

1 The three religions of China—Confucianism, Buddhism, and Taoism
2 Concept of the State in Confucianism
3 Filial piety in Chinese culture
4 The family in Chinese society
5 The Nestorian tablet of China
6 System of education in Confucianist China
7 Ancestor worship in China—its meaning and practice
8 Confucian and Christian morality compared
9 The "Superior Man" in Confucian ethics
10 The *Analects of Confucius*, their significance in Chinese history
11 Doctrine of the Mean in Confucianism
12 The role of music in Chinese religious culture
13 Chinese religious art
14 Confucianism and Marxism in conflict in China today
15 Chinese Communism and religion

Questions for examination

I ESSAY FORM

1 What are the ten books which constitute the basic Confucian scriptural writings?
2 Briefly describe the contents of the *Analects of Confucius*.
3 How did Confucius become the great ethical teacher of China?
4 Describe the religious elements in Confucianism.
5 Analyze the main features of "The Great Plan" of the *Shu King*.
6 Comment on the Confucian "five sources of happiness."
7 Explain the so-called "Method of Heaven."
8 Why is Chinese culture so preoccupied with numbers?
9 What is meant by the Chinese saying that "Heaven's principles do not change"?
10 Comment on the fact that in Confucianism the family is the foundation of the whole social order.
11 Analyze the moral implications of Chinese devotion to one's ancestors, even the most distant forebears.
12 Trace the psychological development of filial piety from childhood to adult maturity.

13 Identify the moral virtues of the Confucian "Superior Man."

14 Compare the two basic virtues of *jen* and *li*.

15 How has Marxism exploited Taoism and Mohism to propagate Communist ideology in China?

II MULTIPLE CHOICE

In each of the following groups, select the letter of the item that does *not* belong.

1 Chinese Universism is a combination of: (a) Buddhism, (b) Confucianism, (c) Hinduism, (d) Taoism

2 Names for God in Confucian literature are: (a) *Tien*, (b) *Shang-Ti*, (c) *Ti*, (d) *li*

3 Harmonization in Confucian terms means: (a) order, (b) conformity, (c) variety, (d) submission

4 The basis of Confucian morality is: (a) fidelity to tradition, (b) worship of ancestors, (c) loyalty to the past, (d) conformity to principle

5 The two qualities of *jen* and *li* include: (a) propriety, (b) manliness, (c) friendliness, (d) self-restraint

III COMPLETION TEST

Write in the space provided the words or phrases that best complete each statement.

1 If the founder of Confucianism was ...., its principal philosopher was ...., and its greatest patron was ....

2 According to Han Wu Ti, Confucianism teaches that .... men should lead in the .... life of a nation; that to become .... a person must be directed by ....

3 Confucianism fared differently under different dynasties. It was most favored by the .... emperors, began to influence European culture under the ...., developed the cult of Confucius during the .... dynasty, became a closed Chinese system under the .... rulers for three hundred years.

4 According to the precept of propriety, a father should be ...., a son ...., an older brother ...., a younger brother ...., husbands should be .... to their wives, wives should be .... to their husbands, rulers are to be ...., and subjects should be ....

5 Confucius taught that the three essentials of good government are .... and .... sufficiency and the .... of the people in their .... as human beings.

6 Mencius taught that people are .... endowed with instincts that are .... People become .... only when these instincts are not .... through education.

7 The cardinal principle of Confucian ethics states that a person should always be .... to remain in .... with the .... of God. If he does this, he will obtain much ....

8 Mencius set down the norm that the root of the empire is in the
............, whose root is in the ...., whose root is in the person of
its ....

9 The rock of Chinese civilization was Confucius' dictum that the duty
of .... to their .... is the fountain from whence all ....
ultimately spring.

10 Two ideologies which early competed with Confucianism were
.... and ....

11 The philosophy of Lao-Tze challenged Confucianism by teaching a
form of Hindu .... and opposing .... of the people.

12 Chinese Communists now quote Yang Chu, and stress his .... in
reflecting the desire for .... in his day. They carefully avoid
mentioning his ....

13 Chinese Marxists cite Mo-tzu in order to highlight the .... side
of society and to insist on the necessity of .... But they fail to
mention the .... of Mo-tzu, which Mencius so strongly criticized.

14 Essential to the Confucian program of fostering the welfare of society is to capitalize on the natural .... of .... respect, cultivate it by a strong .... life, and preserve it by keeping love for
.... dominant in people's minds.

15 The cult of Confucius, practiced for centuries, means that he is
.... as a great .... It does not mean that he is .... as
a .... comparable to ....

IV MATCHING TEST

Write in the space provided at the right the number of the statement
that best fits each item on the left.

1 Supreme Originator	.... *Shu* texts
2 Virile friendliness	.... K'ung-Fu-Tze
3 Mo-tzu	.... Mencius
4 *Analects of Confucius*	.... *Shang-Ti*
5 Lao-Tze	.... Count of Chi
6 Patron of Confucianism	.... *Hsaio King*
7 People's Republic of China	.... *Chun-tzu*
8 Dialectic materialism	.... *Jen*
9 Founder of Mohism	.... *Ti*
10 God	.... *Li*
11 Filial piety	.... *Tien*
12 Superior man	.... Tzu Ssu
13 Trustful confidence	.... Yang Chu
14 Philosophical analysis of Confucianism	.... *Tao Teh Ching*
15 Confucius	.... Mih Teih
16 Law of God	.... Mao Tse-tung
17 The Second Inspired One	.... Marxism
18 First president of the Chinese Republic	.... Chiang Kai-shek
19 Ritual propriety	.... Chu Hsi
20 "The Great Plan"	.... Sun Yat-sen

ISLAM

Topics for discussion and further study

1 Islam as the religion of faith
2 The concept of Christ in the Koran
3 Significance of the Crusades for Islam
4 The five pillars of Islam—their significance in maintaining Moslem solidarity
5 Mohammed as the "Seal of the Prophets"
6 Dietary practices of Islam
7 Literary structure of the Koran
8 Place of Mary, the mother of Jesus, in Islam
9 The *Hadith* (Traditions) about Mohammed and his companions
10 Theory and practice of polygamy in Islam
11 Attitude toward the Jews in the Koran
12 Influence of Moslem scholars on Christian thought
13 Averroes and Thomas Aquinas
14 Religious liberty in Pakistan
15 The pilgrimage to Mecca

Questions for examination

I ESSAY FORM

1 Comment on the meaning and implications of the term *Islam*.
2 What is a Moslem?
3 What was Mohammed's purpose in teaching the Koran?
4 Why did Mohammed first favor and then oppose the Jews?
5 What does the Koran teach about the divinity of Christ?
6 Who was Al Ghazali, and what were his contributions to Islam?
7 What did Avicenna teach about the nature of man?
8 Why did Mohammed flee from Mecca to Medina?
9 Explain the formula for changing dates from the Gregorian to the Moslem calendar.
10 Explain the meaning of the Moslem profession of faith.
11 What was Mohammed's concept of idolatry?
12 What are the historical sources of the Koran?

13 How do you explain the phenomenal growth of Islam?
14 Why has Christianity made so little impact on Moslems?
15 Make a comparative analysis of the main elements in which Christianity and Islam are the same; and the main aspects in which they differ in certain essentials.

II MULTIPLE CHOICE

In each of the following groups, select the letter of the item that does *not* belong.

1 Mohammed believed that Jesus was: (a) the Messiah, (b) the Son of God, (c) the Son of Mary, (d) the Servant of God
2 According to the Koran, man is: (a) immortal, (b) born with original sin, (c) a creature, (d) in need of divine grace
3 Moslems believe that angels: (a) are spiritual beings, (b) messengers of Allah, (c) mediators between Allah and men, (d) enjoy the beatific vision
4 The Moslem faith teaches that Allah is: (a) one and triune, (b) one and unique, (c) one and eternal, (d) one and not finite
5 Islam teaches that Mohammed was: (a) foretold by Jesus, (b) the last of the prophets, (c) the only true prophet, (d) as much prophet as was Jesus

III COMPLETION TEST

Write in the space provided the words or phrases that best complete each statement.

1 The main religions professed in pre-Islamic Arabia were ...., ..., orthodox ...., and ....
2 The followers of Mohammed prefer not to be called .... They call themselves .... and their religion ....
3 Mohammed's flight from .... to .... is known in Arabic as ...., which literally means ....
4 The four essential concepts around which the whole of Islam revolves are .... and ...., ... and ....
5 According to the Koran, absolute .... means that Allah has no .... in the work of ....
6 Two attributes of .... with which almost every .... of the Koran begins are .... and ....
7 Mohammed taught that idolatry is the sin whereby people take their .... as ....
8 Failure to show gratitude to Allah is ...., which means .... in Islam.
9 Assigning partners to Allah is ...., which Islam considers ....
10 The word *Islam* means .... to ...., and acceptance of .... as God's ....
11 Rebellious spirits, according to the Koran, are called .... or ...., corresponding to .... in the Bible.

12 The Moslem term for prophet is .... In the Old Testament, the most ancient prophets were ...., ..., and .... In the New Testament, the greatest prophets were ...., ..., and ....

13 Islam teaches that each great prophet, from Moses to Mohammed, communicated a divinely inspired writing to the world. Thus .... gave the ....; .... gave the ....; .... gave the ....; and .... gave the ....

14 The Holy War, called ...., is enjoined by the ...., but its definite prescriptive character is taught by the ...., which is the traditional sayings of Mohammed.

15 Islam, as complete .... to Allah, allows no room for .... or saying that anything merely .... Everything has been .... by Allah.

IV MATCHING TEST

Write in the space provided at the right the number of the statement that best fits each item on the left.

1	Surrender to Allah	....	*Zakah*
2	Prescribed pilgrimage to Mecca	....	Fatihah
3	Regions bordering on Islam	....	*Subh*
4	Sacred book to be recited	....	*Shahadah*
5	Basic Moslem creed	....	*Dar al-Islam*
6	Object of the *Hajj*	....	*Iblis*
7	Fighter for Islam	....	*Mal'ikah*
8	Greatest messenger from Allah	....	Ar-Rahman
9	Father of all Moslem believers	....	*Taharah*
10	Prescribed Moslem fast	....	*Salah*
11	Witness to the truth of Islam	....	Mecca
12	Leader in a Moslem community	....	Hegira
13	Religious tax in Islam	....	Gabriel
14	Ritual daily prayer	....	Abraham
15	Time for prayer before sunrise	....	Medina
16	Allah as the merciful One	....	*Sawm*
17	Ceremonial cleanliness	....	Al'Ilah
18	Created spiritual beings	....	*Mujahid*
19	Leader of the evil spirits	....	*Qur'an*
20	Major ritual purification	....	*Rakah*
21	Year one in the Moslem calendar	....	Islam
22	Opening verses of the Koran	....	*Shahid*
23	Prescribed ritual bowing	....	*Hajj*
24	The one true God	....	*Ghusl*
25	Hejaz, in Saudi Arabia	....	*Imam*

GLOSSARY OF TERMS

HINDU

Unless otherwise indicated, all the Hindu religious terms are Sanskrit, which was the ancient Aryan language of the Hindus of India. Two forms of the language are distinguishable: early Vedic Sanskrit (to 200 B.C.) in which the four Vedas were written, and Classical Sanskrit (to A.D. 1100) in which the rest of the sacred writings were composed. Today Sanskrit for the Hindus corresponds to Hebrew and Greek as the biblical languages of Judaeo-Christianity.

Advaita Nonduality. Doctrine of monism advocated by Vedanta Hinduism, which holds the Absolute is considered personal by the untutored, whereas it is objectively impersonal. Thus the world and the individual are only relatively or phenomenally real. Sankara taught this theory of nondualistic illusionary pantheism.

Ahimsa Noninjury. Ethical principle forbidding injury or pain to any living thing. In practice it means abstention from animal food, pacifism, straining of water, reverence for the cow, regarding all living beings as kindred.

Asat Nonbeing. Theory which holds that being was originally produced from nonbeing.

Ashramas Life stages. Prescribed periods in Hindu life: celibacy, study, family, asceticism.

Atman Self, soul, ego or I.

Avatar Descent. Applied to a manifestation of the deity in human form.

Avidya Ignorance or nescience. State of mind unaware of true reality.

Ayam atma Brahma This Self is Brahman. Most famous text in Hindu literature (*Brihadaranyaka Upanishad*, 2.5.19). It affirms the identity of the human (Atman) and the divine (Brahman).

Bhagavan Blessed One, highest God. In the *Bhagavad Gita* he comprises all the perfections of Atman and Brahman. He is the origin of all beings and demands supreme devotion.

Bhakti Share, division. Loving devotion to the divine object of contemplation. It is correlative to grace (*anugraha, prasada, pusti, krpa*) which the devotee receives in return for his love of the deity.

Brahma Creative principle of the universe. Main figure, along with Siva and Vishnu, of the so-called Hindu trinity.

Brahman The Absolute. In the Upanishads, union with Brahman is the highest goal of human existence. Term also used (along with *Brahmin*) for the highest caste in Hindu society.

Cit Awareness, consciousness. Best known in the phrase, *sat-cit-ananda* = being-awareness-bliss, a Vedanta definition of beatitude, when a person becomes fully conscious of being.

Dasa Slave. Applied by the Aryans to the darker-skinned indigenous people of India. Also means an evil being or demon.

Deva God. May be used in the plural, along with *devi* (goddess) or *devata* (deity).

Dharma Right, duty, virtue, usage, law, religion, truth. On the social level comprises all the duties imposed by one's position and circumstances. Nearest equivalent to the English "religion."

Gayatri Prayer. Commonly known as the *gayatri mantra* (prayer formula) which every pious Hindu recites frequently: "We meditate on the most excellent glory of that divine Sun (or Source); may That direct our understanding." In Hindu scriptures "That" (*Tat*) indicates the Beyond, contrasted with "This" (*Idam*) which stands for the world of matter and mind.

Guru Teacher. Spiritual preceptor without whom no one can be a true caste Hindu.

Is, Isa, Isana, Isvara Lord. The term vacillates between theology and metaphysics. It is personal and God when it evokes *bhakti* (devotion) and is the impersonal Absolute when merely the object of intellection.

Jiva Life. The individual conscious soul as distinguished from the Absolute Being.

Jnana Knowledge, cognition, wisdom. Insight which gives deliverance from the endless cycle of reincarnations.

Karma, Karman Action, movement, deed. Built-in law of causality or retribution working with equal precision in good and evil deeds and thoughts. It absolutely determines the nature and circumstances of one's next rebirth.

Kshatriyas Members of the warrior or ruling caste, second after the Brahmins.

Mahatma, mahatman Great soul. The superindividual or transcendental self, or the Absolute. Applied to Gandhi as a term of highest respect.

Mantra Hymn, incantation. Pious aspiration expressed in repeated prayerful utterance. Certain holy syllables are considered manifestations of the eternal word and of great mystic power.

Maya Art, making. The power of obscuring or state producing error and illusion. Veil covering reality, illusory experience of manifoldness when only the One is real. Appearance or phenomenon as opposed to reality and noumenon. Can be overcome by knowledge or insight.

Moksha Liberation, salvation. Deliverance from the effects of *karma* and resulting *samsara* (reincarnation). In Vedanta Hinduism, liberation means the discovery of one's own identity with the eternal Absolute. In theistic Hinduism, *moksha* (or *mukti*) is the attainment of happiness in the possession of God, whether in this life through freedom from sin or in the next life through liberation from all evil.

Om Assent. Sacred syllable to be pronounced when beginning prayer or the reading of sacred literature. Repetition intended to concentrate the mind on the object signified, namely Brahman. Also a symbol for the Vedas. Stands for the Absolute. Variant form of *Aum*.

Prajapati Lord of creation. From a polytheistic notion, term later applied to the first principle of creation.

Prajna Realization. Understanding the true nature of self with relation to the Absolute.

Puja Worship. Veneration paid to statues or images of an idol, which represents the body of a deity. A complete *puja* comprises sixteen gifts, including *argya* (offering of flowers, rice, and sandal paste), *gandha* (perfume), *dhapa* (incense), and *nati* (deep bow).

Samadhi Ecstasy. Final stage in the practice of Yoga, in which the individual merges with the object of meditation and attains bliss.

Samsara Going about. Passage of the Ego in the cycle of births and rebirths, transmigration or reincarnation, universally accepted in Hinduism. The concern of every Hindu sect and school of thought is how to escape *samsara* and attain *moksha*.

Samskara Purification. Ritual practice and prayer performed at important moments of human life, for example, birth, initiation, marriage, and death. Term used for the Christian "sacrament."

Sankhya Ancient system of Hindu dualism which assumes two ultimate principles, spirit (*purusa*) and matter (*prakrti*), both eternal and uncaused. Union of spirit and matter necessary for world evolution.

177

Sannyasi Ascetic. Final stage in the four *Ashramas* (q. v.) prescribed for the three highest castes. The first three stages are *Brahmacari, Grihastha,* and *Vanaprastha.*

Sat Being. One of the names of Brahman as Reality, synonymous with *Cit* (Intelligence), *Ananda* (Bliss), *Tajjalana* (Origin and Goal of all beings), *Paramatman* (Self abiding in the heart of every being).

Siddhi Reaching. Success in attaining supernatural powers, for example, clairvoyance and clairaudience, as the highest stage of Yoga. Includes the power of levitation and penetration of matter.

Smriti Recollection. Revelation from Brahman regarded as tradition, as distinguished from *Sruti* which corresponds to the Judaeo-Christian scriptures. Absolutely speaking, the *Vedas* are the ideas in the Eternal Mind, *Sruti* is the material expression of some of these divine concepts, and *Smriti* is the human transmission of what was revealed.

Sudras Fourth and lowest Hindu caste, the laborers who are to serve the other three castes.

Tantra One of many sacred treatises of Mongolian and nonindogermanic Hindu origin. Outside of traditional Vedic tradition, the *Tantras* are deeply speculative, stress cult, and teach the supremacy of the female principle as power or *Sakti.*

Tat tvam asi That thou art. Comparable in importance to *ayam atma Brahma* (q. v.). Expresses the identity of the Absolute and Self, as in the passage: "This finest essence, the whole universe has it as its Self. That is the Real; That is the Self: That you are" (*Chandogya Upanishad,* 6.8.7).

Vaishyas Third caste of Hindu society, engaged in farming and business.

Vedanta End of the Veda. The term has several meanings: (1) the Upanishads as philosophical commentaries on the Vedas, (2) systems of thought developed from the Upanishads, whose central theme is the relation between the world soul (Brahman) and the individual soul (Atman), (3) theories or sectarian interpretations of this Brahman-Atman relationship, of which four are fundamental, namely, that of Sankara, who said God and the soul are identical; Madhva, who said they are different; Ramanuja, different yet identical; and Vallabha, different and yet related by the grace from God to man.

Yoga Yoking. Restraining of the mind or disciplining the activity of consciousness. The purpose of this universally recommended Hindu practice is to gain peace of mind and deeper insight into reality. Three types are: *Karma Yoga* by doing, *Bhakti Yoga* by devotion, and *Jnana Yoga* by mental and spiritual exercise. Eight steps are commonly prescribed: moral restraint (*yama*), self-culture (*niyama*), posture (*asana*), breath control (*pranayama*), control of senses (*pratyahara*), concentration (*dharana*), meditation (*dhyana*), and *samadhi* (trance).

Yogin One who practices *yoga.* In the final stage, he enters into a state of pure spiritual self-consciousness. Unlike the Christian mystic, the *yogin* does not receive God's communication to man; he simply penetrates into the depths of his own Ego.

BUDDHIST

Since Buddhism is derived from Hinduism, many of its terms are also Hindu. In most cases such overlapping is avoided, so that the following list should be taken together with the Hindu glossary.

Moreover, since there are two main forms of Buddhism, Hinayana and Mahayana, the vocabulary and its spelling correspond to these two traditions. Unless otherwise indicated, the Sanskrit term and spelling are given, as found in Mahayana Buddhism. The Pali equivalent, represented by Hinayana, is included when ambiguity might arise or when the Pali has entered the stream of general Buddhist literature.

Amida Buddha viewed as the *avatar* or incarnation of compassion. The spiritual principle of Buddhahood. Object of worship in the Pure Land Schools of China and Japan.

Anagarika Homeless one. Person who undertakes to live a homeless life without actually becoming a monk.

Anatta-vada Theory of egolessness. Doctrine of Hinayana about the non-existence (Sanskrit: *An-atman* = nonself) of the soul. One of the three "Signs of Conditional Existence," along with *Anicca* (impermanence) and *Dukkha* (suffering or misery).

Arhat (Pali = *Arhan*) The worthy one. A person who has completed the eightfold Path to Nirvana.

Asavas Pali term for the natural outflow of desires, which must be stopped in order to attain Arhatship.

Avasa Colony of monks living together within a prescribed area.

Bhikkhu (Sanskrit = *Bhikshu*) Member of a Buddhist monastery. A Buddhist nun is a *Bhikkhuni*.

Bodhi Enlightenment. Spiritual condition of a *buddha*, the wisdom resulting from direct perception of the truth, along with the compassion that the enlightenment produces.

Bodhisattva (Pali = *Bodhisatta*) A person whose being or essence (*Sattva*) is destined for *Bodhi*; or, from another viewpoint, one whose whole nature aspires after *Bodhi*.

Buddha Title in both Sanskrit and Pali applied to one who is Awakened, in the sense of Enlightened. Applied mainly to the founder of Buddhism, it is also referred to his followers who attain Nirvana.

Buddhi Intuition. In psychological terms, the faculty of direct awareness of Reality.

Dhamma (Sanskrit = *Dharma*) Truth. Borrowed from Hinduism, its essential meaning is the Teaching of Buddha. Depending on the context, it may also mean system, doctrine, law, and cosmic order.

Dukkha Unhappiness. Suffering from whatever cause. In Hinayana it refers to all the pain experienced in daily life. In Mahayana it means especially the unhappiness caused by separation or duality, whereas the goal of human existence is union or unity. Theistic Buddhism understands it as suffering induced by separation from the Source of one's being.

179

Guru Hindu name for a spiritual teacher of Buddhism who takes pupils (*Chelas*).

Jiriki Japanese term which means reaching Nirvana by one's own powers, a sort of Buddhist Pelagianism. It is the opposite of *Tariki*, which holds that salvation requires help (grace) from some Other Power.

Karma Same in Sanskrit and Pali. Taken from Hinduism, it means the law of cause and effect as applied to the mind in much the same sense as understood in Hinduism. But in Buddhism there can also be group *Karma*, for example, family or nation, so that the deeds or misdeeds of a group have consequences on the reincarnation of all the members of the group.

Karuna Pure compassion. Along with *Prajna* (Wisdom), it is one of the two pillars of the Mahayana.

Klesha (Pali = *Kilesa*) Defilement. The moral depravity whose elimination is necessary for progress on the Path to Nirvana. Buddhist equivalent of sin.

Koan Problem. Japanese term in Zen for something which cannot be solved by the intellect, corresponding to the Christian "mystery." It also means the exercise for breaking the limitations of the reasoning mind and developing intuition.

Maha Great. Taken from Hinduism, it is a frequent prefix to many terms in Buddhism, for example, *Mahayana* = *Maha* + *Yana* (Vehicle), *Mahavastu* = *Maha* + *Vastu* (Story) which is the Great Story or biography of Buddha.

Mondo Japanese term for the rapid question-and-answer method used in Zen to break through the barriers of conceptual or rational thought.

Nirvana (Pali = *Nibbana*) Supreme goal of Buddhist endeavor. Release from the limitations of separate or separated existence and consequent ending of desire. Attainable in this life. *Parinirvana* is the final *Nirvana*; sometimes identified with the Absolute.

Pali One of the early languages of Buddhism, later adopted by the Hinayana (Theravada) in which to preserve what they considered the authentic teachings of the Buddha.

Pitaka Basket. Corresponds to the term "tradition." Three *Pitakas* constitute the Pali canon of sacred writings: *Sutta Pitaka* (Sermons of Buddha), *Vinaya Pitaka* (Rules of the monastic order), *Abhidamma Pitaka* (Systematic analysis of Buddhist practice).

Puja Gesture of worship or respect, practiced in prayer, usually raising the hands with the palms together. The height of the hands indicates the degree of reverence.

Rajas Restless activity, or passionate anger. One of the Three Fires which cause all human suffering, along with *Dosa* (hatred or ill-will) and *Moha* (mental dullness or infatuation).

Rupa Body. One of the five elements constituting the self, along with sensation, conception, discrimination, and cognition. Also refers to the material of which Buddha images are made, thus *Buddha-rupa* = Buddha statue. This material is revered as the physical body of Buddha.

Samadhi Contemplation. Taken from Hinduism, it represents the last step before Nirvana.

Sangha Monastic order. This is the third of the three articles of the Buddhist faith, whereby a person says, "I believe in *Buddha* (the Teacher), in *Dhamma* (his Teaching) and *Sangha* (his Order)." In accepting the *Dhamma*, a believer subscribes to the Four Noble Truths and the eightfold Path. If he decides to enter the monastery, he begins as a *Pabbajja* (one who leaves home); entering the monastery, he becomes a *Sramanera* (novice), at which time he shaves his head; finally he is ordained monk (*Upasampada*) when not less than twenty years old; all the while he is directed by the *Guru* or master; dedicates himself to follow the *Vinaya* (monastic rules), of which the essential prescriptions of discipline are the *Parimokha* (bond, that which holds the community together) that number 227 in the Pali canon, 250 in Chinese, and 253 in Tibetan Buddhism.

Satori Japanese term in Zen for the state of consciousness which varies in quality and duration from a flash of intuitive awareness to Nirvana.

Shin Pure Land School of Japanese Buddhism which teaches that salvation (*Nirvana*) requires nothing but faith in *Amitabha* (also *Amida*), presiding Buddha of the Western Paradise (Pure Land). No matter how sinful, a person is saved by merely invoking *Amitabha*. Beans are used to count the acts of confidence. Salvation comes entirely from the grace of Buddha.

Stupa Reliquary mound, usually covering one or more relics of Buddha, for example, a particle of his ashes. At the site of each *Stupa* is a *Chaitya* or shrine, which became the temple. Distinct from both is the *Vihara* or monastery (also used as term for a state of mind). *Pagoda* is the common name for Buddhist shrines, which are usually pyramidal in India, octagonal in China and with superimposed stories decreasing in size toward the top, in Japan of wood and square and five stories high with projecting roof.

Tanha (Sanskrit = *Trishna*) Craving or thirst. The basic urge for satisfaction that can be extinguished (or fulfilled) by the eightfold Path.

Tantra Chief competitor to the two main forms of Buddhism. Tantric Buddhism gives initiates access to the *Tantras* or magical formulas unknown to the common people. Also called *Mantrayana* (*Mantra* = spell + *Yana* = vehicle), it emphasizes the female aspect of nature and uses sex symbolism. The most famous *Mantra* is one uttered by every Tibetan, "*Om mani padme hum* (O the jewel in the lotus!)."

Theravada Elders. The Pali term for Hinayana Buddhism, as representing the teaching of the ancient monks of the Southern School. It is preferred by its own followers because Hinayana, they say, has pejorative connotations.

Urna Jewel or small protuberance between the eyes of a Buddha statue, symbolizing the "third eye of spiritual vision," to be attained on reaching Nirvana.

181

Ushnisha Symbolic protuberance at the top of a Buddha image which represents the flame of supreme Enlightenment reached by the founder.

Wabi Japanese term for the mood of serenity. It may be described as "aloofness in the midst of multiplicities," and its features are simplicity in the performance of even complex tasks, yet with an absence of visible skill. Inspired by Buddhist self-discipline, it makes of every human act a means of worship. Best known is the *cha-no-yu* or "tea ceremony."

Wesak (Sanskrit = *Vaisakha*) Lunar month corresponding to April-May. During its full moon are commemorated Buddha's Birth, Enlightenment, and Passing.

CHINESE

Since Chinese Universism includes various religious traditions, and not only Confucianism, it seems better to list all the principal terms commonly used in China with reference to religion.

In view of their number, only a brief definition is given for some of the terms. Also where it seems necessary they are identified with a specific religious tradition, other than Confucian.

Ch'an To sit in contemplation or meditate (Buddhist).

Chen ts'a The true Lord who directs the operation of the universe, but to whose existence there is no clue.

Ch'eng Sincerity. Three meanings in Confucian literature: honesty or sincerity, reverence or seriousness, and truth or being one's true self.

Cheng hsin Setting one's own heart or rectifying one's emotions. When a person is upset by fear, passion, or anxiety, his mind lacks balance. It must be rectified before virtue is possible.

Cheng ming Rectification of names. Words must first correspond to reality if order in social and personal morality is to be achieved.

Ch'i Breath, force, or spirit. The vital energy as expressed in the operation and succession of the active principle (*yang*) and the passive principle (*yin*), along with the five elements or agents of the universe (*wu hsing*), that is, water, fire, wood, metal, and earth. Out of this reaction comes the multiplicity of things in the world.

Chi Subtle power from which all things came and to which all things return (Taoist).

Chi Dou Chiao Christianity. Literally "Christ-Religion." Also *T'ien Chu Chiao*, literally "Heavenly Lord Religion," to designate Catholicism.

Ch'ing Passions. Human nature on its impure side, when stirred by contrary feelings, mainly like and dislike, and the sense of advantage and disadvantage.

Ching Four levels of meaning: (1) Confucian or Taoist religious classics, formerly spelled *King*; also the cardinal standards or directions in Confucian ethics and government based on the classics, (2) reverence or seriousness, according to the Confucian principle, "Seriousness is the basis of moral cultivation, the essence of human affairs, just as sincerity is the way of Heaven," (3) the essence or nature which constitutes things, (4) tranquillity, which Confucianism interprets as the original state of human nature and Taoism identifies with absence of desire or unity of thought.

Chiu ch'ou Nine categories of the Great Plan or Grand Norm of Heaven. Basis of Confucian morality.

Chung The Mean. Inner self or moral being, unmoved by passion. Also objectively the Moral Law or ultimate principle of the universe.

Chun-tzu The superior man, the perfect man, the moral man, the noble man. In Confucius' words, "The superior man (*chun-tzu*) rejoices in the fulfillment of the moral law, whereas the inferior man (*hsiao jen*) rejoices in the fulfillment of his desires."

Hsiao Filial piety. Love of parents, devotion to the source of one's being. It is "the standard of Heaven, the principle of earth and the basis for the conduct of man."

Hsin Mind or heart. The fourth aspect of Nature in Confucian theology. When Nature (*hsing*) is viewed from its goodness, it is the Moral Law (*tao*); when viewed from its essence, it is Destiny (*ming*); when viewed in terms of its Primordial Principle, it is Heaven (*T'ien*), and when seen in its manifestations in man, it is the Mind (*hsin*).

Hsing Human nature understood in the sense of that which is "inborn," or "what is created." It is that which is imparted by Heaven, whereas what is received from other persons or from the world is fate (*ming*). Man's original state of nature is tranquil. When it comes into contact with the external world, it is aroused and becomes feelings (*ch'ing*).

Hsuan te According to Lao-Tze, "The Way (*Tao*) produces things but does not take possession of them. It does its work but does not take pride in it. It rules over things but does not dominate them." This is called Profound Virtue (*Hsuan te*) (Taoist).

Hui hui Moslems. The followers of Mohammed call their religion *Ching Chen Ssu*, meaning "The Pure and True Religion," which they inscribe over the entrances of their mosques.

Hun The spiritual part of man that ascends to Heaven. In Taoism, the Golden Age is *Hun Mang*, when men lived in perfect harmony within themselves, with one another, and with the forces of nature. The same idea is transferred to the eschatological future.

I This term has at least five basic meanings: (1) in Taoism, it is the One which is produced by *Tao* and which in turn produces the Two, *yin* and *yang*, (2) Confucianism considers *I* as "change," often spelled *Yi*, namely what arises from the Great Ultimate (*T'ai Chi*) which is changeless, (3) Neo-Confucians use the term for will, purpose, and motive, (4) Classic Confucianism identifies it with righteousness or justice, and (5) Mencius distinguished it as the objective Moral Law.

I Yuan The One Prime. Identical with the Origin of myriad things including man.

Jen Man. From the root meanings are derived numerous others, for example, goodness as embodied in the Superior Man; moral character in living up to the demands of human nature; maturity of person, shown by a man who "having established his own character, seeks to establish the character of others, and, having succeeded, seeks to make others succeed" (Confucius); kindness and benevolence "without the element of self."

Ju Confucianists. Generally used in the form *Ju Chiao* (Confucianism) to designate this system which (1) emphasizes ethics and social morality, and (2) worships *Shang-Ti* and honors ancestors.

Kuei Man's spirit after death. Correlative term for earthly spirits as distinct from the coexisting heavenly spirits (*shen*).

Kung Respect and courtesy. Neo-Confucianism distinguishes *kung* from *ch'in*. The former refers to expression, whereas the latter refers to the interior sentiment. As such, *ch'in* is synonymous with kinship and the affection based on blood relationship, which was contradicted by Mohists as untenable in the face of the equality of all men.

Lao-T'ien-Yeh Popular name for God. Derived from Taoist sources, it means the Ancient-Ancestor-Heaven, where each term is significant, that is, eternal-originator-transcendent Being.

Li Reason or law. This fundamental concept of Confucian ethics has taken on various interpretations. Historically the term has meant "propriety," on which Confucius wrote that, "The rules of propriety (*li*) are rooted in Heaven, have their correspondences on earth, and are applicable to spiritual beings." Implied in "propriety" is the notion of harmony (*ho*) between the Divine Plan and human conduct, reflected in virtuous actions, ritual practices, and musical compositions.

Miao Borrowed from Taoism, it is the mystery of existence which is unfathomable; the subtle presence of the almighty Creative Power in all things; and may also mean temple or place of worship.

Ming Etymologically it means "name," or "that which designates a thing." Theologically it is Fate, Destiny, or Decree of Heaven. Confucians agree that Fate (*Meng*) and Nature (*Hsing*) are not the same thing; the former is decreed by Heaven, the latter is what actually exists among men. Similarly the Destiny is planned by Heaven, but its realization depends on men.

P'u Taoist idea of man's natural state. Literally "unwrought simplicity," it stands for his inborn powers when these have not been tampered with by any outside knowledge or circumscribed by any rules of morality.

Shang-Ti Supreme Ruler on High, that is, God. As the highest authority, he presides over an elaborate hierarchy of spirits and is the supreme object of veneration. Also called Heaven (*T'ien*), or August

Heaven (*Huang T'ien*), Sovereign (*Ti*), or Heavenly Lord (*T'ien Chu*) which is preferred by Christians.

Shu Number. Based on the Confucian *Book of Changes*, the concept of number enters every phase of religion and morality. To Heaven belong the odd numbers, which symbolize the active principle (*yang*) and tend to increase; to earth belong the even numbers, which represent the passive principle (*yin*) and tend to decrease. To Heaven belong twenty-five numbers, to earth thirty. The total of fifty-five is sacred and fixed. Everything in the world can be fitted into this numerical pattern, and the whole moral system can be thus explained and classified. *Shu* also expresses virtue in relation to others, and may be taken generically for the method of governing a people.

Ta t'ung The Great Unity and Harmony, when Heaven and earth form an organic whole. Applicable to Confucian eschatology.

Tao In Taoism it is the ineffable first principle of being, at once eternal, immaterial, and all-present, which guides the destinies of men. In Confucianism it is the "Way," or the moral law derived from Heaven's Plan.

Te Power. Efficacy which comes from character. Tao inherent in a person, which enables him to do what others cannot do. Also kindness.

Ti God as Lord governing the world, whereas *T'ien* is God as omnipresent and all pervading. Also respect for elders, which may be spelled *t'i*.

Ti chih tse The pattern of the Lord, either as instituted by God or by the highest ruler in the land under divine guidance.

T'ien chu The evolution of nature. Spontaneous change which things undergo from one form to another, the beginning and end of whose changes are like a circle, in which no part is any more the beginning than another part.

Tz'u Parental love. Corresponds to *ti* on the part of children. It comprehends kindness and concern for one's offspring.

Wen Culture. The evidence of moral behavior and religious practice shown in human society.

Wu Creatures. Correlative to *Tsao hua*, Creator. In Taoism, *Wu* also means "Eternal Non-Being" in contrast to *Tao* the First Principle.

Yin yang Passive and active principles, respectively, of the universe. Also the female, negative force and the male, positive force, always contrasting but complementing each other. Forms of *yin yang* are heaven and earth, man and woman, good and evil, odd and even numbers, joy and sorrow, reward and punishment, love and hate.

Yu Desire. Taoists consider *yu* detrimental to happiness, Confucians accept it as natural if under control.

Yung Common, ordinary, universal. To the Confucians, this is "the eternal law of the universe." To the Taoists, "the common and ordinary are the natural function of all things, which expresses the common nature of the whole. Following the common nature of the whole, people are at ease. This is letting nature take its course, . . . This is Tao."

MOSLEM

With almost no exception, Moslem terms are Arabic. They are also rooted in space and time and reflect the deep sense of history which is typical of Islam.

There is another side to Islam beyond the Koran and Moslem piety. Islamic theology is rich and extensive, and has been very influential in shaping the language of Christian culture. With this in view and because Islam built so much on Judaeo-Christianity, many of the terms have special significance for the Christian religion.

Ahmad Prophetic name of Mohammed in the Koran, where Jesus foretells the coming of Islam, "Jesus, son of Mary, said . . . I announce the good tidings of the messenger who will come after me, bearing the name Ahmad" (61:6).

Allah Contraction for *Al-Ilah* = The God. The term is also used by Syrian Christians.

Allahu Akbar Daily prescribed prayer, "Allah is most Great," to be recited with hands on each side of the face.

Ashab Companions. Everyone who personally saw and accompanied the prophet and whose testimony has since become part of Moslem tradition.

Bismillah Invocation which introduces every surah of the one hundred fourteen in the Koran, except the ninth: "In the name of Allah, the Merciful, the Compassionate."

Darwish Persian for the Arabic *Faqir*, mendicant member of a Moslem religious community. Starting as a disciple (*murid*) under the direction of a director (*shaikh* = Persian *pir*), he followed the master's way (*tariqa*).

Fatihah Opening surah of the Koran, recited daily.

Fatwa Legal opinion handed down by *muftis* (Moslem lawyers) on a point of Islamic law.

Fiqh One of several terms for Islamic law: (1) *ilm* as positive knowledge of theology, (2) *figh* as understanding based on theology, (3) *qanun* as administrative rule distinct from revealed law, and (4) *Shari'a* as the whole legal system or "Way." *Fiqh* may also be a statement of the Moslem articles of faith.

Fitra Religious condition of a person at birth, which is variously interpreted from innate Islam to right reason that requires preaching of the Koran to believe.

Hadith Above seventy-three hundred recorded anecdotes about Mohammed, outside the Koran, venerated as part of the Moslem revelation. Validity measured by the witnesses' familiarity with the prophet.

Hajj Prescribed pilgrimage to Mecca for all who are physically and morally able to do so.

Haram Absolutely forbidden. Strict prohibitions like the drinking of wine (*Khamr*). Corresponds to *makruh*, disapproved, like gambling or playing games of chance.

Hijra Mohammed's historic flight from Mecca to Medina.

Iblis Devil. Most likely derived from the Greek *diabolos*. Condemned to hell because he refused to honor Adam, though commanded to do so by Allah. Tempts people to reject Allah.

Ibn Son of. Comparable to Hebrew *ben*. Equivalent terms are *'Abd* (servant or slave) as *'Abd Allah*, the father of Mohammed; and *Abu* = Father of, similar to Hebrew *Abba*.

Imam Leader in the widest sense; then leader of prayer in the mosque; also the spiritual head of a Moslem community.

Iman Faith. The term is almost synonymous with Islam, so that *Muslim* (Moslem) and *Mu'min* (Believer) are found interchangeably in the Koran and in Islamic theology.

Injil Gospel, derived from the Greek *evangelion*. Given to mankind by Jesus, it means the message of Jesus, the entire New Testament, or the writings commonly called Gospels.

Isa Jesus. There are sixteen different titles by which Jesus is described in the Koran, in approximate order of frequency as follows: *Isa*—25 (Jesus, from the Syriac *Yeshu*), *Ibn Maryam*—23 (Son of Mary), *Al Masih*—11 (The Messiah, from the Hebrew *Mashiah*; popularly combined with the prefix *Al-Sayyid*, "the Lord"), *Abd*—3 (Servant, normally as *Abd Allah*, "Servant of God"), *Nabi*—8 (Prophet), *Rasul*—10 (Messenger, distinguished from prophets who came only to Jews, Christians, and Moslems), *Kalima*—3 (Word, in popular Islam expressed as *Kalima Allah*, "word of Allah"), *Ruh*—7 (Spirit, found in Islamic devotion as *Isa, Ruh Allah*, "Jesus the spirit of Allah"), *Aya*—4 (Sign, foretold to the prophets of Israel), *Mathal*—3 (Parable, as example to be followed), *Shahid*—2 (Witness, especially against those who reject the Messiah), *Rahma*—1 (Mercy, in the Koranic passage [19:21] where Allah says that Jesus "is Mercy from us"), *Wajih*—1 (Eminent One, so named by the angel at the Annunciation to Mary), *Min al-Muqarrabin*—1 (One nearest to God, same Annunciation context), *Al Salihin*—1 (The Righteous One, also Annunciation context), *Mubarak*—1 (Blessed, as one having power to give happiness).

Jihad Holy War. Prescribed by the Koran as a collective duty to defend and extend Islam.

Jinn Spirits. Pre-Islamic spiritual beings adopted by Islam, who may be angels, or disembodied souls, or semimaterial creatures who negotiate between heaven and earth.

Ka'ba Sacred shrine at Mecca, formerly place of pilgrimage for Animists. Cubelike structure housing the Holy Stone which pilgrims are to kiss.

Khalifa Caliph. Literally lieutenant of Mohammed and thus head of the Mosels. The last Caliphate was of the Ottoman Turks, from A.D. 1299 to 1922.

Malik Angel. Function is to worship God, relay messages to men, record men's deeds.

187

Manara Minaret. First built in Syria, before A.D. 750. Later became typical of mosques. Used as call-tower, place for observation and signal in case of need.

Masihi Christian, from *Al Masih*, "the Christ." In the Koran, the term *Nasara*, Nazarenes, is regularly used for Christians.

Masjid Mosque. The term means "place of prostration."

Mihrab Niche at east end of the mosque which gives the direction of Mecca to be faced in prayer.

Nikah Marriage. In Islamic law, marriage is a mutual contract for the purpose of legalizing generation. Temporary marriage, *Mut'ah*, is defended by some Moslems from the Koran (4:28) and by others from custom. Concubinage is also defended from tradition.

Al-Qur'an The Koran, "that which is to be recited." Synonyms are: *Al-Furqan*, "the Separation" between believers and unbelievers; and *At-Tanzil*, "the Revelation" sent down from God.

Rabb Lord. Most common name for Allah in the Koran. He is also called *Ar-Rahman*, "the Merciful One"; and *Wadud*, "Loving One."

Ramadan Ninth month of the lunar year, daylight abstinence from food and drink to commemorate the revelation of the Koran.

Shaitan Satan. Either collective or distributive term for the evil spirit who tries to lead believers away from Allah.

Shari'a Islamic Law. The two main sources are the Koran (scripture) and *Hadith* (tradition). Orthodox Islam (*Sunni* = handed down by custom) recognizes four positions or schools of interpretation: *Hanafi* (liberal), *Maliki* (communal), *Shafii* (governmental), and *Hanbali* (conservative).

Shia Sectarian Islam, claiming that only lineal descendants of Mohammed had right to succession. Produced Bahaism. Competitive to the *Sunni*.

Shirk Unbelief. Unforgivable sin of associating anything or anyone with Allah. Christians are charged with *shirk*.

Sufi Ascetic. Nickname from the garment of wool (*suf*), worn by Moslems who sought direct experience of Allah. Early formed religious orders, practiced celibacy, recited Koran in common, meditated, and followed many practices of Christian monks. Outstanding Sufi theologian, who influenced Aquinas, was Al Ghazali (1058-1111). Reacted against Mutazilites (Dissidents) or Moslem rationalists, for example, Averroes (1126-1198).

Yawm al-Akhir Last Day. Synonymous with *As-Sa'ah* (the Hour), *Yawm al-Qiyamah* (Day of Resurrection), *Yawm ad-Din* (Day of Judgment), *Yawm al-Fasl* (Day of Separation), *Yawm al-Jam* (Day of Gathering of Men before God), *Yawm al-Talaqi* (Day of Meeting with God). After the Last Day, there will be only Heaven and Hell. The most common terms for Heaven are: *Al-Jannah* (the Garden), and *Firdaws* (Paradise). Hell is designated as: *Jahannam* (Gehenna), *Al-Jahim* (the Hot Place), *Sa'ir* (Blaze), and *An-Nar* (the Fire).

SELECT BIBLIOGRAPHY

The following titles cover the principal religious traditions of present-day Asia and Africa. They include books which deal with the history, beliefs, worship, and practices of these religions. The majority of titles are concerned more particularly with the theology of the living non-Christian faiths of mankind. Primitive religions are included in order to give an adequate view of man's religious culture.

The list is not comprehensive and new titles appear almost every month. However, those given here are representative and sufficiently extensive to cover the main areas of Afro-Asian religion.

HINDUISM

1 R. Antoine and others, *Religious Hinduism*, Bombay: St. Paul Publications, 1964 (second edition).
2 Jean Chevalier, *Le Veda*, Paris: Planete, 1967.
3 Surendra Dasgupta, *History of Indian Philosophy*, London: Cambridge University Press, 1932-1955, 5 vols.
4 J. M. Dechanet, *Christian Yoga*, New York: Harper, 1959.

5 Paul Deussen, *The Philosophy of the Upanishads*, New York: Dover, 1966.
6 Ainslee T. Embree, *The Hindu Tradition* (Basic Hindu Writings), New York: The Modern Library, 1966.
7 Mahatma K. Gandhi, *Autobiography*, Ahmedabad: Navajivan, 1948.
8 Jan Gonda, *Les Religions de L'Inde*, Paris: Payot, Vol. I, 1962; Vol. II, 1965.
9 Homer A. Jack, editor, *The Gandhi Reader*, Bloomington: Indiana University Press, 1956.
10 J. M. Macfie, *The Ramayana of Tulsidas*, Edinburgh: Clark, 1930.
11 Kenneth W. Morgan, *The Religion of the Hindus*, New York: Ronald, 1953.
12 F. Max Muller, *The Upanishads*, New York: Dover, 1960, 2 vols.
13 Raymond Panikkar, *The Unknown Christ of Hinduism*, London: Darton, 1964.
14 Swami Prabhavananda, *The Spiritual Heritage of India*, London: G. Allen, 1962.
15 Sarvepalli Radhakrishnan, *A Hindu Way of Life*, New York: Macmillan, 1960.
16 Louis Renou, *Hinduism*, New York: Braziller, 1961.
17 Paul Thomas, *Epics, Myths and Legends of India*, Bombay: Taraporevala, 1949.
18 R. C. Zaehner, *Hindu Scriptures*, New York: Dutton, 1966.
19 R. C. Zaehner, *Hinduism*, New York: Oxford University Press, 1962.
20 Heinrich R. Zimmer, *Philosophies of India*, Edited by Joseph Campbell, New York: Pantheon, 1953.

BUDDHISM

21 Kenneth K. S. Chen, *Buddhism*, Woodbury, N. Y.: Barron's Educational Series, 1968.
22 Kenneth K. S. Chen, *Buddhism in China*, Princeton, N. J.: Princeton University Press, 1964.
23 Edward Conze, *Buddhist Scriptures*, Baltimore: Penguin, 1960.
24 Edward Conze, *Buddhist Texts Through the Ages*, New York: Philosophical Library, 1953, First Series.
25 Edward Conze, *Buddhist Texts Through the Ages*, New York: Harper and Row, 1967, Second Series.
26 Ananda K. Coomaraswamy, *Hindouisme et Bouddhisme*, Cherbourg: Gallimard, 1949.
27 Heinrich Dumoulin, *A History of Zen Buddhism*, New York: Pantheon, 1963.
28 Charles Eliot, *Hinduism and Buddhism*, New York: Barnes and Noble, 1954, 3 vols.
29 Alfred Foucher, *Les Vies Anterieures du Bouddha*, Paris: Presses Universitaires, 1955.

30 Richard A. Gard, *Buddhism*, New York: Braziller, 1961.
31 Dwight Goddard, *A Buddhist Bible*, New York: Dutton, 1952.
32 Christmas Humphreys, *Buddhism*, Baltimore: Penguin, 1955.
33 Christmas Humphreys, *The Wisdom of Buddhism*, London: Joseph, 1960.
34 Henri de Lubac, *Aspects of Buddhism*, New York: Sheed and Ward, 1953.
35 Kenneth W. Morgan, *The Path of the Buddha: Buddhism Interpreted by Buddhists*, New York: Ronald, 1956.
36 T. R. V. Murti, *The Central Philosophy of Buddhism*, London: Allen and Unwin, 1955.
37 Bernard Philips, *The Essentials of Zen Buddhism*, London: Rider, 1963.
38 Robert L. Slater, *Paradox and Nirvana*, Chicago: University of Chicago Press, 1951.
39 Daisetz T. Suzuki, *Essais Sur Le Bouddhisme Zen*, Paris: Michel, 1965, 3 vols.
40 Daisetz T. Suzuki, *Essays in Zen Buddhism*, New York: Harper and Row, 1948-1958, 3 vols.
41 Daisetz T. Suzuki, *Mysticism, Christian and Buddhist*, New York: Collier, 1962.
42 Daisetz T. Suzuki, *The Training of the Zen Buddhist Monk*, Kyoto: Eastern Buddhist Society, 1934.
43 Daisetz T. Suzuki, *Zen Buddhism*, Garden City, N. Y.: Doubleday, 1956.

CONFUCIANISM

44 H. G. Creel, *Chinese Thought from Confucius to Mao Tse-Tung*, Chicago: University of Chicago Press, 1953.
45 H. G. Creel, *Confucius: The Man and the Myth*, New York: Day, 1949.
46 E. R. Hughes, *Chinese Philosophy in Classical Times*, London: Dent, 1942.
47 E. R. Hughes and K. Hughes, *Religion in China*, London: Hutchinson, 1950.
48 Leo Sherley-Price, *Confucius and Christ*, New York: Philosophical Library, 1951.
49 Arthur Waley, *The Analects of Confucius*, London: Allen and Unwin, 1949.
50 James R. Ware, *The Sayings of Confucius*, New York: New American Library, 1961.
51 Max Weber, *The Religion of China*, New York: Macmillan, 1964.
52 Liu Wu-Chi, *A Short History of Confucian Philosophy*, London: Penguin, 1955.
53 C. K. Yang, *Religion in Chinese Society*, Berkeley: University of California Press, 1967.

CHINESE RELIGION

54 Wing-tsit Chan, *Religious Trends in Modern China*, New York: Columbia University Press, 1953.

55 John K. Fairbank, *Chinese Thought and Institutions*, Chicago: University of Chicago Press, 1957.

56 W. E. Soothill, *The Three Religions of China*, New York: Oxford University Press, 1951.

57 Y. C. Yand, *China's Religious Heritage*, Nashville: Abingdon, 1943.

JAPANESE RELIGION

58 Masaharu Anesaki, *Religious Life of the Japanese People*, Tokyo: Society for International Cultural Relations, 1961.

59 William K. Bunce, *Religions in Japan*, Tokyo: Tuttle, 1960.

60 Jean Herbert, *Dieux et Sectes Populaires du Japon*, Paris: Michel, 1967.

61 Jean Herbert, *Les Dieux Nationaux du Japon*, Paris: Michel, 1965.

62 Carl Michalson, *Japanese Contributions to Christian Theology*, Philadelphia: Westminster, 1960.

63 Clark B. Offner and Henry Van Straelen, *Modern Japanese Religions*, Leiden: Brill, 1963.

64 George B. Sansom, *A History of Japan*, Stanford, Calif.: Stanford University Press, 1958-1965, 3 vols.

65 P. Wheeler, *Sacred Scriptures of the Japanese*, New York: Abelard, 1952.

MINOR RELIGIONS OF THE EAST

66 J. C. Archer, *Sikhs in Relation to Hindus, Moslems, Christians and Ahmadiyyas*, Princeton, N. J.: Princeton University Press, 1946.

67 R. B. Blakney, *The Way of Life: Lao Tzu*, New York: New American Library, 1957.

68 Witter Bynner, *Lao-Tzu*, New York: Day, 1944.

69 J. Duchesne-Guillemin, *The Hymns of Zarathustra*, London: Murray, 1952.

70 J. Duchesne-Guillemin, *The Western Response to Zoroaster*, New York: Oxford University Press, 1958.

71 E. E. Herzfeld, *Zoroaster and His World*, Princeton, N. J.: Princeton University Press, 1947.

72 James Legge, *The Texts of Taoism*, New York: Dover, 1960, 2 vols.

73 Chimanlal J. Shah, *Jainism in North India*, London: Longmans, 1932.

74 Khushwant Singh, *The Sikhs*, London: Allen and Unwin, 1953.

75 D. L. Snellgrove, *The Hevajra Tantra*, London: Oxford University Press, 1959.

ISLAM

76 Abudullah Yusuf Ali, *The Holy Qur'an*, New York: Murray, 1965.
77 Tor Andrae, *Mohammed: The Man and His Faith*, New York: Harper and Row, 1960.
78 A. J. Arberry, *Revelation and Reason in Islam*, New York: Macmillan, 1957.
79 T. W. Arnold and A. Guillaume, *Legacy of Islam*, New York: Oxford University Press, 1960.
80 Richard Bell, *Introduction to the Qur'an*, Edinburgh: Edinburgh University Press, 1963.
81 El Bokhari, *L'Authentique Tradition Musulmane*, Paris: Grasset, 1964.
82 N. J. Coulson, *A History of Islamic Law*, Edinburgh: Edinburgh University Press, 1964.
83 Kenneth Cragg, *The Call of the Minaret*, New York: Oxford University Press, 1956.
84 Caesar E. Farah, *Islam*, Woodbury, N. Y.: Barron's Educational Series, 1968.
85 A. A. Fyzee, *Outlines of Mohammedan Law*, New York: Oxford University Press, 1949.
86 Louis Gardet, *L'Islam, Religion et Communaute*, Paris: Desclee, 1967.
87 C. V. Gheorghiu, *Vie de Mahomet*, Paris: Plon, 1962.
88 H. A. R. Gibb, *Mohammedanism*, New York: Oxford University Press, 1953.
89 H. A. R. Gibb and H. Bowen, *Islamic Society and the West*, New York: Oxford University Press, 1950, 1957, multivolume series projected.
90 Toshihiko Izutsu, *Ethico-Religious Concepts in the Qur'an*, Montreal: McGill University Press, 1966.
91 R. Levy, *Social Structure of Islam*, London: Cambridge University Press, 1957.
92 D. Masson, *Le Coran* (traduction et notes), Bruges: L'Imprimerie Sainte-Catherine, 1967.
93 D. Masson, *Le Coran et La Revelation Judeo-Chretienne, Etudes Comparees*, Paris: Adrien-Maisonneuve, 1958, 2 vols.
94 Kenneth W. Morgan, *Islam, the Straight Path: Islam Interpreted by Muslims*, New York: Ronald, 1958.
95 Reynold A. Nicholson, *The Mystics of Islam*, London: Routledge and Kegan Paul, 1963.
96 Geoffrey Parrinder, *Jesus in the Qur'an*, New York: Barnes and Noble, 1965.
97 Mohammed Marmaduke Pickthall, *The Meaning of the Glorious Koran*, New York: New American Library, 1967.
98 Daud Rahbar, *God of Justice, A Study in the Ethical Doctrine of the Qur'an*, Leiden: Brill, 1960.
99 Fazlur Rahman, *Islam*, London: Weidenfeld and Nicolson, 1966.

100 Wilfred Cantwell Smith, *Islam in Modern History*, Princeton, N. J.: Princeton University Press, 1957.

101 J. Windrow Sweetman, *Islam and Christian Theology*, London: Lutterworth, 1947, 1955, 2 vols.

102 W. Montgomery Watt, *Islam and the Integration of Society*, Evanston, Ill.: Northwestern University Press, 1961.

103 Muhammad Zafrulla Khan, *Islam, Its Message for Modern Man*, New York: Harper and Row, 1962.

SOURCES AND SACRED WRITINGS

104 Robert O. Ballou, *The Bible of the World*, New York: Viking, 1939, one volume of selections.

105 A. C. Bouquet, *Sacred Books of the World*, Baltimore: Penguin, 1960, one volume of best quotations.

106 William T. De Bary, *Introduction to Oriental Civilizations*, New York: Columbia University Press, 1958-1960, three volumes—one each for the religions of China, India, and Japan.

107 C. R. Lanman, editor, *Harvard Oriental Series*, Cambridge, Mass.: Harvard University Press, from 1895 to the present. Forty-three volumes of texts, mainly Hindu and Buddhist, with commentaries.

108 Max Muller, editor, *Sacred Books of the East*, New York: Oxford University Press, 1879-1910. Fifty volumes of sacred non-Christian books which have shaped the religion of Asia. Complements the *Harvard Oriental Series*.

PRIMITIVE RELIGIONS

109 M. Eliade, *Rites and Symbols of Initiation*, New York: Harper and Row, 1966.

110 M. Eliade, *Sacred and the Profane*, New York: Harper and Row, 1961.

111 James G. Frazer, *The Golden Bough: A Study in Magic and Religion*, New York: Macmillan, 1935.

112 William J. Goode, *Religion Among the Primitives*, Glencoe, Ill.: Free Press, 1951.

113 E. O. James, *Prehistoric Religion*, New York: Praeger, 1957.

114 Robert H. Lowie, *Primitive Religion*, New York: Liveright, 1952.

115 Bronislaw Malinowski, *Magic Science and Religion*, New York: Doubleday, 1960.

116 Paul Radin, *Primitive Religion*, New York: Dover, 1957.

117 William Schmidt, *The Origin and Growth of Religion*, New York: Dial, 1953, one-volume edition of the ten-volume work, *Der Ursprung der Gottesidee*.

118 G. E. Swanson, *Birth of the Gods: The Origin of Primitive Beliefs*, Ann Arbor: University of Michigan Press, 1960.

119 Edward B. Taylor, *Religion in Primitive Culture*, New York: Harper, 1958.

REFERENCES

HINDUISM

1 *Rig Veda*, II, 33.
2 *Ibid.*, X, 121.
3 *Ibid.*, X, 90.
4 *Mandukya Upanishad*, 1-2.
5 *Brihadaranyaka Upanishad*, III, 7, 23.
6 *Katha Upanishad*, I, 2, 14.
7 *Ibid.*, I, 15-17.
8 *Ibid.*, I, 20, 22.
9 *Ibid.*, I, 23.
10 Plato, "Symposium," *Platonis Opera*, II (Oxford: Clarendon, 1910), p. 210.
11 *Svetasvatara Upanishad*, VI, 5-13.
12 *Bhagavad Gita*, XI, 36-37, 41-42, 45.
13 *Ibid.*, XI, 47.

14 *Ibid.*, XI, 52-55.
15 *Ibid.*, IX, 17, 19; X, 8, 20, 39-42.
16 *Ibid.*, X, 28, 33-35, 38.
17 *Ibid.*, XII, 13-19.
18 *Ibid.*, XVI, 16-21.
19 *Ibid.*

BUDDHISM

1 *Dipavamsa*, XX, 20, trans. by Hermann Oldenberg (Pali Text Society, 1879), p. 211.
2 *Digha-Nikaya*, II, 14.
3 *Majjhima-Nikaya*, 63.
4 *Divyavanda* (Cambridge, 1886), p. 355.
5 Pe Maung Tin, *The Path of Purity* (London: Oxford University Press, 1929), 2.223.
6 *Milindapanha*, II, 13.
7 *Ibid.*
8 T. W. Rhys Davids, "The Questions of King Melinda," *Sacred Books of the East* (Oxford: Clarendon, 1890), 35.114.
9 F. W. Woodward, *Kindred Sayings* (London: Oxford University Press, 1924), 4.267.
10 *Digha-Nikaya*, II, 2, trans. by T. W. and C. A. F. Rhys Davids, *Dialogues of the Buddha*, Part II (London: Luzac, 1951), pp. 343-45.
11 *Ibid.*
12 *Ibid.*
13 Santideva, *Bodhicaryavatra*, VIII (C. Bendall, edit.).
14 *Anguttura-Nikaya*, X, 176.
15 *Maha-Prajna-Paramita-Hridaya*, 24 (*A Buddhist Bible*, Dwight Goddard, edit., New York: Dutton, 1952), p. 91.
16 *A Buddhist Bible*, "The Word of the Buddha," IV (Goddard, edit.), p. 44.
17 *Itivuttaka*, 27.
18 *Bodhicaryavatra*, V.
19 *Digha-Nikaya*, loc. cit.
20 Hokei Idumi, "Vimalakirti's Discourse," *The Eastern Buddhist*, III, 2, pp. 138-39.
21 *Digha-Nikaya*, loc. cit.
22 "The Word of the Buddha," VI (Goddard, edit.), p. 46.
23 *Digha-Nikaya*, loc. cit.
24 *Ibid.*
25 *Sacred Books of the East* (Max Muller, Oxford, 1879-1910), XI, p. 114.
26 *Ibid.*, XXI, pp. 44, 118, 120, 121, 302.

27 Milarepa, *Spiritual Testament* (J. Bacot, trans.), p. 285.
28 Santideva, *Bodhicaryavatara*, VIII, vv. 90-91, 113-14.
29 *Ibid.*, 94, 101-02.
30 Daisetz T. Suzuki, *Zen Buddhism* (Garden City, N. Y.: Doubleday, 1956), pp. 134-35.

CONFUCIANISM

1 Max Weber, quoted in H. H. Gerth and C. W. Mills, *From Max Weber: Essays in Sociology* (New York: Oxford University Press, 1946), p. 293.
2 *Shu King* (Books of Chau), Part I, 1.
3 *Ibid.*, IV, 4 (pp. 90-92).
4 *Ibid.* (p. 98).
5 Khung Ying-ta, quoted in *Sacred Books and Early Literature of the East* (New York: Parke, Austin and Lipscomb, 1917), Vol. XI, p. 91.
6 *Sacred Books of the East* (Oxford: Clarendon, 1879-1910), Vol. XXVIII, p. 98.
7 *The Analects*, VIII (*Sacred Books and Early Literature of the East*), *loc. cit.*, p. 293.
8 *The Analects*, II, *loc. cit.*, pp. 274-75.
9 *Hsiao King*, I (SBELE), p. 393.
10 *Ibid.*, IX, p. 400.
11 *Ibid.*
12 *Ibid.*
13 *Ibid.*
14 *Ibid.*
15 *The Analects*, II, 13-14; III, 10-11; IV, 16, 22, 24; XIV, 45; XV, 17-21, 36.
16 *Ibid.*, XII, 22; XIII, 19; XVII, 6.
17 *Mencius* VI, i, 6.
18 *Ibid.*, V, 2, 2-3.
19 *Ibid.*, II, 6, 2-7.
20 *Ibid.*, IV (Part One), 4, 1-2.
21 *Ibid.*, IV (Part One), 3.
22 *Ibid.*, IV (Part One), 5.
23 Mencius, *The Book of Duke Wan*, III, 2, 7-10.
24 *Tao Teh Ching*, I, 4.
25 *Mencius* VI, 1, 6.
26 Yi-pao Mei, *Motse, the Neglected Rival of Confucius* (London: Probthain, 1929), pp. 80-81.
27 V. I. Lenin, *Works* (Moscow, n.d.), Vol. 15, 4th (Russian) edition, p. 374.
28 Mao Tse-tung, *China's New Democracy* (New York: International, 1945), p. 48.

ISLAM

1 *Koran*, Surah XXV, 2-4. Subsequent references to the *Koran* will give only the Surah (chapter) and verse.
2 Surah X, 4-5.
3 Surah XLVI, 3.
4 Surah XXII, 72.
5 Surah XXIII, 93.
6 Surah II, 163-65.
7 Surah XXIX, 52.
8 Surah XXV, 45.
9 Surah XII, 40.
10 Surah XVI, 29.
11 Surah XVIII, 50.
12 Surah VI, 100.
13 Surah IV, 117.
14 Surah X, 29; XXV, 18.
15 Surah XXXV, 1.
16 Surah XL, 7.
17 Surah LXXXII, 10-12.
18 Surah II, 97.
19 Surah LXXXI, 19-21.
20 Surah XV, 28-43.
21 Surah XVII, 95.
22 Surah XIII, 38.
23 Surah XII, 109; XVI, 44; XXI, 7.
24 Surah IV, 64.
25 Surah IV, 105.
26 Surah XIX, 31.
27 Surah III, 73; VI, 89.
28 Surah II, 137.
29 Surah LXII, 1-2.
30 Surah IX, 5, 29.
31 Surah III, 29.
32 Surah XXII, 78.
33 A. A. Galwash, *The Religion of Islam* (Cairo: I'timad Press, 1945), Vol. I, p. 222.
34 Surah II, 155-57.
35 Surah II, 183.
36 Surah LXII, 9-10.
37 Surah IV, 43.
38 Surah I, 1-7.
39 Ali, *Sahifat-Kamila*, quoted in Ameer Ali Syed, *The Spirit of Islam* (London: Christophers, 1953), pp. 163-64.
40 Surah XIX, 33.
41 Surah III, 40-45.
42 Surah XLIII, 57-63.

43 Surah XXI, 91.
44 Surah IV, 155-56.
45 Surah V, 75, 79.
46 Surah XIX, 28-34.
47 Surah III, 36.
48 Surah V, 112-15.
49 Surah LXI, 6.
50 Quoted in Geoffrey Parrinder, *Jesus in the Qur'an* (New York: Barnes and Noble, 1965), p. 96.
51 Ibn-Hisham, *The Life of Muhammad* (New York: Oxford University Press, 1955), pp. 103-04. The original biographer was Ibn-Ishaq, but his work is extant only in the version preserved by Ibn-Hisham (died A.D. 834).
52 Surah III, 59-61.
53 Surah V, 72-75.
54 Ameer Ali Syed, *op. cit.*, pp. 140-41.
55 Fazlur Rahman, *Islam* (London: Weidenfeld and Nicolson, 1966), p. 27.
56 *Ibid.*
57 Surah XLVII, 38.
58 Surah II, 62; V, 69.
59 Surah V, 82-83.
60 Surah IV, 3.
61 Surah IV, 25; XXIII, 6.
62 Surah IV, 28.
63 Ghulam Ahmad Parwez, "Salim," quoted in J. M. S. Baljon, *Modern Muslim Koran Interpretation (1880-1960)* (Leiden: Brill, 1961), p. 114.
64 Surah IV, 3.
65 Ameer Ali Syed, *op. cit.*, pp. 229-30.
66 A. de Zayas Abbasi, *The Islamic Literature*, January 1956 (Baljon, *op. cit.*), p. 115.
67 Muhammad Iqbal, *Jawid Nama*, 1959, p. 127.
68 Fazlur Rahman, *op. cit.*, p. 234.

THE CHURCH'S MISSION

1 Karl Barth, quoted by Nicol Macnicol, *Is Christianity Unique?* (London: The Student Christian Movement Press, 1936), pp. 168-69.
2 Arnold Toynbee, *Christianity Among the Religions of the World* (New York: Scribner's, 1957), pp. 95-96.

REFERENCES

3 *The Sacred Books and Early Literature of the East* (New York: Parke, Austin and Lipscomb, 1917), Vol. XII, p. 382.
4 Eugene Hillman, *The Wider Ecumenism* (New York: Herder and Herder, 1968), pp. 156-58.
5 Toynbee, *op. cit.*, pp. 111-12.

INDEX

201

2363 - Schoolcraft

About this book

Religions of the Orient—A Christian View was designed by William Nicoll of Edit, Inc. It was set in the composing room of Loyola University Press. The typeface is 10/13 and 9/11 Caledonia. The display type is 30 Baskerville.

It was printed by Photopress, Inc., on Warren's 60-pound English Finish paper and bound by The Engdahl Company.